MW00608036

Culture and Customs of the Hmong

Recent Titles in
Culture and Customs of Asia

Culture and Customs of Vietnam
Mark W. McLeod and Nguyen Thi Dieu

Culture and Customs of the Philippines
Paul Rodell

Culture and Customs of China
Richard Gunde

Culture and Customs of India
Carol E. Henderson

Culture and Customs of Thailand
Arne Kislenko

Culture and Customs of Afghanistan
Hafizullah Emadi

Culture and Customs of Pakistan
Iftikhar H. Malik

Culture and Customs of Indonesia
Jill Forshee

Culture and Customs of the Central Asian Republics
Rafis Abazov

Culture and Customs of Mongolia
Timothy Michael May

Culture and Customs of Laos
Arne Kislenko

Culture and Customs of Singapore and Malaysia
Jaime Koh and Stephanie Ho

Culture and Customs of the Hmong

GARY YIA LEE AND NICHOLAS TAPP

Culture and Customs of Asia
Hanchao Lu, Series Editor

GREENWOOD

AN IMPRINT OF ABC-CLIO, LLC
Santa Barbara, California • Denver, Colorado • Oxford, England

Copyright 2010 by Gary Yia Lee and Nicholas Tapp

Library of Congress Cataloging-in-Publication Data

Lee, G. Y. (Gary Y.)
    Culture and customs of the Hmong / Gary Yia Lee and Nicholas Tapp.
        p. cm. — (Culture and customs of Asia)
    Includes bibliographical references and index.
    ISBN 978-0-313-34526-5 (hardcopy : alk. paper)—ISBN 978-0-313-34527-2 (ebook) 1. Hmong
(Asian people)—Social life and customs. I. Tapp, Nicholas, 1952– II. Title.
    DS509.5.H66L44   2010
    305.895'972—dc22   2010015978

ISBN: 978-0-313-34526-5
EISBN: 978-0-313-34527-2

14   13   12   11   10   1   2   3   4   5

This book is also available on the World Wide Web as an eBook.
Visit www.abc-clio.com for details.

Greenwood
An Imprint of ABC-CLIO, LLC

ABC-CLIO, LLC
130 Cremona Drive, P.O. Box 1911
Santa Barbara, California 93116-1911

This book is printed on acid-free paper ∞

Manufactured in the United States of America

The publisher has done its best to make sure the instructions and/or recipes in this book are correct.
However, users should apply judgment and experience when preparing recipes, especially parents and
teachers working with young people. The publisher accepts no responsibility for the outcome of any
recipe included in this volume.

This book is dedicated to

Our wives, Maylee and Jing

Who slept alone many a night
And went out by themselves on countless occasions
While we tinkered away at the PC
And got too lost in our work to see.

Thank you for your forbearance and love.

Contents

Series Foreword

GEOGRAPHICALLY, ASIA ENCOMPASSES the vast area from Suez, the Bosporus, and the Ural Mountains eastward to the Bering Sea and from this line southward to the Indonesian archipelago, an expanse that covers about 30 percent of our earth. Conventionally, and especially in so far as culture and customs are concerned, Asia refers primarily to the region east of Iran and south of Russia. This area can be divided in turn into subregions, commonly known as South, Southeast, and East Asia, which are the main focus of this series.

The United States has vast interests in this region. In the 20th century, the United States fought three major wars in Asia (namely the Pacific War of 1941–45, the Korean War of 1950–53, and the Vietnam War of 1965–75), and each had a profound impact on life and politics in America. Today, America's major trading partners are in Asia, and in the foreseeable future the weight of Asia in American life will inevitably increase, for in Asia lie our great allies as well as our toughest competitors in virtually all arenas of global interest. Domestically, the role of Asian immigrants is more visible than at any other time in our history. In spite of these connections with Asia, however, our knowledge about this crucial region is far from adequate. For various reasons, Asia remains for most of us a relatively unfamiliar, if not stereotypical or even mysterious, "Oriental" land.

There are compelling reasons for Americans to obtain some level of concrete knowledge about Asia. It is one of the world's richest reservoirs of culture and an ever-evolving museum of human heritage. Rhoads Murphy, a prominent Asianist, once pointed out that in the part of Asia east of Afghanistan and south of Russia alone lies half the world, "half of its people and far more than half of its historical experience, for these are the oldest living civilized traditions." Prior to the modern era, with limited interaction and mutual influence between the East and the West, Asian civilizations developed largely independent from the West. In modern times, however, Asia and the West have come not only into close contact but also into frequent conflict: The result has been one of the most solemn and stirring dramas in world history. Today, integration and compromise are the trend in coping with cultural differences. The West—with some notable exceptions—has started to see Asian traditions not as something to fear but as something to be understood, appreciated, and even cherished. After all, Asian traditions are an indispensable part of the human legacy, a matter of global "commonwealth" that few of us can afford to ignore.

As a result of Asia's enormous economic development since World War II, we can no longer neglect the study of this vibrant region. Japan's "economic miracle" of postwar development is no longer unique, but in various degrees has been matched by the booming economy of many other Asian countries and regions. The rise of the four "mini dragons" (South Korea, Taiwan, Hong Kong, and Singapore) suggests that there may be a common Asian pattern of development. At the same time, each economy in Asia has followed its own particular trajectory. Clearly, China is the next giant on the scene. Sweeping changes in China in the last two decades have already dramatically altered the world's economic map. Furthermore, growth has also been dramatic in much of Southeast Asia. Today, war-devastated Vietnam shows great enthusiasm for joining the "club" of nations engaged in the world economy. And in South Asia, India, the world's largest democracy, is rediscovering its role as a champion of market capitalism. The economic development of Asia presents a challenge to Americans but also provides them with unprecedented opportunities. It is largely against this background that more and more people in the United States, in particular among the younger generation, have started to pursue careers dealing with Asia.

This series is designed to meet the need for knowledge of Asia among students and the general public. Each book is written in an accessible and lively style by an expert (or experts) in the field of Asian studies. Each book focuses on the culture and customs of a country or region. However, readers should be aware that culture is fluid, not always respecting national boundaries. While every nation seeks its own path to success and struggles to maintain its own identity, in the cultural domain mutual influence and integration among Asian nations are ubiquitous.

Each volume starts with an introduction to the land and the people of a nation or region and includes a brief history and an overview of the economy. This is followed by chapters dealing with a variety of topics that piece together a cultural panorama, such as thought, religion, ethics, literature and art, architecture and housing, cuisine, traditional dress, gender, courtship and marriage, festivals and leisure activities, music and dance, and social customs and lifestyle. In this series, we have chosen not to elaborate on elite life, ideology, or detailed questions of political structure and struggle, but instead to explore the world of common people, their sorrow and joy, their pattern of thinking, and their way of life. It is the culture and the customs of the majority of the people (rather than just the rich and powerful elite) that we seek to understand. Without such understanding, it will be difficult for all of us to live peacefully and fruitfully with each other in this increasingly interdependent world.

As the world shrinks, modern technologies have made all nations on earth "virtual" neighbors. The expression "global village" not only reveals the nature and the scope of the world in which we live but also, more importantly, highlights the serious need for mutual understanding of all peoples on our planet. If this series serves to help the reader obtain a better understanding of the "half of the world" that is Asia, the authors and I will be well rewarded.

Hanchao Lu
Georgia Institute of Technology

Preface

THIS BOOK TAKES a global approach to understanding the Hmong, a people whose ancestors are known to have lived in China for more than 4,000 years. A glance at the bibliography will show that there are many publications on the Hmong, but this is the first time that a book has been written on them from an international perspective, with special emphasis on the impact of their recent history in Laos since the Vietnam War, and their subsequent settlement in Western countries such as the United States, France, Canada, Germany, Argentina, French Guyana, and Australia. In Southeast Asia, they live in Vietnam, Laos, Myanmar (Burma), and Thailand, with a small, unconfirmed group reportedly migrating to northern Cambodia from Vietnam during the last few years.

A broad international perspective allows us to look at the Hmong more comprehensively through the complex interplay of the many social, historical, economic, and cultural influences that they have been exposed to in their worldwide migration, and at how they manage to maintain their many traditions across national boundaries and great distance. In China, the Hmong are officially classified by the Chinese government as part of the "Miao" nationality that includes three other ethnic minorities: the Qho Xiong, the Hmu, and the A Hmao. They live in the provinces of Hunan and Hubei, Guizhou, Sichuan, Yunnan, and Guangxi, with the Hmong concentrated in the latter four provinces. The total number of "Miao" in China is 9.2 million, of which some 3.1 million are Hmong.

Today, the Hmong in the West are looked on as an example to watch and follow and are the voice for the Hmong in other parts of the world. This is true especially of those living in the United States, where most have settled in Minnesota, California, and Wisconsin. Although they number only a little over 200,000 people, they have made a great impact on other Hmong groups due to their frequent travels to visit co-ethnics in Asia and to their active use of the media (newspapers and radio) to share news and ideas in the Hmong language with fellow Hmong in other countries. They have set up hundreds of Web sites on the Internet to share their culture and history, to do business, to show their talents in the arts and their works in different fields, to publicize issues of concern, and to chat with each other. With access to education, information, and political freedom, they have been the most ardent in advocating justice and fair play for the Hmong worldwide, with frequent representations to the United Nations, the U.S. Congress, and even the European Union.

The Hmong have been living in the United States only since 1975, when they fled Laos after serving as recruits there for the Central Intelligence Agency (CIA)-supported "secret army" with the end of the Vietnam War. Already, however, many of the younger Hmong in America have made inroads into American businesses, civic life, and politics. Americans of Hmong background are now serving as university professors, U.S. Navy and Marine officers, county councilors, state senators, and representatives. Given that many of them did not have the opportunity to go to school until their settlement in the United States, they have made education a high priority, with over 200 now having PhD degrees, close to 3,000 with master's degrees, and many thousands more with first degrees.

The Hmong are thus a diaspora worth learning about and taking notice of. It is for this reason that we wrote this book for all who are interested to know more about them. Based on his recent experience of teaching Hmong studies in the United States, Gary Lee knows only too well the lack of suitable textbooks for a general introductory course. This book is designed to fill this void. We also hope that the many young Hmong who are losing touch with their own people, and who are today studying in high schools, colleges, and universities across the United States and in other countries, will benefit and come to know themselves better after reading this book. To do justice to Hmong society as a whole, in so many different countries across the world, is not easy. We have tried to balance an account of traditional life, which continues in some parts of Asia and is still remembered by the older Hmong refugees, with an account of their modern life and all the changes that have taken place since their resettlement in the West.

To truly know the Hmong, of course, we would like to encourage readers to get to know them in person, to make friends with them, to take part in their festivals and social events, and to continue studying them. That is the best way. This was what a group of American students from the Randall School in Madison, Wisconsin, did during 2002 and 2003. With their teacher, they immersed themselves in Hmong culture by traveling across Wisconsin to visit Hmong communities in seven cities. They studied Hmong history, traditions, and community life. The result is that they came to know many things: "how to dance, how to make egg rolls, and how to say a few Hmong words." Their very positive experience has been recorded on their Web site for everyone to share at http://csumc.wisc.edu/cmct/HmongTour/.

The task of writing this book was shared by the two authors. Nick Tapp wrote Chapters 1, 2, 6, 7, 9, and the Glossary. Gary Lee dealt with the Preface, Chronology, Chapters 3, 4, 5, 8, 10, and the Further Readings. Both authors assembled the Bibliography. In reality, we read and revised our respective chapters extensively based on each other's comments and sometimes made direct inputs into each other's writings. We have both lived and done research among the Hmong in various countries, including Laos, Thailand, Vietnam, China, Australia, France, and Canada. We have studied and published on the Hmong for more than 25 years. We believe our shared experience is broad and hope it is reflected in this book.

We would like to thank Greenwood Press for their invitation to us to undertake the project of writing the book, and especially our editor, Kaitlin Ciarmiello, who gave us the time we needed and whose perseverance, detailed comments on the manuscript, and guidance have allowed us to pull the project through as expected. We also wish to thank most deeply Bryan Thao Worra, the American Laotian poet, for his help with information in the section on modern literature in Chapter 3.

Gary Lee would further like to say a word of appreciation to his parents, whose foresight allowed him to be sent to school at an early stage of Hmong modern history. He is especially grateful to his mother, who now requires constant care in her old age, who understood that his need to finish this book meant that he had less time to attend to her urgent needs. He also wants to show appreciation to Mr. Seexeng Lee for allowing him to reproduce two images of Seexeng's art works and for updating him on the most recent changes to Seexeng's personal information. Mrs. Sayblong Saykao, Melbourne, Australia, was most helpful in lending her beautiful Hmong embroideries and story-cloths to Gary to photograph for this book. Permission to use two figures on Hmong embroidery and jewelry designs by the John Michael Kohler Arts Centre, Sheboygan, Wisconsin, is also warmly acknowledged here.

During the months we spent on the book, our families, relatives, and friends had to put up with the unpredictable temperament of two authors who were faced with a deadline and had little time for them. Their patience is greatly appreciated.

Note on Transliteration
and Hmong Names

THE OFFICIAL TRANSCRIPTION system for Hmong (Romanized Phonetic Alphabet, or RPA) is much like English, except that the ending consonant indicates the tone of the word, as the Hmong language has eight tones, and doubling the vowels means that the word ends in an –ng. So "Hmong" (in a high tone) is spelled "Hmoob," with the –b at the end meaning that it is pronounced in a high, level tone. Also, for historical reasons, the "s" sounds more like an English "sh," and the "x" sounds more like the English "s." In this book, we have mostly followed this spelling system for Hmong words, except where they are very well known under a different spelling, or for the names of people that are spelled as they usually spell them.

The two main cultural divisions of the Hmong outside China are known as the Hmoob Dawb (White Hmong) and the Moob Ntsuab (Blue Mong). The official spelling system, RPA, was developed for White Hmong, who pronounce their name with a puff of initial air through the nose, pre-aspirated, which is why it is spelled "Hm." But the Moob Ntsuab do not have this pre-aspiration of the name, so their name should really be spelled "Moob," not "Hmoob," in RPA, and "Mong," rather than "Hmong," in English. The Moob Ntsuab are also known as the Moob Lees (Mong Leng), and many prefer to be known by the latter name. With respect to those feelings, in this book, we have generally retained the spelling "Hmong" or "Hmoob" for the Hmong people as a whole, since that is how they are so generally known internationally, but when the Moob Lees are specifically being discussed, we have spelled it "Mong" or "Moob" to make it clear that their name is actually not pre-aspirated.

"Ntsuab" means green. In the 1960s, the Moob Ntsuab in Laos made a strong argument that their name should be translated into English as "Green Mong," and this has been accepted since then by many writers. However, more recently it has been felt that this may be derogatory and they prefer to be known as "Blue." For the Green/Blue problem, we have used "Blue" in this book. We hope this causes no confusion. The Blue or Green Mong are the Moob Ntsuab or Moob Lees. Together with the White Hmong and other divisions, they form the global Hmong nation, despite some impetuous claims that they are a completely separate ethnic group.

Abbreviations

BBC	British Broadcasting Corporation
BPP	Border Patrol Police (Thailand)
CIA	Central Intelligence Agency
CMA	Christian and Missionary Alliance
CPT	Communist Party of Thailand
MEP	Missions Étrangères de Paris (Foreign Missionary Society of Paris) Roman Catholic missionary organization, founded in 1659.
NBC	National Broadcasting Company
PLAT	People's Liberation Army of Thailand
RLA	Royal Laotian Army
RPA	Romanized Phonetic Alphabet
SGU	Special Guerrilla Unit
UN	United Nations
UNHCR	United Nations High Commissioner for Refugees
USAID	United States Agency for International Development
USSR	Union of Soviet Socialist Republics
YWCA	Young Women's Christian Association

Chronology

Miao as a name was used for all non-Chinese groups in southern China, with the ancestors of the Hmong probably classified under this name.

The "Miao" were first mentioned in Chinese histories compiled after the third century BCE but possibly dating back to the fifth century BCE as having lived in the basin of the Yellow River in today's Hunan province of China. The Chinese, led by Huangdi or the Yellow Emperor, who is supposed to have reigned from 2697 to 2598 BCE, defeated the Miao led by Chiyou, said by some to be known in Hmong as Txiv Yawg.

The Hmong/Miao continued to resist Han Chinese after Chiyou's defeat, refusing to recognize the legendary Emperors Yao, Shun, and Yu the Great[1] who founded the Xia Dynasty (2100–1600 BCE).

A strong tribal alliance known as the San-Miao (Three Miao) had appeared in Chinese reports, with one of its chieftains controlling the region between Lake Donting and Poyang. Shun sent Yu to exterminate them, drove their chieftain to San-wei, and kept him there.[2] The two groups continued to fight during the first centuries of Chinese rule.[3]

Despite some scattered mentions in Chinese historical records in the Tang and Song dynasties (618–1279), the ancestors of the Hmong were not referred to again in official dynastic histories until the Yuan dynasty (1271–1368), when their rebellions against the Han Chinese were frequently cited.[4]

EARLY MODERN PERIOD (1368–1918)

Under the Ming dynasty (1200–1644), the Miao were frequently subdivided into the "Raw" (Sheng) and the "Cooked" (Shu). Sheng Miao were those who refused Chinese assimilation and thus remained seen as "barbarians." Shu Miao were those who became more integrated and assented to Chinese rule.[5]

Under the Qing dynasty (1644–1911), use of the term "Miao" came to be more restricted to groups of specific people such as Bai (White) Miao, Hei (Black) Miao, Qing (Green/Blue) Miao, Hong (Red) Miao, and Hua (Flowery) Miao—roughly distinguished by the color of their women's costumes, although it was still often used as a general term to cover many other groups. Major "Miao" rebellions (which also involved other peoples, even Chinese) broke out against the tightening of Chinese rule in Guizhou and Hunan provinces in 1733 to 1737, 1795 to 1806, and 1854 to 1873. The last revolt coincided with the revolt of the Panthay Muslims in Yunnan province (1851–1864), in which Hmong were probably also involved. After their suppression and the burning and looting of their villages, many Hmong started fleeing to countries in Southeast Asia.

1868

There were 10,000 Hmong reported arriving in Tongkin (northern Vietnam) from Guizhou province.[6] Some movements may have taken place earlier than this, however. Hmong believe they began settling in Laos as early as 1810 to 1820.

Other groups eventually crossed to Laos and Thailand about 1880.[7]

Many Hmong also moved southward in search of agricultural lands due to population pressure from the Chinese and the incentive to grow opium as a cash crop, which was introduced by the British and French governments and in China as early as 1842.[8]

Other Miao/Hmong groups, living further up north in Guizhou, Hunan, and Hubei, did not move further south, due to the difficult terrains through which they had to travel to reach Tongkin and strict Chinese military control of their areas. Thus, the majority of the

Miao/Hmong remain in China. It is only the Hmong who left China to move to neighboring countries (apart from a small group of Hmu in northern Vietnam).

1880	Hmong reported living in Nan province, Thailand.[9]
1887	French Indochina (Indochine Francaise) was formed after France exerted its presence and annexed Cambodia in 1863, Tongkin (northern Vietnam) and Annam (central Vietnam) in 1883, and Laos in 1893 as French "protectorates"/colonies.
1896	French colonial tax was introduced in Laos, leading the Hmong in Nong Het to ambush French tax collectors at Ban Khang Phanieng. Negotiations with French authorities resulted in the first official position of kiatong (canton chief) in Laos given to a Hmong, Moua Chong Kai.
1916	French tax was increased: widows and single people over 18 years of age also had to pay. The Hmong were told to grow more opium for the French monopoly to sell to finance their budget in Indochina under the Opium Purchasing Board.

MODERN PERIOD
(1918–1974)

July 1918 to March 1921	Pachay Vue led the war/revolt of the "insane" or Rog Vwm against the French.
1921	Lo Bliayao was made Kiatong of Nong Het after he helped the French to put down the Pachay revolt. Lyfoung was his personal secretary (being the only literate Hmong at the time) after the latter's marriage to Lo Bliayao's daughter, Lo May, in 1918.
1928	There were two Hmong settlements in Phitsanulok and Lomsak provinces, Thailand.
1929	Hmong settled in Tak province, Thailand.
December 8, 1929	Birth of Vang Pao, who was the only Hmong to attain the rank of General in the Royal Lao Army, and was a staunch supporter of the French and American war against communism in Laos from 1961 to 1975.
January 1933	Lo Bliayao urged many Hmong Tasseng (subdistricts) not to deliver their opium to the French—further causing a rift between him and French authorities.

1935	Death of Lo Bliayao. His position of Kiatong was replaced by a Tasseng position and was given to Lyfoung. The Lo clan became embittered by the loss. Faydang, one of Lo Bliayao's sons, made representations to the Lao Royal family in Luang Prabang.
	Thirty-six Hmong listed as receiving officially sponsored education with Hmong attaining the Certificate of Primary Education for the first time.
1936	Road linking Luang Prabang, Laos, to Annam (in Vietnam) completed, using Hmong corvée labor.
1939	Lyfoung died; his Tasseng position was given to his son, Touby.
1940 to 1945	Japanese occupation of Indochina: Touby and his Hmong supporters helped hide French officers on the run from Japanese troops.
1944	Vang Pao left school to work as an intelligence collector for the French under Touby Lyfoung.
November 1945	Faydang Lo Bliayao made contact with Ho Chi Minh's Viet Minh—the northern Vietnamese anti-French colonial movement.
1946	France re-occupied Laos with the help of Touby and his supporters.
1948	Touby was instructed to form Hmong *maquis* (rural guerrilla forces) with French support.
1939 to 1954	Support for the Viet Minh: large number of Hmong in northwest Vietnam sided with the communist Viet Minh (Ho Chi Minh's independence movement against the French before and after WWII) because of support from the French for the Black Tai overlord (Deo Van Long) in the Hmong area who forced Hmong to learn Tai and also levied heavy taxes on them.[10]
1951 to 1952	Chao Quang Lo, a Hmong hero from northern Vietnam,[11] helped the French fight against Chinese supplying the Viet Minh forces in Vietnam.
1946 to 1954	Fay Dang and his supporters helped the Viet Minh and the Lao independence movement Pathet Lao to harass French positions in northeastern Laos.
1947	Faydang made first contact with Lao Issara ("Lao Freedom") leaders, Souphanouvong and Sithone Kommandan,

and later joined them in opposition to the French and Touby Lyfoung.

Hmong became recognized Lao citizens.

Vang Pao was a police officer in the French Colonial Army.

1948 to 1949	Vang Pao attended military training school in Luang Prabang and later in Vientiane.
1949	Chinese Communist Party under Chairman Mao gained power in China with participation of Miao/Hmong and members of other minority nationalities. France gave partial independence to Laos.
1950	Fay Dang was made minister in the Pathet Lao's First Resistance Congress. The French gave Touby the position of Hmong district governor in Xieng Khouang.
1950 to 1952	Vang Pao attended the French Military Academy at Dong Hen, Savannakhet, southern Laos.
1954	Laos gained full independence from France.
1955	Toulia Lyfoung was elected to the First Lao National Assembly, which among other things abolished the taxes levied by the French.
1957	Touby was elected to the Second Lao National Assembly and made Minister of Social Welfare.
1958	Vang Pao was promoted to captain. Thai government banned opium cultivation by Hmong and other hill tribes, and began various programs to control the clearing of forests and watershed damages.
1959	Vang Pao promoted to major. Pop Buell, a retired farmer from Indiana, began working with Hmong in Lat Huang, Xieng Khouang, Laos.
1960	Neutralist Captain Kong Le took over the Lao government in Vientiane in a coup d'état and ordered Vang Pao to surrender but he refused on the grounds that Kong Le did not have approval from the King for his action. Vang Pao was promoted to Lt. Colonel with the right-wing Royal Lao Army.
1961	Beginning of the recruitment of Hmong into the armed wing of Communist Party of Thailand (CPT) with many young men and women taken to Laos and China for military training.

1962

Geneva Agreements for a neutral Laos signed by 14 nations. Vang Pao promoted to brigadier general and his irregular forces increased from 9,000 to 18,000 men, mostly Hmong but also other hill tribes people. They were assisted by Thai mercenaries under command of Thai regular officers.

CPT radio station, "Voice of the People of Thailand," started broadcasting in Hmong, further helping in the CPT recruitment of Hmong into its People's Liberation Army of Thailand (PLAT).

1963

Vang Pao moved his headquarters from Pha Khao to Long Cheng, and was given his first medal by the King of Laos. His irregular troops increased to 20,000 men.

1964

Vang Pao promoted to major general, and his military region came under heavy attacks from the communist Pathet Lao and North Vietnamese troops. More than 90,000 civilians became displaced from their homes into refugee centers, with material support from United States Agency for International Development (USAID).

1965

Vang Pao's SGUs (Special Guerrilla Units) increased to four battalions (40,000 men), with U.S. Ambassador in Laos running the covert operations directly.

Hmong population in Thailand was estimated to be 53,031 with 24,681 living in Phetchaboun province; 9,454 in Nan; 5,728 in Chiangrai; 5,609 in Tak; 4,725 in Chiangmai and smaller groups in other parts of the northern provinces.

1967

Hmong uprising (known as the 'Red Meo Revolt') began in Thailand when the government fire-bombed a Hmong village suspected of harboring communists.

1968

Vang Pao visited President Johnson in Washington, D.C. Hmong involved in the war in Laos now totalled 120,000 (RLA, SGU, others) with 18,000 killed.

1969 to 1970

Vang Pao and his troops took the Plain of Jars back from the communist Pathet Lao. U.S. Congress learned about the covert war in Laos for the first time.

1972

Vang Pao established many schools in his area of command. His headquarters, Long Cheng, came under heavy attack from the enemy.

1973	Paris cease-fire agreement was signed between United States and North Vietnam for complete withdrawal of American troops from Indochina. From 1964 to 1973, 2 million tons of bombs were dropped in Laos.

The United Nations Program for Drug Abuse and Control was initiated in Thailand to encourage opium growers to adopt other cash crops and to stop opium cultivation.

POST-MODERN PERIOD
(1975–PRESENT)

1975	Lao civil (secret) war ended with Hmong toll of 30,000 troops and 50,000 civilians killed, and 200,000 refugees.
May 4, 1975	Vang Pao resigned his post and left Long Cheng with his family and close associates for Thailand, then the United States.
1975 to 1978	First wave of Hmong refugees from Laos resettled in United States, France, Australia, Canada, Argentina, and Germany.
1979	PLAT had around 11,000 to 12,000 anti-government fighters in Thailand, including many Hmong and their families.
1980	Thai government ordered the forced destruction of Hmong opium fields by the military, marking the end of opium production in Thailand.
1981	Vang Pao in the United States formed the United Lao Liberation Front to recapture Laos from the communist Pathet Lao, with branches in other western countries.
1982	Thai government declared amnesty for all CPT members, including the PLAT. Thousands of PLAT fighters—many of them Thai students—surrendered their arms and returned home.
1983 to 1985	Remaining hardcore PLAT in Phitsanulok Province were militarily defeated, with the help of remnants of ex-Kuomingtang troops from the Golden Triangle and former CIA Hmong soldiers from Laos who were now refugees in Thailand. Many former Hmong PLAT soldiers surrendered and were resettled in various parts of the Thai highlands.

1991	Laos, Thailand, and the United Nations agreed to repatriate Hmong refugees in Thailand to Laos.
1995	The closing of all UNHCR refugee camps in Thailand forced 16,000 Hmong unwilling to resettle in Western countries to seek refuge at Wat Tam Krabok, Saraburi province.
1997	Hmong veterans of the Lao civil war were recognized by the U.S. government for their contributions during the Vietnam War.
2000	Hmong numbered 186,000 in the United States, mostly first-generation refugees from Laos.
2001	Mee Moua, a Minnesota lawyer, was the first Hmong woman to be elected as a U.S. senator.
2003	Cy Thao was the first Hmong to be elected to the U.S. Congress as a state representative (Minnesota).
2005–2006	Resettlement of final group of Hmong refugees occurred from Laos at Wat Tham Krabok, Thailand, to the United States and Australia. The Hmong in Laos numbered 460,000, 7 percent of the total population.
2007	June 4: arrest of Vang Pao and nine other associates in California for attempt at the "violent overthrow" of the government of Laos, a country now "at peace" with the United States. July 12: Vang Pao was released on bail, after many demonstrations by Hmong all over the United States.
2003–2008	Laos named leaders of Hmong background to prominent government positions: Panee Yatouthao as Deputy Chair of the National Assembly, Chaleun Heu as Minister for Justice, Ly Cheng as Minister Assisting the Prime Minister in Rural Development, Lytou Bouapao as Deputy Minister for Education, and Tong Yeu Thao as Deputy Chair of the Neo Hom Xang Xat.
September 2009	All charges against Vang Pao were dismissed by the court in Sacramento, California, but not those against his former co-accused.

NOTES

1. Geddes 1976, 3.
2. Lin 1940, 271.

3. Savina 1924, viii.
4. Schein 2000; Wiens 1954.
5. Diamond 1995, 100.
6. Lemoine 1995.
7. Culas and Michaud 2004, 71.
8. Ibid., 67.
9. Geddes 1976, 29.
10. Culas and Michaud 2004, 78.
11. Mottin, 1980a, 59.

1

Introduction—Diaspora, History, Identity

THE HMONG ARE dispersed into many parts of the world from their original homeland in southern China. The Hmong population today totals nearly 5 million worldwide if we add the following to the 3.1 million in China: 787,604 in Vietnam; 460,000 in Laos; 124,000 in Thailand; some 2,000 to 3,000 in Myanmar; between 200,000–300,000 in the United States; 15,000 in France; 2,000 in Australia; 800 in Canada; 1,500 in French Guyana; some 600 in Argentina; and 92 in Germany.[1] This dispersion means that the Hmong have been influenced by many neighboring cultures and affected by many diverse socio-economic factors that have brought changes to their society and culture.

Because the Hmong are found in so many parts of the world, it is not possible to describe all the geographic locations in which they live in detail, because these locations are numerous and very diverse. The economic system they adopt also varies from one country or region to another. Except for those in the countryside in Asia who still carry on subsistence agriculture, those living in cities and in Western countries are engaged in very different modes of employment such as factory workers, storekeepers, market gardeners, businesspeople, teachers, nurses, and other professions. So it is again difficult to discuss the Hmong economy as a single system embraced by the majority. Here we introduce the Hmong diaspora, showing how it has arisen from its historical migration to and settlement in different countries in Southeast Asia and the West, and how Hmong economic practices and social life have varied according to their different geographical locations.

THE HMONG—A DIASPORIC COMMUNITY

The Hmong today clearly form a diaspora, defined as a dislocated ethnic collectivity without a territorial base.[2] Like other diasporic groups, they have a history of dispersal, myths and memories of a homeland, alienation in their new host countries, a desire to return to the homeland with continued support for it, and a collective identity defined by this latter relationship.[3] While more than 3 million of them are currently living in China, their original homeland, close to 1 million live in neighboring countries such as Vietnam, Laos, Thailand, and Myanmar as a result of population pressure in China, Han Chinese occupation of their native territories, and oppression. This dispersal started in the early nineteenth century and continued until the late 1950s, when many who had worked with the French colonial authorities fled Vietnam for Laos following the French military defeat by the Viet Minh in 1954. However, the largest global Hmong diaspora was formed after 1975, when the American defeat in Vietnam and the Lao civil war culminated in the displacement of more than 180,000 Hmong from Laos itself into refugee camps in Thailand. Most of these refugees were eventually resettled in Western countries such as the United States, France, Canada, Australia, Argentina, and Germany. The Hmong are today spread all over the world.

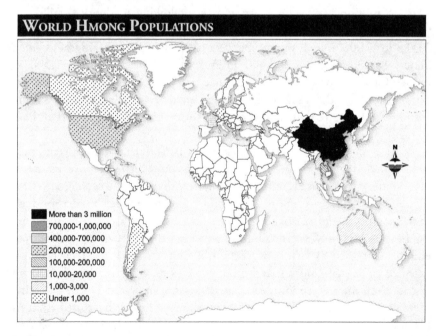

Map showing Hmong populations throughout the world. (For more precise population numbers, see page 1).

The Hmong fall somewhere in between what Armstrong calls a "proletarian" and a "mobilized" diaspora: they are disadvantaged like a proletarian diaspora, but at the same time have an elite that is fairly active and manipulative within both their community and the broader society in which they live, like a mobilized diaspora.[4] The Hmong also form what has been called a "victim diaspora." Cohen identifies other types of diaspora such as business/trade, labor, professional, imperial/colonial, or cultural ones.[5] The Hmong diaspora shows all the features identified by Cohen as characteristic of diasporas, with some features more dominant than others: (1) a dispersion from an original homeland, often in traumatic circumstances; or expansion from a homeland for work or colonial purposes; (2) a collective myth about the homeland and a commitment to its maintenance; (3) the development of liberation or return movements; (4) a strong ethnic group consciousness; (5) an ambivalent and sometimes troubled relationship with the host society; (6) solidarity with co-ethnic members in other countries; and (7) the possibility of contributing to and enriching the host society, culturally or economically, "with a tolerance for pluralism."[6]

Many Hmong still look back to China as their original homeland, but those who now live in the West see Laos as more important, because it figures more prominently in their memories as they or their parents were born or grew up there. They left it with a great sense of loss and trauma, and were dispersed as refugees into different corners of the globe, not by choice but by force of circumstances. The poignancy of their situation is illustrated by the Hmong who now live in French Guyana. Although many have been resettled there since 1977 from the Thai refugee camps, sponsored by the French government to open up the local jungles for farming, many older Hmong still feel like Ly Dao Ly, aged 50. Looking at his thriving tropical fruit trees in Cacao, he said, "Sometimes I imagine that I am seeing the mountains of Laos in those green hills."[7] Their homeland of Laos was taken away from these former Central Intelligence Agency (CIA)-supported soldiers by their long-standing enemy, the communist Pathet Lao, with the support of Vietnam and the assistance of other Hmong factions in the country. Many of these former refugees find it difficult to accept their life in exile, and have formed or joined political movements to try and regain control of their old homeland, despite the impossibility of realizing such a dream.

THE HMONG FROM CHINA—IDENTITY AND HISTORY

The Hmong have a rich culture and a long history in China and Southeast Asia. Their society is organized around patrilineal surname groups.

Every Hmong is born into a family with one of 18 or more surnames similar to those of the Chinese people and may only marry someone who does not have the same surname. In particular places where the Hmong live, the members with the same surname form a clan and much social interaction tends to take place with the other members of that clan, which can also act as a kind of mutual assistance group. Their traditional religious and medical system unites elements of ancestor worship with shamanism and beliefs in a wide variety of spirits, although many today are Christian and some are Buddhist. Ancestors, especially in the male line, are very important to most Hmong, and traditional families hold rituals at particular times of the year to honor and respect their departed relatives. In times of illness or crisis a shaman or traditional ritual specialist may be consulted for diagnosis and help, and such shamans tend to occupy a respected position within Hmong society. Throughout recorded history the Hmong have been peasant or tribal farmers in the mountainous regions of Indochina (the northern parts of Laos and Vietnam), Thailand, and Burma, and throughout adjacent parts of southwestern China, particularly in the Chinese provinces of Yunnan and Sichuan, Guizhou, and Guangxi. They have generally cultivated their crops through a system of shifting cultivation, in an economy oriented toward subsistence needs and self-sufficiency, which yet has often had important relations with local markets.

The Hmong language serves as an important index of their identity and is related to very few other languages. Although some linguists classify the language as part of the Sino-Tibetan language family, others see it as part of a Tai-Kadai group related to the Tai and Thai languages. Still others, however, affirm that the evidence is not yet sufficient to locate Hmong firmly within any particular language group, so that it is best thought of as forming one of a group of languages shared with the Yao (Iu Mien) and She peoples. Together with the A Hmao people, the Qho Xiong people, and the Hmu (or Khanao) people, the Hmong form part of a much wider group of loosely related peoples in China who are today classified officially by the Chinese government as the "Miao." In history, the term "Miao" (Meau or "Meo" in its Southeast Asian variant term) had strongly derogatory overtones. Most Hmong outside China resent the term and do not wish to be known by it.

However, the term "Hmong," because it is not a Chinese word, could not be written in traditional Chinese characters, so all the historical records that are available in China speak only of the "Miao," and never of the "Hmong." At times this term was used very widely indeed, to include all the ethnic minority peoples in the southern parts of China. Today in China the term has changed its formerly unpleasant-sounding meaning, and the

Hmong in China are now quite happy, and often proud, to be called "Miao." The Miao are one of the officially approved 56 nationalities (*minzu*) of China, 55 of which are minority nationalities, the Han Chinese being the one majority. Because of their minority status, these minority nationalities receive special benefits in the form of educational subsidies, preferential employment policies, and lower pass marks for college and university entrance, besides exemptions from the "one-child one-family" family planning policy. So "Miao" in China is not a term of abuse, but rather an official category, grouping the Hmong together with some other loosely related peoples. People in China apply to be recognized members of the category, and consider themselves fortunate if they are recognized in this way.

Early references in the Chinese historical classics, compiled around the time of Christ but referring to earlier versions that were probably composed five or six centuries before the Christian era, mention the Miao, under whom we assume some ancestors of the Hmong were included, as a rebellious and savage people. They were said to have been defeated by the ancestors of the Han Chinese and banished from the central plains by the legendary founders of the Chinese state in the third millennium BCE. There are brief references to them from 221 BCE to 207 CE, but then the term disappeared entirely from all the records for several centuries. It did not reappear again, except for a very few isolated mentions after 618 CE, until the twelfth century CE.[8] From that time on, although the term was often widely applied to all the non-Han southern populations, ancestors of the Hmong today were almost certainly included in these references to the Miao.

The Han Chinese population in southern China expanded immeasurably after the introduction of maize and potato from the New World to China in the sixteenth century. Southern China, a maze of ethnic heterogeneity and linguistic diversity at that time, was increasingly settled and colonized by Han Chinese troops, officials, farmers, miners, and traders from the central and northern regions. As the Han Chinese population expanded into what is today the southern parts of China, natural resources, in particular land and water, became scarcer and scarcer in relation to those who sought to use them. Fierce conflicts and struggles began to develop over which groups should use them and who should control them. It is possible that it was at this time that some groups of Hmong were forced up into the inhospitable mountains to practice what is known as shifting cultivation of dry-field crops such as barley, wheat, millet, buckwheat, and upland rice. The ancestors of the Hmong prior to this time may have been more settled agriculturalists, cultivating irrigated rice in the plains. However, shifting cultivation (known as cultivation "by the sword and fire" in the Chinese records) has always been associated with the Miao in China since the very earliest records we have of their cultivation practices. At lower altitudes in largely mountainous southern China it was possible to plant varieties of rice which do not require irrigation by the shifting cultivation method, while other cereals were grown higher up. In what is known as the pioneer type of shifting cultivation traditionally practiced by the Hmong, the virgin forest is burned and crops sown among the ashes by hand. After some 12 years of continuous planting on these patches of land in the forest, the soil fertility gradually begins to decrease, the crops do not grow well, and so the village or settlement as a whole must move onward to find new forest to clear for new cultivations. Sometimes these moves were extensive, of up to 100 miles.[9] The original land is left fallow and should without population pressure revert to secondary forest, so the system can also be seen as one of fallow management. The traditional Hmong economy was not only agricultural, but also included important elements of animal husbandry, hunting, and fishing in mountain streams or rivers. Wild game used to be plentiful in the forest, while pigs and poultry such as ducks and chickens have always been commonly raised by Hmong families in Asia.

Early Western colonial writers and ethnographers of the Hmong in the Chinese borderlands pointed out many similarities of their social customs to the very earliest practices ever recorded in China, particularly the love duets sung between young girls and boys at the New Year and the courting

Traditional Hmong farming environment. Courtesy of the authors.

game of catch, which takes place at that time. Sometimes in the older literature the Hmong were referred to as "aboriginal Chinese."[10] Their versions of their history have only been recorded quite recently, since the language had no form of writing until 1959 when the Romanized Phonetic Alphabet (RPA) for Hmong was invented through collaboration between Roman Catholic and Protestant missionaries in Laos. In these orally transmitted histories, Hmong stories and legends speak of a long history of loss, deprivation, and exploitation, which their ancestors certainly underwent. Many of these oral legends tell how the Hmong lost their lands and their sovereignty to the Chinese, often because of deceptions and trickery by the stronger and more dominant Chinese.[11] The widespread story of the loss of writing (which other people besides the Hmong near the Sino-Tibetan borderlands with India also have) tells of how the Hmong once had their own form of written language.[12] According to various tales, it was while they were being chased by the fierce Chinese across a huge river that these precious Hmong writings either were dropped, eaten up by horses, or eaten by the people because they were hungry. Therefore, now it is said the Hmong are clever in their hearts (*siab*, livers), while the (Han) Chinese are only clever in books.[13]

The history of the Hmong—both in China together with other ethnic groups and more recently since 1900 in Vietnam, Laos, and Thailand—has been a long one of discrimination and impoverishment, of domination and resistance. Throughout the course of this history, the Hmong as a people have struggled fiercely to maintain their own language and identity, and by and large, succeeded despite overwhelming odds against them. Geddes mentioned that theirs has been an unparalleled history comparable to that of the Jews who lost their homeland and were widely scattered in history, and yet managed to retain a strong sense of their cultural identity.[14] A history of exploitation and persecution is related in many Hmong historical legends and is supported by available historical materials. The expansion over the past 1,000 years of the Han Chinese people into southern China where the ancestors of the Hmong lived was characterized by the dispossession of minority peoples, forcible extortion of taxation and corvée labor from them, and often trickery and deception that resulted in the most fertile lands falling into the hands of the Chinese. There are many historical accounts of these processes, and also of repeated Miao rebellions in Chinese history that showed their desire to retain their independence and their fertile lands. The fact that the Hmong lived in the most remote mountain fastnesses, where the land was least fertile, and practiced shifting, rather than permanent-field cultivation, itself speaks of a long historical process in which stronger state-based people became dominant at the expense of peoples without writing and without the abilities to defend themselves against encroachments from the outside. Since Hmong society has a classically segmentary or tribal organization based on lineages and clans of equal weighting, without a centralized form of government or control, this kinship system, which we emphasize in Chapter 10, has been seen by some as accounting for their ability to resist the might of historic states in Asia. It has also been seen as a source of the strength and resilience with which they retained their culture and language[15] despite all the forcible attempts to make them Chinese, Vietnamese, Lao, or Thai that are so well documented since the eighteenth century. As early as the eighteenth century in Guizhou province of China, Chinese administrators discussed setting up schools to "civilize" the minority people they saw as barbarians and ways of introducing them to wearing Chinese clothes, speaking Chinese, and adopting Chinese manners generally. Yet, probably because of their clan or lineage system, the Hmong have survived such historical pressures, to remain a remarkably homogeneous ethnic group today.

Rebellions and fierce clashes between the Miao, who traditionally had no political organization above the village level, and the Chinese are recorded throughout written Chinese history. Wiens lists many of these occurring from the twelfth century onward.[16] In the eighteenth and nineteenth centuries, almost constant campaigns of suppression or "pacification" were recorded taking place against the Miao, particularly in the Guizhou and Hunan provinces of today. Particularly violent and major Miao rebellions took place in 1733 to 1737, 1795 to 1807, and 1854 to 1873.[17] These major uprisings against the tightening of Chinese rule and the various iniquities and extortions associated with it included various ethnic minorities in China. But almost certainly they also included ancestors of the present-day Hmong who played a major role in them.[18] These rebellions were very savagely suppressed by the imperial Chinese forces. Western travelers like Margary and McCarthy traveling through these regions shortly afterward left good accounts of the ravages suffered, with villages razed to the ground and whole populations slaughtered.[19] So these oral legends of a history of persecution and oppression by the Chinese have some basis in real historical facts, and have become important in forming the consciousness of the global Hmong today, because they often see themselves as a people in exile from their rightful lands and homes.

THE EXODUS FROM CHINA

Particularly dense areas of Hmong settlement in China today are in Wenshan autonomous district on the Vietnam border; Bijie, a county in northwest Guizhou province; and the area adjoining the provinces of Guizhou, Sichuan, and Yunnan. But many Hmong live in scattered and dispersed villages throughout the four southern provinces of Guizhou, Yunnan, Sichuan, and Guangxi, where their villages are interspersed with the villages of other ethnic groups. The population of the Miao in China today is 9.6 million; ethnic Hmong speakers account for up to a third of these.[20] Hmong in Vietnam, Thailand, and Laos tell of having originated from a place in China called (in Hmong) *Paj Tawg Teb*, or "Flower Blossoming Country." The older (pre-revolutionary) Chinese name for Wenshan, as it is now known, was Kaihua, which also means "Opening Flowers," and probably this is the area the ancestors of most Southeast Asian Hmong migrated from.

Unlike almost all other Miao groups only the Hmong left China, from the eighteenth century onward, to migrate into the neighboring mountains of northern Indochina. From here they slowly infiltrated into Thailand and also into some parts of Burma (Myanmar), where some small groups still remain. After the failure of their various nineteenth-century insurrections, the Hmong and related A Hmao people suffered terrible exploitation and discrimination at the hands of local Yi landlords and Han Chinese settlers in the region of southern China.[21] From this time onward, large numbers of Hmong began to arrive in Yunnan, Tongkin (as the northern part of Vietnam was then called), and the northern Laotian states. Migration swelled particularly after the defeat in 1864 of a major rebellion in southern China, the Taiping rebellion, in which some Hmong were almost certainly involved, and in 1868 as many as 10,000 Hmong are recorded as arriving in Vietnam from Guizhou province of China.[22] From around 1850, northern Vietnam was plagued by bandit armies of marauding Chinese rebels who were in flight from the central Chinese authorities they had rebelled against. These "banner" armies, as they were known, employed ethnic minority members including many Hmong, as their troops, couriers, porters, and grooms. Some of these armies were then hired by the central Vietnamese state in Tongkin to suppress their own local rebellions in Vietnam, and to act as a balance against the growing influence of the French, who were soon to colonize this entire region of Indochina, including present-day Laos, Vietnam, and Cambodia.

In northern Indochina, the Hmong moved into new nation states whose borders eventually took shape toward the end of the nineteenth century under the impact of the French colonization of Vietnam, Laos, and Cambodia, and the British colonization of Burma. Prior to colonization, these colonial areas had been very loosely administered, if they were administered at all, often with a local ruler paying tributary allegiance to a number of stronger states.

Historically, there was a particularly close relationship between the Southeast Asian Hmong and Yunnanese Chinese who had also immigrated into these regions. This relationship was based partly on the opium economy, which had emerged throughout southern China after the Opium Wars in which Western powers forced the Chinese to permit the import of opium in exchange for gold, silk, and tea. To avoid these imports, the Chinese administration in the late nineteenth century encouraged the home growing of opium, which rapidly spread through the mountainous areas where the Hmong lived. The Hmong developed an integrated highland economy throughout the region, well described by many writers of the past; dry (unirrigated) rice was cultivated on the mountain slopes by methods of shifting cultivation and in the winter months it was rotated with crops of maize and the opium poppy that was used as a cash crop. This was combined with the animal husbandry of pigs and chickens, some fishing, hunting wild animals, and gathering wild products in the forest.[23] Horses were kept as pack animals. Land was farmed by local patrilineal descent groups, who were often several closely related families such as the families of brothers and perhaps a first cousin. Opium was sold to Chinese traders and paid for with the silver that the Hmong used for bridewealth payments or in credits of rice before the harvest, because rice production was chronically insufficient. Wealth was stored in the form of silver and mostly worn. Silver was an important need when a young man got married since his family was expected to make a large marriage payment to the family of the bride. In the last years of the nineteenth century, Hmong shifting cultivators started to move into the uplands of northern Thailand along routes from Laos and from Burma.[24]

THAILAND

The Hmong population of Thailand is currently around 124,000, and around 450,000 in Laos (2005 census), perhaps only 2,656 in Burma, and close to 1 million in Vietnam.[25] Thailand was the only Southeast Asian country never to be colonized by Europeans, although neighboring Burma and Malaysia were colonized by the British, and Vietnam and Laos by the French. Traditional borders were extremely porous, and movement across them was common. Until 40 years ago, the Hmong in Thailand were able to retain their traditional lifestyles as upland village cultivators, establishing villages mostly in the mountainous foothills at about 3,000 to 5,000 feet above sea level. As large populations of Thai people moved up into the hills to farm from the 1970s onward, the land available for shifting cultivation became increasingly scarce, and extensive construction of roads, mining concessions, and forestry enterprises further deforested the region and led to the virtual end of the traditional forms of shifting cultivation by the 1980s. However, it is still quite common for individual households, or sections of villages, to move to other locations near already settled Hmong villages elsewhere. Opium, previously a Royal Thai Government monopoly, was officially banned in Thailand in 1958. However, its cultivation was still tolerated for more than two decades, often at the whim of a local official. This led to the invidious position for many Hmong households of being allowed to cultivate it by local officials in return for bribes that some officials used to supplement their meager official salaries.

In 1967, heavy-handed government efforts to eradicate communism sparked a full-scale ethnic Hmong rebellion in northern Thailand, after a Hmong village that had refused to pay the last of several successive attempts at extortion was burned down.[26] Hmong villages suspected of harboring communists began to be indiscriminately napalmed, and this kind of overreaction by government forces, assisted by U.S.-funded and trained paramilitaries (the Border Patrol Police), ironically drove many Hmong into the arms of the Communist Party of Thailand (CPT). For some 15 years, the Hmong in Thailand were divided between those who remained in areas controlled by the government and those who had fled away from government restrictions deeper into "the jungle," as it was known, to join the communists, who had taken up an armed struggle against the government. This only ended in 1981 to 1982 with a general amnesty and reconciliation, and the peaceful surrender of the CPT to the government. Since that time, the Hmong in Thailand have mostly given up their old dependence on the production of opium and moved into new market gardening enterprises of flowers and cool-climate fruits, vegetables, and corn for sale in lowland markets. However, new drugs such as heroin, ice, and methamphetamines have now become the scourge of many highland villages, and new problems have surfaced over the Hmong use of fertilizers and pesticides, which are necessary to support their new crops. For many years, Thai government efforts, assisted by many international development programs, aimed to make the Hmong give up their shifting cultivation practices, because they were seen as harming the forest (although the forest was in fact mostly being removed by large-scale loggers, roads, and other central government interventions). However, now that the Hmong have largely abandoned shifting cultivation and are trying to produce commercial crops for the market on settled cultivation lands in replacement of opium, they are often attacked for the chemical fertilizers and pesticides they now must use.[27]

Despite these problems, and continued discrimination in Thai society against ethnic minorities, many of whom still lack citizenship rights or proper tenure rights to the lands they cultivate, Thai Hmong villages today continue to show some of the aspects of a much more traditional Hmong lifestyle. At the same time as this, though, there are increasing numbers of Hmong living in urban areas, engaged in new jobs such as teachers, traders, agricultural officials, and in the police or military service. Thus, there have been great changes among young Hmong people in Thailand in almost every aspect of life.

VIETNAM AND LAOS

Vietnam and Laos, together with Cambodia, were part of the French colonies of Indochina. The history of the Hmong in Vietnam and Laos was not as peaceful as it has generally been in Thailand. In both countries, the Hmong were involved in and fragmented by the conflict of global ideologies that became the Vietnam War. In many ways their global situation today, in the United States, France, Australia, and elsewhere, can be traced back directly to this momentous conflict. In northern Vietnam, Hmong fought on both sides in the First Indochina War (1946 to 1954), as the communist forces of Ho Chi Minh battled the old French colonial rulers after the ending of World War II and the Japanese occupation of Vietnam. Hmong were crucial in the tremendous defeat of the French by the communist and nationalist forces at Dien Bien Phu in May 1954.[28] As lords of the rugged mountain borderlands where much of the struggle was fought, the Hmong performed well on both sides as fighters, guides, porters, and spies. Often they tried to avoid any political involvement and adopted a neutral stance. Some villages crossed to Thailand and back several times to avoid visits by either communists or royalists. Yet avoiding participation in this way was impossible in the end because of their strategic locations along the borders and also because of their primary involvement, mainly as producers rather than traders, in the economy of opium, which is now known to have funded the military efforts on both sides.

Prior to the Revolution of Laos in 1975, when Laos became a socialist country (at the same time as the U.S. retreat from Vietnam), there had already been some 30 years of civil war between opposing forces in Laos. There were three main political parties. The socialist Pathet Lao, who were strongest in the northeastern provinces of Phong Saly and Sam Neua, a dense area of Hmong settlement, were closely allied with the Vietnamese communists and received military, tactical, and logistic support from China and the Union of Soviet Socialist Republics (USSR). Besides these, there were the neutralists, more liberal-leaning people who favored some sort of compromise with the communists. And then there was the royal government of Laos, which was the recipient of massive amounts of overseas economic and military support from the United States and from the South-East Asian Treaty Organization (SEATO), which included many other countries such as Australia and Britain. The Hmong were caught up in this nationwide conflict partly owing to clan conflicts that stemmed back to the 1930s. In 1917, Lo Bliayao, a local Hmong leader, had been nominated by the French colonial authorities to be the chief of Nong Het, which was a large Hmong area in Xieng Khouang province (near Vietnam). However, Faydang, his son, lost this position in 1939 to a member of the Ly clan, Touby Lyfoung, who was in fact his affinal relation, being the son of old Lauj Bliayao's own son-in-law, Lyfoung, who had married Faydang's sister. Touby had been educated in the French educational system and was a sophisticated figure, more approved of by the French than the previous leaders. A major feud broke out between the two families of the Lis (Ly/Lee), who generally supported the colonial government at that time, and the Lauj (Lo) clan of Lo Bliayao, who later supported the communist Pathet Lao and their allies in neighboring Vietnam, the Viet Minh, in their conflict against the French. During World War II, the country was occupied by the Japanese and a fierce underground resistance was mounted against them. Faydang, already alienated from the French regime by this time, supported the Japanese, but his relative Touby helped French military officers in the resistance and organized a Hmong militia against the Japanese that was later instrumental in freeing Xieng Khouang from the Japanese.

After the war ended, Touby and his militia turned to suppressing the communists in defense of the returned colonial government; they beat back Viet Minh attacks on Nong Het and subsequently, in 1946, Touby was appointed as the county governor for all the Hmong in Xieng Khouang province in 1946. This was the highest official position any Hmong in Laos had so far achieved. Later he rose still further, to become a deputy minister and a minister in the restored Royal Lao Government (RLG). Meanwhile, his maternal uncle Faydang also rose high in the ranks of the insurgent Pathet Lao, eventually becoming a Politburo member. Hmong stories tell of how Touby's father, Lyfoung, had constantly beaten his wife (Faydang's sister), so that she committed suicide in 1922. They also tell how her Lauj father and her Lis husband were buried on opposite sides of the same mountain. In the system of geomancy that the Hmong (like the Chinese) use, this burial on opposite sides of the mountain signals their endless opposition. It is sometimes said that this was the original cause of the huge conflict between the two families of the Lauj and the Lis, which eventually polarized the entire Hmong community of Laos between support for the rightists and the communists. At this time globalization had already reached the Hmong, with their involvement in a conflict ultimately between China and the USSR on the one side, who supported the Viet Minh and Pathet Lao in Vietnam and Laos, and on the other side the United States, besides Great Britain, France, Thailand, Pakistan, the Philippines, Australia, and New Zealand (the members of SEATO).

A few Hmong had already gone abroad, prior to the Revolution of 1975, under various educational and training programs, to the United States, France, and Australia, while some Hmong on the other side had been sent by the communists in Vietnam and Laos to the other socialist countries including the USSR, China, Czechoslovakia, and even East Germany for further training and education. In many ways, the exodus of Hmong from Laos to Western countries after 1975 arose from the inter-penetration of local interests, conflicts, and divisions with national and international ones that occurred at this time.

A soldier who had originally served under Touby became commander of the Second Military Region in Northern Laos and a general in the Royal Lao Army in 1964. This was General Vang Pao, a member of the Vang clan, and the Hmong soldiers he led played a very important part in the (ulti-mately unsuccessful) defense of Laos against the communists. The troops he led are often referred to as a "secret army," but in actual fact only some of the battalions he led were trained and funded from special funds of the CIA; the rest were members of the regular Royal Lao Army. The Hmong in both the former French colonies of Vietnam and Laos attained levels of po-litical participation that they have to this day never achieved in Thailand; elite Laotian Hmong, for instance, attended French schools and were edu-cated overseas.

However, the Hmong community in Laos was shattered and fragmented by warfare in a way that never occurred for the Hmong in Thailand. Satura-tion American bombing in the 1960s devastated most Hmong areas in Laos, and enforced relocations and flights from conflict zones after 1961 led to thousands of Hmong becoming displaced persons within their own country of Laos even before they left Laos and became refugees beginning in 1975. According to Hamilton-Merritt, among the total displaced population in Laos of 370,000 at this time, 32 percent were Hmong.[29] Well over 12,000 Hmong (out of a total Hmong population in Laos of some 300,000) are estimated to have died in these conflicts on the RLG side[30]; some estimates consider a third of the Hmong were casualties, but these may be too high.

The Exodus from Laos

In May 1975, Vang Pao finally left Laos, accompanied by several senior cabinet and military leaders of the former government, following a two-year period of provisional government that had seen the progressive withdrawal of American support and increasing communist Pathet Lao influence in the country. Some important Hmong leaders at that time, including Touby Lyfoung, Lyteck Lynhiavu, and Yang Dao, tried to convince the Hmong to stay on in the new Pathet Lao-controlled Laos. However, it soon became clear that anyone involved with the former government, particularly Hmong, would be disfavored under the new regime. And disfavor was soon to turn to outright persecution. About 5,000 were estimated to have left in the spring of 1975, when some hundreds of the Hmong elite and lucky others were airlifted by American and Hmong pilots out of Long Cheng, which was a huge Hmong settlement and military settlement north of Vientiane, the capital; by the end of the war it had a population of 50,000, sometimes referred to as the first Hmong city. Some of these were able to go straight to France under a parole agreement between France and Laos; others joined relatives who were already studying abroad.

After the flight of their leaders and fearful of the implications of the new accommodation that had been reached with the Pathet Lao, Hmong from the large settlement of Long Cheng (which had been Vang Pao's headquarters), began walking toward Ban Sorn, which was the last major Hmong settlement toward the south, from where they could reach the Mekong River and, they hoped, a new life of freedom in Thailand. This movement has been well described in a number of accounts and is still vividly remembered by many Hmong refugees today; whole families traveled together with all they could carry of their household belongings, in a movement of tragic exodus that has become so characteristic of the history of twentieth-century population displacement. Less than half of them actually made it to Thailand; many fell victim to ambushes and arrests, became sick, or particularly the very young and the very old died of hunger and fatigue on the way. Then the rumor spread that Ban Sorn was a trap set by the Pathet Lao for them, and the Hmong headed toward Vientiane, in an effort to reach Thailand.

On May 29, however, a terrible and unforgotten massacre took place; Pathet Lao soldiers fired openly on a crowd of several thousand Hmong refugees at Hin Heup bridge across the Nam Ngum River, the point of access to Vientiane. Controversy still rages about the ultimate responsibility for this. It was a time of enormous confusion, with families separated and lost, hiding in the mountains and forest, or fleeing toward the Thai border during the night. Many felt betrayed by the flight of Vang Pao and their leaders, although many still trusted that somehow Vang Pao would come to their rescue in the end. The United States authorized the admission of the first group of 3,466 Laotians from the Thai refugee camps to the United States in August; Vang Pao and his immediate followers were safely resettled in the United States by December.

For those left behind in Laos, a nightmare period soon began of arbitrary arrests and so-called re-education sessions under the Pathet Lao regime, which was formally installed as the new government in December 1975. As a result, many of the Hmong who had decided to stay or had been unable to flee were forced to take refuge in the mountains within Laos itself, abandoning their homes and livelihoods. A vigorous Hmong resistance movement grew up that received some support from elements of the military and paramilitary in Thailand and, there should be no doubt about this, some elements within the U.S. military. Although most Hmong felt the United States had abandoned them and their struggle for the freedom of Laos at this time, there were also many old-time American military and intelligence officers—some but not all stationed in Thailand—who felt loyal to their Hmong friends and continued to support them with advice, training, and funds. As the Pathet Lao increased its own activities against Hmong dissidents in Laos, so the numbers of Hmong fleeing to Thailand also increased. The first group of 2,500 Hmong refugees arrived in Nong Khai refugee camp in May 1975. By the end of 1979 (when nearly 3,000 refugees crossed the Mekong in a single month), the number of refugees in these camps along the Thai border with Laos was nearly 60,000.

THE THAI REFUGEE CAMPS

In the camps, the Hmong encountered a new kind of life, and a new kind of culture emerged. Although the wars in Laos had disrupted traditional Hmong farming life for many years, and many Hmong within Laos had already become nurses or pilots, soldiers, factory workers, or mechanics, as refugees in Thailand their traditional life and culture was entirely devastated. The Hmong have always prized their independence and their self-sufficiency. Now (like some of those who had been displaced people in resettlement zones in Laos during the war) they were dependent on others for food and had no way to make a living or support themselves.

In the beginning, there was a holding camp at Panat Nikhom, Thailand, and altogether five main refugee camps along the border with Laos, where Hmong and other highland refugees from Laos, such as the Mien (Yao) and Tai Dam (Black Tai) or Khmu, were housed. Families sometimes stayed in these camps for years, even a decade or more; there were many there who were simply fearful to leave and embark on completely new lives in Western countries, or felt they had to remain with elderly parents or ailing relatives who were too ill to travel. Many Hmong were born and brought up in these camps, in an atmosphere remembered by those who visited the camps at that time of gloom, grief, and regret for the lost past in Laos. The camps were officially run by the United Nations High Commission on Refugees (UNHCR) in coordination with the Thai government's Interior Ministry, who actually administered them.

Therefore, although the UN provided funding and some oversight, the camps were largely in the hands of Thai administrators. From the start, it cannot be said that the Thai government welcomed the refugees, even though the location of refugees along the strategic border of Thailand with Laos provided a potential weapon and bulwark against their new communist neighbors. Many refugees lived in constant fear and insecurity owing to the Thai government policy of arbitrary closures of camps and relocations of refugees from one site to another. Most of the agencies helping with educational and health work in the camps, such as World Vision, Christian and Missionary Alliance (CMA), Young Women's Christian Association (YWCA), and Catholic Relief Services, were Christian, and many Hmong were converted to Christianity at this time, although Christianity had been quite common among the Hmong in Laos previously. Some Hmong in the camps were either involved in or tacitly supported the Lao resistance movement, which was itself made up of several major factions,[31] so that the camps themselves became places of conflict, deeply factionalized between various religious movements, a new messianic movement that had first emerged in Long Cheng in 1967, and differing political persuasions. Together with Sao Ya (Xauv Yaj), Lis Txais became the leader of the new messianic religion that looked forward to the birth of a new Hmong savior, or claimed he had already been born; the strange mournful music he composed and his reconstructed legends of the Hmong past, mixed with Buddhist and Western themes, permeated life in the camps.[32] New arrivals in the United States dropped for a while from 1983, and many simply refused to be resettled in the West.

In some cases this was for personal reasons, but also it was because of persistent rumors of the horrors of life in America and France; Vang Pao's advice (or instruction) was for his followers to stay in the camps to support the resistance, which, he believed, would eventually liberate Laos. The UN repatriation program sent some Hmong, deemed to be economic rather than political refugees, back to their homes in Laos, but there were terrible rumors about what happened to them there; hardly anyone wished to join these programs because often there was no land available for them to farm, they were discriminated against, or, it is said, they were sent to re-education camps and killed.

By 1977, approximately 104,000 refugees from Laos had arrived in Thailand. More and more Hmong refugees fled Laos over the next four years owing to their increasing harassment under the Pathet Lao government and the use of Vietnamese troops to suppress them, in addition to a spreading famine and general hardships within the country. Further flights were fuelled by the rumors of "Yellow Rain," the chemical bombing of Hmong villages and settlements.[33] In 1978 the total of Laotian refugees in Thailand, including lowland Lao as well as other highland minorities, was 57,000. Lee reported that there were 48,937 registered Hmong in the refugee camps in March 1980, a month in which there had been 998 new arrivals.[34] A figure of approximately 50,000 remained quite constant in the following years.[35]

The figures cannot be entirely accurate, since the UN classed the Hmong with other highlanders (such as the Iu Mien) as "Highland Minorities," while other figures give a total of all Laotian refugees including the lowland Laotians themselves; however, the real figures are very close to those given here. And it should be added that quite a significant number, officially reckoned in Thailand at some 32,000, quietly filtered out of the refugee camps, either through marriages with Hmong already living in Thailand or through some other means, to join relatives in Hmong villages in Thailand. Moreover, approximately 30,000 of the old fighters and their families took refuge in the vicinity of the notorious Thai Buddhist temple of Wat Tam Krabok; their relocation has been for years a matter of ongoing concern, and it was only in 2006 that the last of the 16,000 of these who had been accepted for resettlement were finally found new homes in the U.S.

Let us look at this massive outflow of Hmong to the West from the point of view of some of the receiving countries. A further 8,000 Laotian refugees were approved to settle in the United States in 1977, and altogether 46,700 "Lao Highlanders" (90 percent of whom are estimated to be Hmong) had been resettled in the United States by the end of 1980. Numbers of admissions decreased after this, with less than 4,000 received in the United States in 1981 and 2,500 in 1982; in 1986, which marked the end of this process of mass immigration, 3,670 admissions were made. Hmong refugees were dispersed across the world in what has now become a global diaspora. The overwhelming majority by far went to the United States, where the major areas of settlement are now in California, Minnesota, and Wisconsin (although there are many other significant Hmong communities in Denver; Chicago; Providence, Rhode Island; North Carolina; and elsewhere).

In 1982, there were 6,000 to 8,000 Hmong in France and the colony of French Guyana, up to 500 in Australia (originally 340 were settled there), 200 in Canada, 100 in Argentina, while a smaller number were resettled in China.[36] The U.S. Office of Refugee Resettlement in Washington, D.C., estimated that by 1983 there was a total of 61,000 to 64,000 Hmong settled in the United States. From 1975 to 1985, 520,000 Southeast Asian refugees had been resettled, nearly 70 percent of whom were in the United States. More than 90,000 Hmong had been resettled in the United States by 1990, 7,000 in France and French Guyana, 650 in Canada, and 350 in Australia. Smaller numbers went to Argentina, New Zealand, Sweden, Germany, Japan, and China. For instance, five Hmong families (comprising only 23 people) were resettled in Germany in 1979 after their original plan to resettle in Argentina (which currently has a Hmong population of some 250) failed. Now their population has grown to 16 families (92 people) owing to natural increase as well as the arrival of two Hmong students from the previous communist country of East Germany after it was reunified with West Germany in 1990; they subsequently went back to Laos and Thailand (respectively) to find Hmong brides, whom they brought back to Germany with them, making up nine out of the total 92 Hmong population of Germany.[37]

Besides their historical marginalization and persecution in China and slow movement into the mountains of Southeast Asia, this recent refugee exodus out of Asia has proved an indescribably traumatic experience for many individual Hmong, and perhaps for the Hmong community as a whole. Whole families were broken up by the process of resettlement, so that many refugee families in the United States may have some close family members in France, others in Laos or Thailand, or other "third countries" like Canada or Australia. Life in the refugee camps meant a slow induction into Western values for the Hmong, particularly because of the impact of Christian missions and international aid agencies like Oxfam. Birth rates in the camps were extremely high, as there was a strong desire to repair the population devastated by the warfare in Laos; nearly half of the camp population were children. Divorces and separations, previously very rare in Hmong society, increased. Traditional gender relations started to change dramatically; the men had little to do, but the women still maintained their roles as household keepers and carers of children, besides engaging in the new trade of stitching "story-cloths" and other items of costumes for the new tourist trade in hill tribe materials; these were sold both to visitors to the camps and through a network of Hmong relatives in Thailand. Women's status has continued to improve for the better in the new life in Western countries with new opportunities for education and employment, and radically decreased birth rates.

A GLOBALIZED HMONG PEOPLE

In their new lives in the West there have been many individual success stories despite the difficulties and tragedies of global dispersal. There are now flourishing Hmong grocery and retail stores, transnational businesses, local housing and credit associations; there are Hmong-language newspapers, online journals, and several academic or community centers for Hmong studies and international conferences devoted to the Hmong; there are Hmong rock bands and a growing trade in Hmong-language videos. Local Hmong activities, like gathering matsutake mushrooms in Oregon, are linked into the world economy.[38] There are Hmong-language Web sites and others in English offering general information on the Hmong, their historical background, and culture; and there are Hmong radio stations and phone-in chat shows. Hmong culture has always placed a very high value on education, and increasingly members of the younger generation in the United States and Canada have been gaining master's or doctoral degrees in a range of subjects, although these success rates are not reflected as well in France or Australia.

Differences have emerged between the generations and the genders, as what commonly happens after the first generation of new immigrants is born into highly developed countries. Often younger people show little interest in Hmong traditions, language, or history, to the great concern of many in the older generation. So efforts are underway to actively teach and transmit the important aspects of Hmong social traditions; in many Hmong locations outside Asia, as well as in Thailand, centers have been set up where Hmong cultural knowledge is taught, for example, in the form of language classes, the wedding songs, or the playing of the reed pipes (*tshuab qeej*). In China some state-employed academics have established courses in Miao history and culture to attract wealthy American Hmong students, although generally there is not much Hmong content to these classes. There is a strong feeling that such knowledge, which may formerly have been passed from father to son, or master to apprentice, may soon be lost, so that its urgent transmission is becoming a matter of collective endeavors.

CONCLUSION

In 2002, there were more than 1,427,564 Hmong living outside China, with 190,000 outside Asia and probably 1,241,656 in Southeast Asia. More than 170,000 are in the United States. Not all Hmong abroad have been able to revisit their home countries in Laos, Thailand, Vietnam, or China, yet the awareness of these homelands is generally still strong among the Hmong in their new lives outside Asia. The Hmong have had a long and a noble history, although much of this is not recorded. They have also been noted for their love of independence and equality, which arises from the segmentary tribal nature of their social structure based on patrilineal clans. Most commentators have remarked on their remarkable achievement of maintaining their strong sense of ethnic and cultural identity despite a history of persecution and oppression by the members of stronger and more powerful states. Divided between several nation-states in modern Asia (Thailand, Laos, Vietnam, Burma, and China), there is a strong awareness of the importance of Hmong cultural traditions and the value of the past. Since the flight of Hmong from Laos after 1975, their global dispersal as refugees from the conflicts of Indochina has led to new forms of consciousness, new ways of living, and new understandings of themselves and others.

NOTES

1. See Lemoine 2005.
2. Armstrong 1976, 393–94.
3. Clifford 1997, 247.
4. Armstrong 1976, 393.
5. Cohen 1997.
6. Cohen 1996, 515.
7. Romero 2008, 1.
8. Ruey 1962.
9. Geddes 1976.
10. Granet 1930.
11. Tapp 1989.
12. See Blackburn 2007.
13. Tapp 1989; Pollard 1919; Hudspeth 1937.
14. Geddes 1976, 10.
15. Lemoine 2008.
16. Wiens 1954.
17. Jenks 1994.
18. Lombard-Salmon 1972; Jenks 1994; McMahon 2002; Sutton 2006.
19. Margary 1876; McCarthy 1879. See also Anderson 1876; Clarke 1911.
20. Lemoine 2005.
21. Pollard 1919.
22. Lemoine 1995.
23. Geddes 1976.
24. Much of this historical overview follows Tapp 2004, which in turn partly followed Tapp 1989 but is greatly expanded and revised.
25. In the case of Burma an extrapolation has been done (see McKinnon and Michaud, 2000).
26. Race 1974.
27. See Forsyth and Walker 2008.
28. McCoy 1972.
29. Hamilton-Merritt 1980; 1993.
30. Lee 1982.

31. Lee 2005a.
32. Tapp 1989.
33. Seagrave 1981; Evans 1983; and Yang Dao 1982.
34. Lee 2008.
35. See Yang Dao 1982; Feith 1988; and Lee 2008.
36. Yang Dao 1982.
37. Tou Yang 2003.
38. Tsing 2008.

2

Thoughts and Religion

THE HMONG TRADITIONALLY believe in the existence of the soul in the human body and the force of spirits in objects in nature. As noted by Graham in China, they

worship no gods or idols, have no temples . . . While they believe in demons that cause disease, they do not worship them, but endeavor to exorcise them or drive them away. It may be said that they worship their ancestors. However, they do not regard their ancestors as deities, and assert that their worship simply includes feelings and acts of commemoration and reverence.[1]

Because of these beliefs, the Hmong organize their social relationships into gender and kinship categories based on the patrilineal ancestral cult of specific groups. Their conception of existence consists of mutual interaction between the living descendants and their dead ancestors, the latter having the power to aid or punish the former who must revere their memories and respect their wishes. Hmong kinship structure is, therefore, really a ritual structure with religious rites and beliefs specific to each category of relationships such as the household, the lineage, the subclan, and the clan.[2] Each category carries its own proper ritual prescriptions and social performances. A household is more than just a shelter and the people living in it. It is a kin group as well as a place for worship, and an appropriate domain for its living members and for the spirits of the dead relatives on the male side.

SHAMANISM AND THE SOUL

In most traditional societies, it is not possible to separate the fields of law, medicine, politics, and religion as sharply as we do in modern societies. Often a single social institution has legal, medical, political, and social functions as well as being religious. This is the case with Hmong shamanism, which is a system for curing illness and other forms of social unhappiness and disharmony, through which the main philosophy of human existence and traditional psychology of the Hmong is expressed. Shamanism is found in traditional societies all over the world and in its classic form exists in Siberia.[3] Shamans are traditional religious experts who have the ability to diagnose illness and cure suffering or other misfortunes such as drought or famine. The shaman is believed to have the ability to enter into the Otherworld by trance or possession and communicate with the spirits there. In some societies, shamans have acted as traditional political leaders and in that way act to express the legal voice of the group; they are believed to have the special gift of seeing deeply into the unknown and revealing the causes of disease and misfortune through their abilities to transcend the normal limitations of time and space.

A contemporary shaman and his assistant. Courtesy of the authors.

The Hmong practice a classic form of shamanism that is clearly of great antiquity. When a person is ill, or a person suffers repeated misfortunes for which there is no ready explanation, or a family is constantly quarrelling or afflicted by misfortune, a shaman may be consulted. Shamans may be men or women, although men are more common, and the position is one of some standing in the society. How does one become a shaman? Shamanism is conceived of as a duty or vocation to help others, rather than oneself or the members of one's own family. The position of a shaman cannot be inherited as such, since shamans are chosen by their shamanic or *dab neeb* spirits. The Hmong often say that you cannot learn to be a shaman, because it is the spirits of shamanism, known as *neeb*, who choose you. The tutelary spirits choose you as a new shaman by making you ill in a strange way for a long time, or as the Hmong sometimes put it, "biting" (*tom*) or "touching" (*yuj*) you. If you are ill in this way, you will go to a shaman to find out what is the matter with you, and then, instead of a normal kind of malady that requires a shaman's intervention to cure, it may be diagnosed that this is no ordinary illness, but one caused by the shamanic spirits of an ancestral line who are afflicting you, because they want to make a shaman out of you.

After an illness is diagnosed as being the result of the intervention of such spirits, there follows a period of apprenticeship to a master shaman (who need not be a member of the immediate family of the person involved). After this the shamanic spirits are divided at a special ritual of initiation between the master (*Xib Hwb*) and the apprentice shaman. The new shaman can then begin to practice as a proper shaman, with his or her own altar, which is kept at the new shaman's home, and a temporary altar set up at the house of a patient when a shamanic ritual is performed there. The altar acts as "home" for the spirits that possess the shaman when he or she is in trance. A shaman, unlike a spirit medium, remains in control of his possessing spirits, and although the Hmong shaman is technically possessed by his *neeb* spirits, he (or she) is the master of them and commands them on his journey to rescue the lost soul of a patient. In trance, the shaman calls on his cavalcade of spirits to guide him. In fact, he calls on all the powers of the cosmos to aid him. The general powers a shaman, or shamaness, calls on in trance include great Hmong deities such as the deity Saub and legendary figures such as the First Couple, and *Pog Ntxoog*, the Sun, the Moon, and the seven stars of the Pleiades, many beasts and birds, such as the tiger, elephant, dragon, dog, eagle, hawk, swallow, woodpecker, bee, and the "digger" wasp. Other powers called on include the great masters of Chinese blacksmithing and of medicine, personifications of the shaman's tools, domestic spirits such as *Txhiaj Meej* (xiameng) and *Xwm Kab* (xue ka), the ancestral spirits of the Hmong, the Chinese, the *Mab* (ma) people, and many other powers including the line of shamanic masters. The shaman wears a veil to symbolize his blindness to this world, while the candle upon his altar symbolizes his inner, or spiritual, sight in the other world.

Shamanic spirits are quite separate from ancestral spirits. Shamanic spirits (*dab neeb*) operate in a specific sphere as healing spirits with their own domain. They float between the world of the living and the sick, and do not reside in the afterworld of the dead as is the case with the ancestral spirits. The shaman may diagnose a sickness as caused by ancestors who need an offering of food, but that is only as it is indicated by what the shaman has seen or experienced in his trance.

In the majority of cases, a sickness is *not* diagnosed as the result of the shamanic spirits seeking a new shaman, nor as a result of ancestral displeasure. A sickness is usually diagnosed as caused by an ancestor seeking food offering or by evil nature spirits who have been offended by the sick person or otherwise wish him harm. In most cases of trouble, disease, or affliction, a family asks a shaman to find out what is the cause of the trouble. He will do this, after a preliminary divination session in which he throws the divination horns (made traditionally out of the end of the horns of a water buffalo or goat, but sometimes out of wood). He is invited to come to the patient's house and enter a trance in front of a temporary altar to the shamanic spirits that he will set up. These divination horns (*kuam*), used at many rituals, are very important, because they are the main and most common means of communicating with the supernatural. They are often thrown (*ntaus kuam*) to determine whether the course of a ritual has been successful and whether an offering has been accepted by the offended spirits or not. The outcome depends on whether the flat or rounded sides of the two horns, conceived of as a male and female couple, match or not when they fall on the ground. At the simplest level, if they land with both their convex (rounded) sides facing upward, this is *yaj* (yang, a sign that the worlds of spirits and of men are in communication and the ritual can proceed). If they land with their convex sides facing downward, this is *yeeb* (yin), and the two worlds are not in communication. If one is up and the other down, the message is not clear and the horns must be thrown again until it is clear. Depending on the precise positional directions of the horns, further diagnoses may be made.

When in a trance the shaman will dance and sing seated on a long wooden bench, from which he sometimes performs acrobatic backward leaps. The bench is known as his "horse" (*nees*), although in ordinary language it is called the *rooj neeb* or shaman's bench, and it appears as if he is riding a cantering horse. Other implements of the shaman include a sharp sword for cutting the evil spirits, the hood to cover his face while in a trance, bell rings he wears on his fingers, a circular rattle shaken in the right hand, and a gong that is beaten by his assistant as he enters a trance and as he leaves it. The shaman performs two sessions, the first being a diagnostic session (*ua neeb saib*), the second being the curing ritual proper (*ua neeb kho*), which is performed after some time when and if it is observed that the patient is showing any signs of initial recovery after the initial diagnostic inquiry. This curing session is *only* undertaken after the patient has shown some signs of recovery from his or her illness, as predicted by the shaman after the first divination or diagnostic session. If no recovery takes place, it means the diagnosis is not correct, and a different shaman may be sought.

As in most Asian societies and many places elsewhere, the body is believed to be inhabited by a number of souls, commonly known as *plig* (pli). Nobody is very sure how many there are or what parts of the body they are attached to, but there are many of them. Some Hmong believe there are seven, some 32 like the Thai people, but most people agree there are at least three of them. Life and health depend on their being attached securely to the body. Some of these souls are a little like mischievous children, and they may wander about, particularly at night when their "owner" (the body) is asleep, whereupon they may get lost, fall down a hole, or even be captured by wild forest spirits. It is the shaman's job to ride his "horse" into the otherworld to see what has happened to the patient's wandering soul. Once he finds it he can rescue it, persuade it to return, or sometimes bargain, trick, or cajole evil spirits who may have caught it to eat, to return it. If a soul stays away a long time from its body, the owner will get sicker and sicker, and eventually die, as the soul seeks to be reborn elsewhere.

The *plig* (or *ntsuj*, as it is sometimes called) is imaged in terms of various poetic metaphors that relate the Hmong self closely to the natural world and the universe as a microcosm. For example, the *ntsuj duab, ntsuab hlauv* is often spoken of, or the soul of shadow and (possibly) iron; then there is the *ntsuj xyoob, ntsuj ntoo*, or the soul of bamboos and trees. There is also the *ntsuj qaib, ntsuj os* (of chickens and ducks), and then the *ntsuj nyuj rag* or spirit of the galloping bull. It will be observed that these types of *plig* mirror very closely a division of the natural world into animal, vegetable, and human spheres.[4] Shamans may talk of other varieties of the soul. It is particularly the chicken-like *plig* that is easily startled and likely to wander away. Parts of the body, too, are thought to be associated with specific *plig*.

While the shaman is performing his mystical operations in the Otherworld in the curing session, the patient will sit anxiously behind him, and usually a chicken or a pig that the shaman has specified has been tied up ready for its sacrifice. Its soul is often seen as a substitute for the soul that has wandered from the sick person. The shaman chants in a mixture of Hmong and antiquated Chinese, a long chant that may take up to two hours, while he or she is in a trance, conjuring up his or her possessing spirits and asking him or her to aid in his search for the lost soul. There are specific rituals designed to block the route to rebirth, to prolong one's "license for life," or to prevent a *plig* from seeking rebirth away from its owner's body. At the end of the trance the shaman is usually exhausted, requiring his assistant to quickly rub his back for him. On coming back to the real world of the living, he will report to the family on what he has seen or done in relation to the soul of the sick person in the Otherworld. They will then eat together, at which point he will receive a small payment for his service and return home.

What is most important is that the patient is the center of attention. Indeed, this is a kind of psychodrama in which the whole family takes part, although they may seem to ignore the shaman and go about their normal business in the house while the shaman chants and bounces up and down vigorously on the wooden stool. Sometimes the shaman will diagnose that the souls of a family have wandered off in different directions, and will perform a special ritual to bring them back together again. This is the case where there is a lot of family disharmony or where a number of family are sick on and off without any apparent reasons.

There is a simpler household ritual to bring back the soul of a sick child called the "calling the soul," or *hu plig*, which is part of the non-shamanic rites that the head of a household or an elder skilled in this ceremony may perform. The person doing the soul-calling does not need to be a shaman. A shaman is only consulted if the sickness is more serious. So shamanism is a health care system as much as it is a religious one. Since shamans may be called on in cases of domestic or community disharmony, it may be said that shamanism has some legal or political functions, too, although this is normally incidental to their main roles since their presence at a dispute settlement is not mandatory. The advice of a shaman is treated with respect, and in the past shamans were often also leaders in war.

Now that many Hmong have become Christians, or even Buddhists, and a younger generation is growing up in the United States and elsewhere who often question the beliefs of their elders, the question is often asked as to whether shamanism actually works. This is a question that could not have arisen in the traditional setting, where the belief system remained unique and unchallenged by other forms of belief. But Hmong shamanism, like most traditional belief systems that form part and parcel of everyday social practices and life, is very difficult to test in this quasi-scientific way, because many times patients recover and it is always impossible to go back and find out whether the patient would have recovered, if shamanism had not been practiced.

Even in traditional Hmong society, shamanism is usually used together with forms of herbal medicine, and then it becomes very difficult to sort out what cure is the result of which intervention. Although many people in Hmong society know some herbal medicines, there is also a form of herbal medicinal knowledge that is passed on somewhat like shamanism, but through women only, who "divide the spirits of herbal medicine" (*faib dab tshuaj*) with an apprentice who wishes to become a herbalist. Herbalists, however, are not chosen by the *dab tshuaj*, and so they are unlike possessive shamans. Anyone can learn to be a herbalist from a senior herbalist, who will then teach the person not only medicinal herbs but also how to maintain the *dab tshuaj* so as to ensure that the herbs will have real health potency. Patients who wish to use the service of an herbalist have to pay a small fee, supposedly to obtain the blessing of the herbal spirits. Now that modern biomedicine is available even in fairly remote Hmong villages in China and Vietnam, it is common for Hmong all over the world to use modern medicine, medicinal herbs, and some shamanic rituals together to ensure health. Hmong in traditional villages sometimes say the best cures are when you first go to a shaman, then to the hospital, then to the shaman again. And sometimes they say that although modern medicine is good for the body (*cev*), shamanism is good for the soul (*plig*), showing a kind of mind-body dualism uncommon in traditional thinking. In the United States and other Western countries where there are not many Hmong shamans and herbalists, however, people usually see a doctor first when they become sick, and only have recourse to traditional healing when all else in the modern health system fails to help.

The Hmong also make use of various justifying explanations to support their beliefs. For example, the reason why shamanism does not always work can be explained with reference to the story of the First Shaman, *Siv Yis*, who was supposed to be summoned back to earth by humanity after his ascent to heaven because so many people were sickening and dying. But everyone overslept and (in one story) in a rage *Siv Yis* threw his instruments of shamanism down to earth and went back to heaven, where various people picked them up and used them, but they were never as effective as when he had first used them.

Some Hmong believe that knowledge deteriorates over historical time, so that people and conditions today can never match those of the past, and over the ages knowledge is gradually whittled away. There is a general awareness of the loss of traditional cultural knowledge, particularly in the new urban settings of Asia and in Western countries. As with other people, it is very often thought by the Hmong that in the remote past, things must have been better than they have become today, and many of their legends and stories of the past confirm this occurrence.

GODS AND SPIRITS

The Hmong world is a spiritualized one that has not become disenchanted. The natural world, from farming tools and the house to mountains and forests, has spirits associated with it. The Otherworld is thought of as populated by spirits. Particular activities, like hunting, have spirits associated with them. And Hmong mythology and folklore often present the stories of epic spiritual figures. There are some particular named spirits, such as *Zaj Laug* (the Old Dragon or Dragon King), *Poj Ntxoog* (an evil forest ogre), semi-legendary personages such as *Yaj Yuam*, the Heavenly Archer who shot eight out of the nine suns down, and personifications of nature such as *Xob* (the winged God of Thunder [and lightning]), and *Nkauj Hnub Nraug Hlis* (the Lady Sun and Lord Moon). There is also a category of spirits of accident and disaster, or malign influence, known as *vij sub vij sw*, and other spirits associated with specialized activities like herbal medicine, blacksmithery, and hunting. While hunting, for instance, the spirits of the woods or hunting must be propitiated (*ntawg dab neem*) and to have good spirits to help one in hunting is known as *muaj neem zoo*. And some special terms must be used instead of everyday ones in order not to upset these spirits. But the main division of spirits (*dab*) for most ordinary Hmong is between the tame ones (*dab nyeg*), who include the household spirits (*dab teev* or *dab vaj dab tsev*), and the wild ones (*dab qus*). The shamanic spirits (*qhua neeb*) form a separate category. The wild ones (including the spirits that aid hunters) live in the forest and nature that traditionally surround Hmong villages, and they can be malevolent. They may haunt particular crags and rocks or trees where one must take care not to walk, and some of them, like the *ntoo xeeb*, or tree spirit, must be propitiated so that they act as protective spirits for the locality. The tame or friendly ones include the ancestral (*dab txwv koob* or *dab niam dab txiv*) and household spirits who preside over specific parts of the house, particularly the hearth and the house-posts, but also the loft and the door. At the New Year all the household spirits are paid respects, and the shaman also honors his or her shamanic spirits.

Although *Siv Yis* was a legendary mortal who had extraordinary healing powers and was the founder of shamanism, he is pitted in the Hmong thinking against a malevolent deity known as *Ntxwj Nyug*, who together with *Nyuj Vaj Tuam Teem* is responsible for issuing licenses or mandates for life on earth, and revoking them or overseeing their expiry. The model here is one of classical Chinese bureaucracy, on which much of Chinese religion is also based. *Nyuj Vaj Tuam Teem* is often pictured as seated behind a majestic writing-desk, issuing and canceling licenses for life with a mighty quill pen. Although *Nyuj Vaj Tuam Teem* may have some relationship with the Chinese Jade Emperor, and the Indian god Yama too may have influenced Hmong beliefs,[5] because the Hmong have not been uninfluenced by neighboring peoples during the course of their long history, *Ntxwj Nyug* is an entirely indigenous Hmong spirit, who inhabits a mountain grotto above 12 ascending mountains in the Otherworld and keeps a herd of heavenly cattle who graze beneath it and whose souls are the souls of living mortals he has captured and made his own. It was when *Ntxwj Nyug* was observed to be killing people as fast as they were born that *Siv Yis* arose to challenge him with the arts of healing. And so the struggle continues today between the forces of death and the forces of healing.

There is also a benevolent Hmong deity, *Saub* or *Yawm Saub*, but he is what is called a *deus otiosus* or an absentee god, somewhat similar to the idea of the ancient Greeks and Romans. That is, he is a deity who was around to help people at the dawn of time but is now generally absent. He may be called on in times of need and sometimes reappears at points of crisis in the course of history. He was responsible for finding seeds at the dawn of time and causing the first hen to lay eggs, and he advised the couple who survived the flood what to do to re-create humanity. What he is not is a Creator, for, like the Chinese, the Hmong have felt no need to explain the origins of the earth in personal terms. But the origins of life itself and many other things are explained in the song that is sung by a ritual expert (who is not necessarily a shaman) when somebody dies, the *Qhuab Ke* or song of "Opening the Way," a prime example of Hmong oral literature.

DEATH AND THE FUNERAL RITES

In traditional Hmong society, as in most tribal societies, morality was relative to the social context. The seriousness of crimes such as murder and incest depended on how closely related to the perpetrator the victim was in terms of clan membership. Of course, thinking about this has dramatically altered under the impact of modernity, but still social status and degree of relatedness remain very important in Hmong society, and one is largely defined according to one's position in society. Although there have never been any hereditary political positions of leadership in Hmong society, seniority and male gender continue to be privileged. So in the case of death, if an infant child dies who has not yet received a name because the traditional name-giving ceremony performed three days after birth has not been completed, very little ritual, if any, would traditionally be required.[6] Social membership and acceptance as human only comes once a name has been given. For a man, full social membership depends on marrying and having children, particularly sons. A woman's status still depends largely on her marriage. Ritual often mirrors social status. Elaboration of death rituals is linked directly to social status for the Hmong, so that a wise elder man, with many sons and grandsons, who dies, deserves the fullest, longest, and most splendid funeral possible. Kinship is always central.

Besides paying respects to the ancestors and practicing shamanism, the funeral and the New Year are the main occasions for the most elaborate Hmong rituals and beliefs. It is on these occasions that, as it were, Hmong culture is on display. At death in a traditional village three gunshots are fired and messengers are sent out to all surrounding villages to alert relatives and friends who begin to arrive to pay their respects at the dead person's house. A funeral may last from three to 10 days, depending on the status of the person who has died. The corpse is kept inside the house until the last day and is fanned (to keep flies away from it) by the daughters and daughters-in-law, in the case of an elderly individual, for instance. First it is washed by the sons and dressed in a special suit of death clothes made and kept for this occasion. Roles are divided up for the funeral—ideally there should be two people to beat the wooden drum with cowhide made specially for each funeral and hung from the main post of the house, two people to serve and cook the food, two people to chop the firewood, two to make the coffin, two to carry the water from the well to use in the house, two masters of ceremony, and so on. And the ritual expert who will sing the song *Qhuab Ke*, "Opening (or Showing) the Way," must be invited, as well as the two players of the reed pipes (the *qeej*) who circle the drum as they play. The song is sung on the night of the first day of the funeral, after the washing the corpse. Ritual expertise in this song and its accompanying rites is thought of as quite different to the ritual expertise of shamanism; it is often said that while the master of the *Qhuab Ke* deals in death, the shaman's job is with ensuring life. Expertise in the *Qhuab Ke*, therefore, is not the same as being a shaman; if a shaman performs the *Qhuab Ke*, he does not do so in his capacity as a shaman. The *Qhuab Ke* can be learned and practiced by anyone with a good voice and memory.

In many versions of the song it is told how at the dawn of time the frog *Nplooj Lwg* was trampled to death by the ancestors of humanity because he had lied to them about the size of the earth (he had said it was no larger than the sole of a foot, the palm of a hand); in his dying breath he curses mankind to know sickness and death. From that time on leaves would wither and trees would grow thin, the world of spirits (*yaj ceeb*) and the world of people (*yeeb ceeb*) would be separated, and no longer would people be able to return to life 13 days (the Hmong week) after their death as previously. The soul of the deceased is led in the song back to the land of his original ancestors through a series of ordeals over the 12 mountains of the Otherworld, where it will dwell for a while before being reborn. After the song is over, individuals will come up to the corpse, which is set on a raised bier against the uphill (altar) wall of the house, take the hand of the dead person, and lament (*nyiav*) in a keening singsong with words that are often beautifully spontaneous sung poetry.

Each day of the funeral, the hosts must ritually offer breakfast, lunch, and supper to the dead person, and also actually serve all those who come. The reed pipes (*qeej*) are blown at each meal and also at other key occasions during the funeral such as the marking of the final expiry of life, the raising of the bier, and the sending off of the coffin. Each piece has its own tune, and the notes of each tune correspond to words that are not spoken. The *qeej tu siav*, or chant of expiring life, for example, is played immediately after the *Qhuab Ke* is over; as the corpse is raised onto its bier, the *qeej tsa nees* is played; and later, as it finally leaves the house, the *qeej sawv kev* is played. A table is set up to collect the money, incense, spirit-paper, and wine offered by those who come to the funeral, and special offerings are expected from each category of relative; each son should present a bull, for instance, and there should be at least one offered by the sons-in-law, and one collectively by the daughters. For a woman's death an extra bull is represented to represent her dowry. All the dead man's debts must be reckoned up and paid before burial or he will not be reborn well. On the last night of the funeral the counseling chant of *txiv xaiv* is recited, especially among the Blue Mong, a moral lament reminding the living of their obligations to the dead and to themselves to do good in life.[7] The chant is a sort of debriefing in poetry for the descendants of the dead person, and the mourning family will kneel in front of the chanter and the body, holding burning incense to be blessed in the name of the deceased. It can take more than 10 hours to finish.

After this final ritual, the body is carried out on a rough stretcher made of two poles through a specially made hole in the wall, since it is inauspicious to use the front door for this purpose, and a procession led by the drummer and piper, the chief mourner (often an oldest son), and a daughter-in-law representing affinal relations waving a burning brand, will take the corpse to the place outside the village for some final rituals of *tshwm tshav* (open air showing of the body). Some Hmong clans do not have this open-air session. It is here that the number of cattle to be given as offerings to the dead are killed, the meat cooked and divided to be given away to various kinship categories of the deceased throughout the course of the day before the body is taken to its resting place for burial; the *qeej* is played here, too, and the drum beaten before it is finally discarded. For the burial, where the landscape is appropriate, the Hmong often use the system of geomantic divination known as *looj mem* by the Hmong or *feng-shui* by the Chinese to select the most appropriate gravesite that will ensure good fortune for his (or her) descendants.

The funeral is not the end of the matter for the deceased or for their living descendants. Thirteen days after death, a special ritual (*xi plig*) is held at home by the family of the deceased to welcome back into the house the part of the soul of the deceased that stays around the grave after the funeral, before dispatching it back to the gravesite. At this ritual, the dead person is represented by a winnowing basket upturned and draped with a shirt and a turban, because there is no body or coffin in the house now. And some time after death, notionally three years but often sooner, there should be another mortuary ritual known as *tso plig* (letting go of the soul), which is the very final release of the part of the soul that is to be reborn. Many of the rituals of the funeral are repeated and the body is again represented by a winnowing tray. In case of trouble in the family or repeated sickness, a further ritual still may be performed some years later for the soul of the deceased known as the *ua nyuj dab*. This is the ceremony of the bull offering, in which a bull

Tso Plig, a soul release ritual being performed in Sichuan, China. Courtesy of the authors.

is killed and its meat is offered to the soul of the deceased to provide it with food in the Otherworld, should this be diagnosed as the cause of the trouble or sickness by a shaman. Some of these customs (*kev cai* or *kab ke*) vary among different descent groups, who may indeed distinguish themselves precisely according to such differences, particularly according to how many bowls of meat the bull is divided into for the offering at the *ua nyuj dab* ceremony, and different styles of burial. As we said at the beginning of this chapter, kinship is a ritual structure.

Outside Asia and in modern conditions in urban settings in Asia, these rituals are very much truncated and abbreviated. In the United States one does not see much of the liquor-drinking and smoking characteristics of the Asian Hmong funeral, and because of federal health and safety regulations corpses are prohibited from being kept in the house so that often a proper funeral home is hired for the purpose of a funeral. For the same reasons, the *tshwm tshav* or open air display of the body on the last day of the funeral is also no longer practiced. In American cities with a large Hmong population, funeral homes are even bought and operated by the Hmong themselves, so that many rituals are carried out more or less in their traditional forms. Slaughterhouses have also been bought where animal sacrifices can be legally performed. Funerals are much shorter than in the past, and often have to be accommodated to match the different architecture of modern houses. This is partly because modern transport allows relatives from distant cities to come quickly, whereas in the past in the hills of Southeast Asia and China, people had to travel on foot and it took many days to convey messages about a death, so that by the time everyone arrived, it would be already be a week or more. Sometimes makeshift substitutes have to be used, such as for the traditional cowhide drum, for instance. The discussions that often take place at funerals about the correct way to proceed, however, are a feature of traditional funerals, too, for the funeral is regarded as an opportunity for the younger men to learn the rituals of death and retired elders will sometimes interrupt the proceedings to instruct the ritual practitioners about correct procedure. Christian Hmong follow very different practices, and in Western countries it is difficult to have geomantic divination for burials wherever one desires because the deceased have to be buried at officially approved cemeteries, whether the site is an auspicious one or not.

PAYING RESPECTS TO THE ANCESTORS AND TO THE HOUSEHOLD SPIRITS

As noted, the Hmong organize their social relationships into gender and kinship categories based on the patrilineal ancestral cult. Apart from death, all religious activities that are not *ua neeb* (shamanism) are known as *ua dab* (propitiating the spirits), and these are closely connected with the ancestral worship that is the pillar of the Hmong's religious beliefs. This in turn is closely linked with the importance of the kinship system in everyday life. One of the most visible ritual objects in a home is the household altar (*dab xwm kab*), which is on the wall of the main room in a traditional house. The *dab xwm kab* is the god of good fortune and is maintained as part of the household spirits (*dab teev, dab vag dab tsev,* or *dab hauv tsev*) to help bring a good harvest, to prevent money leaving the house, and for the successful raising of domestic animals. The *dab xwm kab* altar is particularly honored at the New Year. The ancestral spirits (*dab txwv koob* or *dab niam dab txiv*) must have occasional offerings of rice, chicken, soup, and wine, served in small bamboo or china cups, with incense and spirit-paper, made generally at weddings, funerals, and at the New Year, too. Offerings to ancestral spirits are also made at the first harvesting of dry rice, maize, and (for some descent groups) the first cucumber known as *dib* in Hmong. On the last day of the Old Year (the thirtieth day of the twelfth lunar month), rice is offered to the ancestral spirits with a sacrificed chicken, and a soul-calling ritual is held. These offerings to the ancestral spirits are made on the dining table.

Although the Hmong are not always clear about this, a person is often believed to possess three souls or three parts of the soul: the first stays at the gravesite after death, the second is sent to join the ancestors during the mortuary rituals of a dead person and remains associated with the family through ritual offerings and other ceremonies, while a third is sent on the path toward rebirth during the elaborate funeral and mortuary rituals. It may be because nobody can be sure when a rebirth has taken place that ancestors are worshipped in the household while it is also believed that they are reborn. It is the soul that joins the souls of the ancestors that is given offerings of food and paper money to use in the Otherworld. In every *laig dab*, or feeding of the ancestral spirits ritual, the names of these dead persons for three generations are invoked and their souls called to come and join in the offering. Ancestors beyond the ascending three generations are summoned generally, without their names being spoken. The ancestral spirits must be paid respects in order for the living to obtain good health and to prosper. Some descent groups also perform other rituals for the ancestors such as the *npuas tai* (ceremony of the pig *tai*) ritual, in honor of a deity who saved the Hmong during the great crossing of the water out of China, a ritual sacrificing a pig, held behind closed doors in the evening when only Hmong can be spoken and only men can take part.

Household spirits besides the *dab xwm kab* include the *dab txhiaj meej*, or spirit of wealth and richness, represented by five coins attached to a red cloth with a piece of white cloth or paper beneath it protruding with jagged edges below it above the lintel of the main door; the *dab roog*, who resides within the framework of the main door, protecting all entrances to the home, and is particularly associated with the marital couple; the *dab ncej tas* or spirit of the house central pillar, which expresses the essence of ancestral unity, besides the *dab nthab* or protective spirit of the granary loft. There are also the important *dab qhovcub* or spirit of the main hearth, and *dab qhovtxos* or spirit of the side oven where pigswill is made, which can also be used for major feasts.

There are many other rituals that would take too long to describe here, some of which form part of other rituals, such as *khi tes* or the tying of wrists with hemp (or today, woollen string) after a soul-calling, and *pauj yeem* or the fulfillment of a promise made to a spirit of an offering if a particular wish or request (*fiv yeem*) is fulfilled. There are also ritual taboos and prohibitions such as where a married daughter-in-law may go in a house, or not mentioning the name of the deceased during a funeral. The *khi tes*, sometimes also called *khi hlua* (string tying), can be performed on a number of occasions, in the same way that the Lao and Thai also do. For example, wrists may be tied before undertaking a long and difficult journey or on return from one, and the recovery from a traumatic event such as an accident or a severe illness.

The Hmong sometimes say that, although all their other rituals may be shared with other peoples or may change in the course of time, the only two rituals that have never changed and are quintessentially Hmong, are those of *laig dab* and *hu plig*. *Laig dab*, feeding the ancestral spirits, is something like a thanksgiving, since as we have seen it is conducted after the harvests, as well as at the New Year and at a wedding (the *laig dab* is done in a very different context after someone has died, since it is then for feeding the soul of the person who has just passed away).

Hu plig, or calling the soul, is a common household ritual that can be performed by the head of any family, often for a child who is sick, but not so seriously that it is thought advisable to consult a shaman. It can be performed at any time of the year, and in different forms it is conducted to call the soul of a child when it is three days old, and to summon the soul of a newly married woman to her new home three days after her arrival there. In most cases the household head performs the everyday form of this ritual standing by the door and calling for the soul to return with some incense, a trussed chicken, an egg, a bottle of alcohol, and some uncooked rice. After the sacrifice of the chicken at this and other rituals, the tongue, skull, and other parts of the chicken are examined for omens of good or ill fortune. A variant of the ritual may be performed outside the house or the village, if it is thought that the soul of the child has "fallen" at a particular spot where it may have been frightened or shocked, for instance. A miniature rough wooden "bridge" may be constructed at such a crossroads for the fallen soul to cross over on its return to the village. On occasions, a special *hu plig* is held to call back the souls of all the family together, for example on New Year's Eve when the souls not only of humans but also of their domestic animals and crops are summoned to remain in the house. From time to time, a family may hold a *khi tes* (hand tying) ceremony accompanied by the *hu plig*, for a sick member who has recovered, or for someone about to go on a long journey. After the food has been prepared and the *hu plig* is completed, all those present will tie a small thread of cotton around the person's wrists to wish him or her good health and fortune. This ceremony may be done for a whole family, and is a ritual also practiced by other Southeast Asian and Chinese peoples. The string is a protective symbol, like the silver neck ring or *xauv* Hmong men and children often wear, to secure the soul firmly to the body lest it may wander and by its absence bring sickness or misfortune to its owner.

Above all, traditional Hmong believers are pantheists, believing in a variety of spirits inhabiting parts of the natural universe and also inhabiting the body of the person, who is a microcosm of the universe. Ancestor worship, shamanism, and the rites of death, to say nothing of the techniques of divination and magic (*ua khaw koob*), which are not seen as exclusively Hmong since they were often learned from Chinese Taoists, all relate to a powerful belief in the forces of the natural universe, and for the need for human life to be in accordance with those natural forces and with society.

THE INFLUENCE OF BUDDHISM

In Thailand during the 1960s, the Thai government, as part of an integrated program aimed at assimilating the hill tribes of northern Thailand, began a program of missionary Buddhism known as the Thammacarik program under which Buddhist monks were sent out to remote areas of Thailand to preach to and convert the Hmong and other ethnic minority members.[8] Buddhism began to make inroads among the Thailand Hmong and a fair number of individual conversions were made. However, Hmong religious beliefs do not necessarily exclude adopting other beliefs, so that many Hmong who respect Buddhist beliefs are not themselves practicing or committed Buddhists in the same way as is the majority of the lowland populations of Laos and Thailand. Thus, they would not see attending a Buddhist temple or temple festival as necessarily challenging their own beliefs. Although Theravada Buddhism is the national religion in Thailand, as it was in pre-socialist Laos, this form of Buddhism has coexisted for several centuries with older beliefs in spirits and ritual practices dating back to Hindu influences that predated the arrival of Buddhism in the region around the thirteenth century. So Thai and Lao Buddhism do not usually preclude the belief in many kinds of spirits and in some cases can coexist with Hmong beliefs.

Moreover, Buddhism has occupied a particularly important role in the societies of Thailand and Laos. The Buddhist temple used to be the center of the Thai or Laotian village, and every young Thai or Lao man was expected to become a monk for a short period in his life before being considered to have attained maturity. Before the arrival of modern systems of medicine and education in the region from the 1920s onward, the temple was not only the locus of medicine, so that villagers would come to the monk to be treated for a variety of illnesses, but also the only place where an education was taught. It was also an important route for young men who wished to rise above their stations as villagers and embark on a career, so that it was and always has been an important avenue of social mobility for uneducated Thai and Lao villagers who would otherwise have had no chance to become literate or improve their station in life. In this same sense it has been important, too, for Hmong and other ethnic minority members who became Buddhists in name, because it has often provided the best way to learn Thai (or Laotian) and become literate for those who otherwise had no access to schooling. At one major temple in Chiangmai, Wat Sri Sodha, allied with a famous temple in Bangkok, many Hmong became monks every year.

In Theravada Buddhism monkhood is not necessarily a permanent status; one can ordain as a monk for a year or several years, three months as many young men do during the Buddhist Lent period, or even for only three days. But some of these Hmong continued to stay in the Buddhist Order after they were ordained, and some went back to their villages equipped with a new knowledge of the outside world, and fluent if not literate in the language of the majority people. During the 1970s and 1980s, becoming Buddhist was also an important way of expressing one's loyalty to the Thai king and the country of Thailand, so that at a time when Thailand was riven by conflicts between communists and royalists, some Hmong chose to become Buddhist as a way to express their loyalty to the country they were living in.

In Laos, too, as an aspect of becoming more like the dominant Lao people, some Hmong, particularly those of elite or well-off families, may choose to adopt some Buddhist beliefs and practices without necessarily becoming true Buddhists, for they still maintain their beliefs in, for example, the importance of having a traditional Hmong funeral or paying respect to the ancestors at the Hmong New Year. Buddhism, then, has been able to some extent to co-exist with Hmong beliefs, and its adoption has been relatively gentle, but this has not been the case with the adoption of Christianity by the Hmong.

The Impact of Christianity

Christianity impacted the Hmong community quite early in China. Not only were Roman Catholic missionaries from the Paris Foreign Missions Society (MEP) working in the areas of Guizhou, Yunnan, and northern Vietnam where the Hmong lived, but also Protestant missionaries, particularly from the Methodist churches and from the interdenominational China Inland Mission began working among the Hmong and A Hmao peoples from the last quarter of the nineteenth century in both Yunnan and Guizhou provinces. They were not as successful in Guizhou, but in Yunnan several mass conversions were made by one of the first missionaries, Samuel Pollard from Cornwall, attached to the Bible Christian movement that later merged into the United Methodist Mission. Pollard (and his son Walter) left several accounts of his work in China at this time and the deprived and desperate position his Hmong and A Hmao converts were in after the failure of their various uprisings against harsh Chinese rule. In some cases he interceded for them against wicked or corrupt Chinese landlords and magistrates. It was Pollard who, with A Hmao helpers, designed the first script for any Miao language, a form of writing that is still being used by the A Hmao of Yunnan province.[9] There can be no doubt that converts at this time were in a desperate economic and political position and welcomed the teachings of Christ as a beacon of hope in their misery.

However, from the start there were confusions and misinterpretations of understanding, which, according to Pollard's own writings, caused him considerable grief and upset. Many of the converts took the words of the Bible too literally, believing that the Day of Judgment was already at hand, and that the Messiah, whom they identified as a Hmong one, was shortly to be born. The pronunciation of Jesus as "Yesu" sounded a little like the name of the Hmong deity *Yawm Saub*, so they became confused. In one case a Miao woman claimed to be the sister of Christ and went around winning converts. And it is more than probable that, hearing that Pollard had bought a Book that was specially for them, as he put it, and coupled with the fact that he was designing a form of writing for their language into which the Bible could be translated, many converts believed that this was the fulfillment of the prophecy that one day the lost form of Hmong writing would be restored to them. Without going too much into history here, these movements and mass conversions of Hmong to Protestant forms of missionary Christianity have continued to occur at regular frequent intervals in Vietnam, Laos, and Thailand up until the present day. In the midst of the unhappy wars in Laos in the 1960s, for instance, three Hmong men traveled about the country claiming to be the Holy Trinity and seeking to convert other Hmong.[10] Around the same time the Communist Party of Thailand tricked many Thailand Hmong into leaving their villages and fleeing to what turned out to be a communist base in Chiangrai province by spreading rumors of the birth of a Hmong Messiah there.

The impact of Christianity on the Hmong has been dramatic, unlike the slow adoption of Buddhist values and practices, and it has differed somewhat between different churches and sects. In general the Catholic missionaries have taken a more long-sighted view of Hmong culture and custom and in many cases actively encouraged or sponsored the documentation of traditional Hmong practices such as the death rituals and shamanic ceremonies. Protestant missionaries such as the Presbyterians who worked in Thailand have generally adopted an approach that is much more culturally intolerant, often burning household altars and forbidding any kind of ancestral or funeral practice. And different sects have adopted different approaches; for example, the Seventh-Day Adventists were known for not allowing even the consumption of pork in northern Thailand. In the last two decades further changes have taken place in the spreading of Christianity, because most pastors now are Hmong themselves, unlike the fairly recent past when the missionaries were almost all American, French, or from other Western nations.

In Vietnam, and to a lesser extent in Laos, Christianity is still disapproved of by the socialist authorities, and in Vietnam the increasing Hmong adoption of Christianity in recent years has been seen as a sign of their wishes for subversion and has been savagely repressed with the slaughter of household animals belonging to Hmong Christians, their arrests, and even their executions. The Chinese government, too, keeps a very careful watch on mass adoptions of Christianity by the Hmong in its border provinces. The Hmong response to this persecution has been in some cases flight (several families disappeared into Burma from Yunnan for this reason in the 1990s), and particularly in Vietnam, even suicide. The Christian faith has a very strong appeal, partly because it originated from Western missionaries, whom the Hmong have traditionally identified as powerful advocates who would deliver them from oppression by other local dominant groups. Christianity also teaches about the second coming of Christ, which meshes with Hmong mythical belief about the coming of a Hmong king to unite all Hmong under his rule as it did with the converts made by Pollard. In such cases Christianity may be seen by converts as a part of their culture and traditions, an aspect that offers them hope in the face of oppression.

The kinship-based clan or lineage is important in Hmong society at every level and there is a customary need to perform ancestral and shamanic rituals at times of life crisis and at particular points in the annual calendar to affirm and maintain that identity. However, once an individual or even a family or group of families converts to Christianity, it becomes virtually impossible for communal social activities, such as those at weddings, funerals, or even the New Year, to be performed together any more. Villages in Thailand and elsewhere have become severely fragmented by these issues. It is fair to say that families, lineages, and whole communities have been riven by divisions between Christians and non-Christians.[11] There are cases of shamans converting to Christianity, or of fathers whose sons refuse to follow them, or of children converting for reasons of strong faith against the wishes of their parents.

Many younger Hmong also convert on the pretext that the Hmong traditional rituals that each married male has to perform for his family are too difficult to learn, or are not relevant to their modern needs. However, in many cases these conversions are matters of genuine faith and belief and arise from a feeling that the older Hmong beliefs are superstitious or based on fear, as pointed out by Dowman.[12] Often a succession of unfortunate events such as illness or crop failure is pointed to as the result of the conversion, or refusal or failure to convert. In Canada, the United States, and elsewhere conflicts over the adoption of Christianity have become endemic. In these countries it was often local churches that sponsored the arrival of Hmong refugees after 1975 and some converted out of a sense of obligation to the sponsors, while others came into conflict with their sponsors as occurred with the sponsorship of Hmong families by the Mennonites in Canada.[13] In Australia the conversion to Christianity of a Hmong shaman who had been sponsored to come to the country owing to the shortage of shamans caused deep resentment as the individual concerned was seen as reneging on his commitment and using the conversion to avoid his community obligations. For a Christian, perhaps the most serious issue is the inability to take full part in the funeral rituals for the soul of a deceased relative or parent. However, debates and disagreements have also centered on other ritual events and practices such as customary weddings and the traditional practice of bridewealth payments.

An important contributing reason to the rifts that have developed within the Hmong community over the adoption of Christianity has been that some Christian denominations, especially in the United States, are so rigid in their teachings that they dismiss all Hmong traditional practices as paganism, so that their Hmong converts are forced to cut off all ties with their relatives and clan members who remain faithful to the Hmong traditional system. Some sects see all traditional rituals as tainted by demons, and converts are not allowed to join in any feasts arising from these rituals. This kind of cultural intolerance further erodes mutual obligations between family and clan members, because the more fundamentalist Christian Hmong may refuse to provide help with family celebrations or community events that involve some religious activities. Despite this, some of the bigger Hmong churches are active with their own missionary work among fellow Hmong in China and Southeast Asia, both through conversion in the field and through missionary radio broadcasts from the United States and the Philippines.

One must not forget the agony of individual decision-making that the adoption of Christianity involves in many cases, besides the communal conflicts drawn attention to here. Cases of conversion back and forth several times are very common. Many Hmong may wish to become Christian or leave their ancestral belief system behind, but feel constrained by the presence of an elderly parent or relative for whom the absence of a traditional funeral would be a calamity. Where a girl from a traditional family marries a Christian Hmong, or a brother converts against the wishes of his father, the personal traumas caused can be tremendous. At Hmong New Year in the United States, Christian Hmong also hold a family feast but combine it with Christian songs and blessings, while some hold the feast in a restaurant or hotel. It has become more of a private, family celebration than a public event, and may not be held on the exact date.[14]

The issue in the wider sense comes down to one of Hmong identity and how being Hmong is to be defined in the future. The introduction of Christianity often challenges this very identity, the traditional leadership structures and often the traditional authority of men in the family, so that it involves not just relations between men and women, but also relations between the younger generation and their elders, and the traditional respect owed by wives to their husbands as by youth to their elders. So the issue of the adoption of Christianity becomes conflated with other changes in the relations between genders and generations that are taking place in the new lives of the Hmong today, not just in the United States or other advanced economies, but also in the rapidly modernizing society of Thailand and the more urbanized parts of Asia where Hmong families and individuals live. Many members of the older generation may feel that the younger generation are losing their Hmong culture and therefore their "Hmong-ness" by not being able to speak Hmong, adopting ways seen as non-Hmong and turning their backs on traditional customs. But others, not only among the younger generation, feel that it is possible to remain Hmong while adopting new ways and customs, and that being Hmong may and indeed should be defined in different ways from those of the past.

Besides membership of the Catholic Church, many Protestant groups, including the Christian Missionary Alliance, the Assembly of God, the Baptist, Lutheran, and Pentecostal churches, Mormons and Jehovah's Witnesses,[15] there are small groups of messianic Hmong who seek to revive the traditions of their people in new and unexpected ways, such as a group of four families in Australia who have retreated to the mountains of the Atherton Highlands to practice a new faith with newly designed rituals that they see as traditional and as a way of remaining Hmong in the face of pressures to become Australian. And there is a small community of Hmong in Portland, Oregon, who converted to the Baha'i faith in Laos, where some believers still remain.

Despite these conflicts and divisions, the overwhelming majority of the Hmong today remain attached to some degree or other to the more traditional beliefs of their ancestors, and even those in Western countries often try to maintain traditional practices of ancestor respect and shamanism as best they can. Behind these beliefs there is a strong substratum of wisdom and belief in the harmony of nature and the need for humans to live in appropriate accord with the natural world that remains an encouragement and inspiration for many Hmong people.

ENVIRONMENTAL RITUALS

With the new ecological awareness spreading through Thailand, some rituals have become more formalized and systematic than they were in the past. For instance, it has always been the case that, particularly on the founding of a new village or around the New Year, rituals were performed for the protective spirits of the locality, known as *thwv tim thwv xeeb* (lords of the land) or *xeeb teb xeeb chaw* (spirits of the land). In many upland areas of northern Thailand, particularly those linked through the Hmong Environmental Network, it has now become statutory for the whole village to perform a special ritual for these spirits of the locality at the New Year, represented by the *ntoo xeeb* or spiritual inhabitant of a particular tree near the village.

Fiv yeem, in the form of a promise to a locality spirit to safeguard a particular part of the forest, has also become more closely associated with ecological concerns. As Leepreecha showed, these revived rituals have much in common with the recent practice of ordaining trees now performed by Thai people to make a point about the need to safeguard and care for forested lands.[16] The *ntoo xeeb* ritual of the Hmong involves the sacrifice of a pig or a couple of roosters, chanted prayers by a ritual expert, and a communal feast. Individual families can also come forward to make particular requests to the *ntoo xeeb*, for example, for the birth of a child.[17] The *thwv tim* is generally thought to reside in a rock or tree near the village, while *xeeb teb xeeb chaw* is a wider and more general category of the spiritual guardians of the territory. Following the ritual, the forest around the *ntoo xeeb* is protected by the village, so that the ritual has the function of reminding villagers of the importance of forest preservation, and displaying to the outside world that the Hmong, too, care about the environment and natural forest cover. Concurrently with these reformulated ritual practices, a practice of *teev hau dlej* (paying respects to the headwaters) by the Blue Mong is also increasing in the area.[18]

In such reformulated and reshaped rituals we can see not only the traditional importance of values of respect for and harmony with the natural environment found in Hmong geomantic practices and the spiritual aspects of their vernacular architecture, which we describe in Chapter 6, but also something of the powerful dynamism of Hmong ritual, its capacity to adjust to and accommodate to new living situations and conditions. It is this, indeed, that makes it a "living tradition."

NOTES

1. Graham 1926: 304.
2. Lee 1994–1996.
3. See Eliade 1964.
4. See Mottin 1984 and Lemoine 1986.
5. Lemoine 1972b; 1987.
6. See Symonds 2004.
7. See Chindarsi 1976.
8. Keyes 1971.
9. See Parsons and Parsons, "Songs and Stories and a Glossary of Phrases of the Hua Miao of South West China," http://www.archives.ecs.soton.ac.uk/miao. Accessed 18 May 2010.
10. Barney 1957.
11. See Leepreecha 2001.
12. Dowman 2004.
13. Winland 1989.
14. Kou Yang 2007.
15. See Ibid.
16. Leepreecha 2004.
17. See Huang and Sumrongthong 2004.
18. See Wanitpradit and Badenoch 2006.

3

Oral and Written Literature

HMONG LITERATURE, BOTH traditional and modern, is found among the Hmong in Asia and those who migrated to Western countries. As the Hmong only developed a form of writing and became literate in their own language since the late 1950s, most of their traditional literature has been oral in forms and delivery method such as folktales, incantations, music, and singing. Although mainstream societies may see Hmong literature as marginal, Hmong oral literature can be considered as national literature for the Hmong people. A national literature is one where most of its texts are seen as representing its users and are used by them as a group either in their everyday life or during special occasions such as New Year celebrations, funerals, and weddings.

ORAL LITERATURE

The Hmong are related to three other sub-groups in China: (1) the Qho Xiong in Western Hunan, (2) the Hmu or Khanao in Southeastern Guizhou, and (3) the A Hmao in Northwest Guizhou and Northeast Yunnan. Each group speaks its own language, within each of which there are many dialects. All four groups form what is known as the Miao nationality in China. All these language groups possess diverse and rich oral traditions with many legends and myths that have been passed down orally for generations. Although this chapter focuses on the Hmong, it will also discuss the literature of the other three groups because they share some similar cultural features; but more importantly, they wish to be identified as members of the same nation, whether they are known as Miao, Hmu, Qho Xiong, Hmong, or A Hmao. When circumstances call, they will readily switch identities, even if they cannot communicate with each other because they speak different languages.[1]

In Chapter 1, we discussed the Hmong story of how they lost their original writing or *ntawv* as they were crossing a big river out of China, pursued by the avenging Chinese, and how important this story of the lost writing has been to some Hmong in their adoption of Christianity. Three variants to this story are that the horses ate the writing, it was accidentally dropped in the great river during the flight, or the Hmong swallowed their precious writings to save them from being swept away by the fast-flowing river, leaving the Hmong "clever in their livers" (hearts) instead of in books like the Chinese.

Still another story tells of the Hmong having to hide their writing in their embroideries so that their pursuing Chinese oppressors would not recognize the writing and destroy it. Hence, the Hmong now call their writing *ntaub ntawv* or fabric writing. A new system of writing, which models its alphabets on the intricate designs of Hmong embroideries, was invented or rediscovered in 1988 in Ban Vinai Refugee camp in Thailand, inspired by this story. A primer with many illustrations from Hmong embroideries was published in 1992. Its proponents believed that they had now restored the Hmong lost writing, and took it with them when they moved to live in the United States to propagate it there. Nao Der Xiong (Nom Dawb Xyooj), who lives in La Crosse, Wisconsin, is now the leader of this group. Another script with many followers in the messianic movement in Laos from the late 1950s until today is the unique Pahawh (*phaj hauj*), inspired by the "Mother of Writing," Shong Lue Yang. This was not based on any myth of lost writing, but many people have taken it as restoration of the lost writing of the Hmong.[2]

The Hmong are one of the few people who have stories that help explain the lack of a unique traditional writing and justify their continued tradition of passing cultural materials orally through memorization from one generation to the next instead of committing them in writing in books. These stories attest not only to the Hmong's firm belief about the existence of their own writing, but also their strong awareness of the value and the link between literacy and power so clearly shown by the literate Chinese majority in relation to the many ethnic groups around their borderlands. Unlike countless minorities without writing and stories to justify it, these Hmong myths show that they have for centuries been in close contact with a literate, powerful, state-based civilization. The Hmong have thus evolved means to explain their own position as an oral people and their deprivation of power and knowledge because of it. The loss of their writing is always explained by association with the Chinese, either as a more clued older brother or as the pursuing enemy. It is as if they are saying that because of the Chinese, they have lost their writing and, by extension, their king and country. The stories point to the Hmong's consciousness of the political strength and privileges that go with having a writing system, as well as strong connections with other peoples around them.

The Hmong's lack of writing means that they have a very developed oral tradition with many rich texts and a diverse range of literary genres. Among the White Hmong and the Blue Mong of Laos and Thailand, oral literature in the form of poetry and narratives include: (1) traditional songs, particularly the kind known as *kwv txhiaj* or *lus txaj*, (2) wedding chants or *zaj tshoob*, (3) folktales or *dab neeg* narratives, and (4) funeral chants such as the *Qhuab Ke* ("Showing the Way"), the *Txiv Xaiv—Hais Xim* ("Last Counsel"), the *Nkauj Plig* ("Soul Chanting"), and the *Qeej Tuag* or reed pipe obsequial music. In Western classifications, traditional singing would count as music, even though the words of songs form a prime example of traditional oral literature, which will be examined as forms of music later. For the same reason we shall consider the funeral airs played on the *qeej* as music, even though each note relates to a word and therefore also has an oral meaning. But it should be noted here how important these are as part of the oral tradition of the Hmong.

In this chapter, before turning to recently written literature, we will explain folktales, wedding chants, the two main funeral chants that contain the essence of Hmong oral culture, and the beautiful *Nkauj Tuag* and *Nkauj Plig* funeral songs that, although sung, are full of plaintive oral meanings. We also look briefly at epic poems and proverbs.

Folktales: *Dab Neeg*

Like other people with an oral tradition, the Hmong have folk stories of all genres: love, war, fairies, ghosts, evil-minded stepmothers, and the mistreated orphan who later makes good. Folktales were the primary form of entertainment in Laos before the advent of television and videos. A generation ago, young children would ask their elderly family members to tell them stories at night after dinner before they went to sleep. For many, it was not only entertainment but also a kind of lullaby to send them to sleep. For this reason, folk stories were very well known, and storytelling was a well-appreciated art. There is a saying that Hmong folk stories can only be told at night. Why is it that you are not allowed to tell such stories during the daytime? This taboo seems to have been carried over to America since Johnson and his assistants could not get the Hmong to tell them stories during work hours so they could be recorded.[3] But the Hmong would tell stories at night if they were left a tape recorder. Johnson asked why. For some Hmong, he says, storytelling during the daytime was not allowed as it was feared it might make the characters in the stories come alive. Since many of these characters are ghosts or little ghostly figures (*poj ntxoog*), the Hmong had no wish to see them in real life. The truth, however, may be that the Hmong are too busy with farming or other work during the day, and evenings are the only time they can sit down and entertain young ones with stories.

During the last 40 years, Hmong folk stories have been recorded by a number of researchers and published in Hmong and English. The best known recent collections from the Hmong in Thailand and Laos include those by Bertrais, Johnson, Livo and Cha, Numrich, and Vang and Lewis.[4] An older but very comprehensive collection from the Hmong of Sichuan in China is that of Graham with a staggering 752 stories.[5] A more recent collection of Miao epic poems and stories from Guizhou, China, was compiled by Jin Dan and Ma Xueliang with translations into English by Bender.[6]

Hmong folk stories are not only beautiful but also most informative about Hmong history and culture. They are also didactic in that they aim to teach about good and evil, right and wrong, and the triumph of love over hatred, courage over cowardice. A very good example is the story of the re-creation of humanity after the Great Flood. The Hmu of Guizhou, the A Hmao, and the Hmong all have similar legends, although there are a few differences in the details. The story, in outline, tells how the Miao/Hmong and their many clans came into existence after a great flood killed all the people on earth, leaving only a brother and sister who survived in a wooden drum. In one version by the Hmu of Guizhou, the brother, Jang Vang, became restless and lonely after "he saw no one to love."[7] He sought advice from the cotton bamboos and was told to "find your sister and talk of love."[8] The sister tried all she could to resist his advances, but he used different measures to persuade her until her hands were caught in a fish trap set by him and he would not help with her release until she called him "husband." After the union, she gave birth to a lump of flesh with no arms and no face, only "eyes . . . like a fish wrapped in paddy grass."[9] Angered by such a calamity, the husband cut the child up into pieces and spread the pieces over nine hills. The scattered pieces of flesh "turned into many, many peoples, turned into myriads of persons" of different races such as the Dong, the Lolo, Chinese, and other races.[10] In another popular version from the Hmong of Vietnam, Laos, and Thailand, the pieces of flesh were scattered around outside the house of the brother and sister (and not over nine hills). The next morning, little huts with smoke coming out of them sprang up from the spots where the fleshy pieces fell. Each hut had a couple in it. The piece of flesh that was left in the goat house (*tsev tshis*) gave rise to the Lee (Lis) clan. The Vang (Vaj) clan came from the piece left in the garden (*vaj*), the Moua clan from the one in the pig sty (*nkuaj npuas*), the Thao (Thoj) from the one on the slope (*ntav toj*), the Yang (Yaj) from the one on the hemp tree (*ntoo maj*), the Chang (Tsab) from the one on the granary (*txhab*), and so on.[11] Another version of the story also adds that the fleshy pieces further turned into insects, birds, bulls, buffaloes, and rodents.[12]

In Hmong folklore, the brother and sister who marry are the survivors of the flood described in the *Qhuab Ke* funeral song. In a very common version they ask *Saub* what to do, and he tells them to go to the top of a mountain, and roll down the opposite sides of it the two large circular stones that make up the upper and lower parts of the grinder of the Hmong rice-mill (known as the male and female stones, *niam zeb txiv zeb*, in Hmong). If the two millstones come together at the foot of the mountain, they can marry. If they end up on opposite sides, they cannot. They end up marrying because the two pieces of stone do meet together, but the fruit of their incest is a shapeless lump of flesh that they are advised to carve up. From each piece springs the ancestor and the ancestress of each of the Hmong clans. It is a story forbidding incest, since it has such horrible results, and it also explains the origins of the clans, and why the members of each clan must marry the members of another clan, not the "brothers" and "sisters" in the same clan.[13] Many folktales are more light-hearted than this, however, dealing with the antics of ordinary folk or animal fables like Aesop's fables.

Thus, folktales can inform about history and culture, and act as guidance for behavior, as well as entertain. In their traditional village settings, the Hmong use these stories as:

- Evening entertainment: sharing tales around the fireplace or in bed to put children to sleep at night.
- Teaching materials: showing what can result from good and evil, right and wrong, kindness and cruelty.
- History (*kwv huam*): the creation of humankind, the origins of living things on Earth, the origins of social customs and relations between Hmong and other people.

An oral tradition requires almost superhuman skills of memory since sometimes very long passages and narratives have to be remembered purely by heart. So the bearers of the Hmong oral tradition tend to have phenomenal memories. Moreover, the telling of folktales is a dramatic performance in itself. Sadly, storytelling today has almost become a lost art. As more Hmong young children go to school and spend their evenings studying, few have time or the interest to listen to stories from their elders. Gradually, many of the folktales become forgotten as the older people get older and no longer remember most of them. Another factor contributing to the erosion of folk storytelling is the impact of new forms of entertainment, although sometimes an old folktale can have a new lease on life by being made into a movie. Folk stories have been replaced by movies, television, and books so much so that few people now know these folk stories by heart. Even Hmong in the villages in Southeast Asia and China prefer to watch movies on compact discs and television, where they can see story characters in the flesh rather than having to imagine them as they listen to a storyteller. Some of the more popular ones have been made into feature films that are well received by older Hmong consumers around the world.[14] Folk stories in the form of instant moving images on film not only entertain but bring alive a long oral tradition that used to rely on the imagination. Oral stories are now being replaced by visual reconstructions that members of the audience can see with their own eyes and readily identify with. We will examine these new visual forms of art later. Despite this innovative way of telling Hmong folk tales, however, many young Hmong people prefer to watch Jet Li, Jackie Chan, Bruce Willis, and other Hollywood action movie stars, thereby further diminishing their knowledge of Hmong heroes and folktales. This is especially true of those living in cities in Laos and Thailand, or those who are born and raised in Western countries.

Epic Poems

An epic is a long narrative poem in elevated language, celebrating the heroic feats of a legendary hero or people in the mythical past. Many cultures possess epic poems. According to Bender, the Hmong/Miao of Guizhou (the Hmu) possess a form of poetic epic that they sing during New Year and at other special events.[15] The A Hmao of Yunnan also have epics in which they sing of their legendary leader Chiyou and their defeat by the Chinese.[16]

The Hmu epic singing, in Southeast Guizhou, consists of a pair of singers who narrate the story by replying to each other, or provoking each other as if they are in a competition. Sometimes, one singer may take one particular role or theme. There may also be a third singer who serves as chorus, or joins in to prod the others. They may sing on a stage or in any public places surrounded by onlookers, and may take a few days to complete their performance. Among the many epic poems of these Guizhou Miao, Bender lists: (1) "Song of Gold and Silver": how these precious metals were invented, (2) "Song of the Ancient Sweet Gum": how seeds came to be used to grow crops, (3) "Song of Butterfly Mother": creation of the Miao people, (4) "The Great Flood": second creation of the human race, and (5) "Westwards, Upriver": the first migration of the Miao people.

The Hmong of Southeast Asia have many folk heroes whose stories are told in folktales, but mostly in the form of simple prose narratives. However, they do not today have epic poems, whether for public performance or for evening storytelling. They seem to have lost this form of performing oral literature, although other related groups maintain them. In China, there is a long tradition of public performances of epic singing in the form of opera or street performances by itinerant troupes,[17] but it is unlikely that the Hmong would have been influenced by this.

Wedding Chants: *Zaj Tshoob*

We shall consider the social significance of Hmong weddings in later chapters; here we are only concerned with the important occasion a Hmong wedding provides for the performance and transmission of oral literature. A Hmong wedding can last from two to four days, depending on how complicated the negotiations are between the families. Wedding chants are poetic incantations that are an integral part of the Hmong wedding ceremony. These are verses that are sung to their own special tunes, normally by the go-betweens or *mej koob* involved in progressing the wedding negotiations on behalf of the groom's party and the bride's family. Each party to the wedding, the bride's side and the groom's side, has two of these go-betweens whose roles are: (1) to conduct the wedding step-by-step, (2) to negotiate with the other side about what they want for the wedding: bridewealth, feast, and restitution for any past grievances that may have been caused by relatives of the groom to relatives of the bride; and (3) to convey any special requests and messages from the bride's side and/or parents to the groom's parental representative.

The *mej koob* are strictly negotiators and facilitators. They do not make decisions, but are only messengers conveying decisions from one side to the *mej koob* of the other side, who will then in turn convey the message to their parental representatives. At various stages of the wedding process, the *mej koob* sing the wedding songs, and each wedding song marks a further stage in the process of the wedding. This begins with: (1) giving the wedding umbrella to the *mej koob* at the groom's house before the wedding party's departure to the bride's house; (2) asking to be allowed to enter the house of the bride's parents; (3) thanking the bride's parents for their welcome; (4) asking for the wedding table to be set up; (5) teaming up with the *mej koob* on the side of the bride's parents; and (6) getting a reply from the *mej koob* on the side of the bride's parents. Particular oral narrative songs are associated with each step of the wedding; sometimes the go-betweens, if they are good and talented, will engage in a game of wit and repartee, chanting complex songs sometimes with riddles to which the other side has to reply in kind, thus entertaining everyone involved. For example, it may be asked if the visitors intend to take the branch, the trunk, or the leaves and flowers of a tree. The answer should be that it is the flowers and leaves they wish to take, meaning the girl (the trunk means the parents, the branches mean the girl's brother).

Many other songs are sung until the wedding is concluded at the bride's house. On the way back to the groom's house, songs are sung before having lunch (*noj su*) at the side of the road. More singing is done after arrival at the groom's house. To be a *mej koob* means that all these wedding songs have to be learned, as they are used at every stage of the wedding ceremony. Between each song, they are invited to take a sip of rice alcohol. A *mej koob* needs, therefore, to be a good drinker as well, and some Hmong men have been known to die young from alcohol poisoning or liver disease after spending a lot of time being wedding negotiators.

The *mej koob* chanting at a wedding. Courtesy of the authors.

Funeral Chants

Besides the major and important chants considered here and the *qeej* funeral music, which we will look at later, many of the chants at rituals are in a kind of plainsong, and therefore also musical, such as the chant for the calling the soul (*hu plig*) ritual, or the *laig dab* (verses used for offering food to the ancestors), as recorded by Mareschal.[18] This chapter will discuss funeral chants regarded as an essential part of Hmong oral literature.

"Showing the Way": Qhuab Ke

The *Qhuab Ke* song is a major part of the funeral rites and one of the most important expressions of the Hmong oral tradition. It is the first ritual that opens a Hmong funeral. Its aim is to guide the soul back to the land of the ancestors. The ritual performer would have informed himself of all the places where the dead person has lived and carefully guides the soul of the latter to them during the chanting of this song to show them gratitude before being taken to the ancestors in the Otherworld. Prior to this final journey, the chanter sings to the dead person about the creation of the world, the origin of crops, and why death first came to the human world. Like the reed pipe funeral music, the *Qeej Tu Siav* or "Song for Expiring Life," which replicates the *Qhuab Ke* wordlessly, the *Qhuab Ke* gives the soul of the departed explicit instructions on how to navigate its way through various stages of the perilous journey, and how to find the original ancestors at the end.

These instructions include several steps, sometimes followed by physical actions performed by the chanter in the real world as he sings. For example, in step, the chanter will wash the face of the dead with a facial towel dipped in water; and in step, he will slip a pair of hemp shoes onto the feet of the deceased. The steps are:

1. Getting water from *Ntxwg Nyug*'s garden to boil and wash the dead person's face—so all "brothers and sisters can see him clearly";
2. Getting the yeast from *Ntxwg Nyug*'s cliff to make wine in "one day and two mornings" to be used to "show the way for the dead . . . to meet his ancestors";
3. When the soul gets to the mountain of giant caterpillars (*nrawm kab ntsi*), stepping over carefully using the hemp mortuary shoes given to the dead person;
4. What to do at the dragon and tiger rocky mountain and valley;
5. When the Chinese ask for his clothes, to say that they are all torn and soiled with blood, the reason for making holes in these clothes at this time;

6. When asked to stay at a spot where people skin onions, to tell them that his fingers are all sore and bleeding so he would be spared, the reason for tying red strings on the dead person's fingers at this time;

7. Following the soul-guiding chicken faithfully, as it will lead the way to the ancestors, the reason for killing a rooster, called pillow rooster, *qaib rau ncoo*, for the dead at this time;

8. After climbing the 13 steps to get to *Teem Txwv*, the heavenly place of the ancestors, go and get the "mandate of life" paper from *Nyuj Vaj Tuam Teem* so the dead person could come back to be born again "so you will have a good life"; and

9. Remembering to descend on earth and be reborn—coming down one step a day for 13 days.[19]

At the end of the *Qhuab Ke*, the chanter will be the first to start wailing out loud, crouching next to the body. Putting his hands over his face, he communicates words to the dead person through the wailing (*nyiav*) that express his grief. Other mourners will then join him and the first keening session will start, followed by other sessions at appropriate intervals.

Advice and Blessing Funeral Chant: Txiv Xaiv

The *Txiv Xaiv*, literally "Master Selection" or "Chosen Blessing" and sometimes also known as *hais xim* (telling poetry), is another funeral chant that plays a fundamental part in the Hmong tradition of oral narrative. It is the most treasured and the most anticipated part of a Hmong funeral, especially in the case of the funeral of an elder in the family.[20] It is a very long poetic depiction of the journey of the soul of the dead to the Otherworld, offering counsel and good wishes to the descendants who are gathered to pay respects to the departed at the funeral. It is recited during the last night before the burial the next day, and it can take up to 10 hours to complete, sometimes longer. It is delivered orally from memory by the chanters on behalf of the dead person who speaks through them. The older and the more prominent the dead person was, the more numerous the blessings and thus the longer the chanting.

The aim is not only to listen to useful advice but also for the mourners to pay their last respects to the dead person. The chanters, who take turns and work in pairs, will indicate to the mourners when to bow and pay respects at intervals during the recitation. The performance is done by at least two chanters, and sometimes up to six. Today when culture has become a commodity, how long the chanting is also depends on how much money is paid by the family to the performers and how much chanting the family wants to hear. Like all other funeral ritual performers, the

Txiv Xaiv chanters were traditionally paid with the meat from the sacrificial bulls killed for the dead person. Today, however, they are paid in cash, especially in the United States. Their fees can range from $800 to $2,000—again depending on how popular a chanter is and how much of the long chant the family wants him to sing. The chant also varies slightly in content from one chanter to another, because each chanter learns from a different teacher. Like the difference in the verses or words used, the tune is also different from one region to another, although not across dialect groups. In the version used by the White Hmong in Thailand, many of the words are Blue Mong words, although the tune is the same: it is explained that this is due to the fact that the *Txiv Xaiv* was originally learned from the Blue Mong, although it may be that a more archaic form of White Hmong language, closer to Blue Mong, is being used.

Unlike the *Qhuab Ke*, very little study has been done on the *Txiv Xaiv*, so we will describe it here in some detail.[21] It has been collected and transcribed under the general title *Kab Ke Pam Tuag: Cov Zaj* (Funeral Rites: Chants and Recitations) under the direction of Fr. Yves Bertrais.[22] The *Txiv Xaiv* is divided into seven parts: (1) offering gratitude or *Cob Tshav Ntuj*; (2) opening the target or *Qhib Phiaj*; (3) inviting the guests or *Hu Qhua*; (4) making offerings or *Cov Zaj Cob*; (5) asking for blessing and chasing the soul or *Taij Kom thiab Raws Plig*; (6) giving blessings or *Foom Kom*; and (7) putting down the table or *Tuam Rooj*, to end the chanting. Each part has a number of chants. There are thus many sections in the *Txiv Xaiv* chanting, starting with the performers thanking all relatives and well-wishers who come to pay their respects and show their love to the dead (*tuaj hlub tus tuag*). From there, the chant touches on why humans die and where they go after death. Before reaching the end of its heavenly journey, the soul of the dead, through the performers, turns back to the Earth (*ntiaj teb* or the world of the living) and gives the descendants counsel or advice (*foom kom*) on how to be good and successful in life.[23]

The *Txiv Xaiv* has many aspects that are similar to those of the Hmong traditional songs we will consider in the following chapter: (1) the number of words in a verse depends on the tune/metrics used, and (2) verses are put together with the same patterns of repetitive words, with paired words used for rhyming or parallelism. The *Txiv Xaiv* remains the most popular Hmong oral tradition, and no funeral for an elderly Hmong ever takes place without the "Blessing Chant" being carried out, regardless of the financial cost. However, it is now believed that many of its metaphors are out of synchronization with modern life and should be replaced by more appropriate imageries. For example, in giving advice to the descendants crouching in front of the coffin of the deceased on the last night of the funeral, the chanters urge them to grow hemp and make materials so they can have clothes to wear. Although this may have been the case 50 or 100 years ago, today most Hmong do not grow hemp or make their own clothing materials anymore; they buy them from shops. Making cloth from hemp continues in some parts of Vietnam and China, but for the great majority of Hmong even in Asia it has become irrelevant. The hemp and cloth-making metaphors for hard work and self-dependence have become alien to most present-day young Hmong who have never seen a field of hemp plants or how cloth is woven on a loom from their yarn. It would be better, it is felt, to use modern figures of speech about cars and factory work, education and success rather than agriculture and farming, which have been given up by city-dwelling Hmong people, especially those living in Western countries. Here we can see how some parts of the oral tradition of the Hmong may be felt to be unimportant in modern life, but there is still much in the oral tradition which speaks to deep feelings about life and death and the world that are still important and meaningful for many Hmong.

Death and Soul Chanting: Nkauj

During the funeral, a series of chants are sung to the deceased at intervals, interspersed between the playing of the funeral *qeej* music. Unlike the *qeej* funeral music, however, these verbal chants are not imperative; they are sung only if a chanter, known as the *Txiv Nkauj*, can be found. Otherwise, they can be dispensed with. Depending on the social status of the dead person, all of the funeral and soul chants may be sung, or only some essential ones.

There are several funeral *nkauj* such as: (1) *Nkauj tu siav*: expiring life chant; (2) *Nkauj tsa nees*: raising the funeral bier; (3) *Nkauj cob tsiaj*: offering animals as sacrifice; (4) *Nkauj hlawv ntawv*: burning the paper money; (5) *Nkauj tshai*: inviting the soul of the dead to breakfast; (6) *Nkauj su*: lunch offering; (7) *Nkauj hmo*: dinner offering; (8) *Nkauj laug hnub laug hmo*: passing the time of day and the time of night; and (9) *Nkauj hais hnub tshwm tshav thiab sam sab*: chanting for the (last) "open" day that includes *nkauj hlawv ntawv*, chant for burning the paper money, and *nkauj sawv kev*, chant to take the dead to the gravesite.

Like the *qeej* songs delivered through the reed pipe instrument, these verbal chants are known by their individual names in the order of the funeral process. They are usually referred to only by these names, although the generic name of *Nkauj Tuag* (death chants, a taboo term the Hmong try to avoid using) has been used for them.[24] The same chants are known as *Nkauj Plig* when used during the "soul-release" ceremony (*tso plig*), which is performed some time after the burial, when the soul of a dead person is invited back to the house so that it can be finally "released" to be born again. The similar *nkauj plig* are sung for breakfast, lunch, and dinner, and for burning the spirit paper money.[25]

These death or soul chants have some of the most haunting melodies in Hmong oral literature. Like the "life expiring" *qeej* music, they talk about the parting of a loved one from the living, the sending of the soul back to the ancestors so that the living will forever be separated from the dead person. Unlike the words of the *qeej* funeral music signified through the *qeej* tunes, the words of the *Nkauj* are recited out loud in a tune peculiar to them. They are in a different scale and rhythm to the airs played on the *qeej*. They are delivered together with the funeral reed pipe music, so that the soul chanter alternates with the reed pipe music player, performing the same songs. The *qeej* player and the singer face each other when it is time for the chanting: after each burst of the *qeej*, the singer sings an equivalent stanza. As we shall see when we look at the actual *qeej* tunes later, the names of the stanzas in the two performances are thus very similar.

The *Nkauj* chants are composed like most of Hmong oral poetry—by pairing words that have the same meaning together in very simple metrical patterns that emphasize the tune of the chanting. The verses must contain the same number of words so that the same tune can be repeated from one verse to the next. Using parallelism, the same set of words are repeated in each verse to keep the metrical patterns, with only the last words of a verse changed to rhyme with the next verse. To hear these chants is akin to taking the journey oneself, as they use everyday objects (such as flowers) and animals (like the rooster, insects, crickets, the snake) as metaphors for life and sickness or ominous signs of death. Their aim is to explain why death occurs and what procedures are to be followed to complete the journey back to the land of the ancestors.

Proverbs: *Paj Lug*

The Hmong have other forms of oral literature besides those expressed in folktales, musical chants, the riddles of the wedding go-betweens, or the words of the traditional songs considered in the next chapter, such as *lus txhiaj txhais* or guessing puzzles, and *paj luj* or proverbs. Both are phrased in metaphorical poetic language. Although the guessing puzzles are used mostly with children as a recreational activity, proverbs are used mainly for serious occasions, such as resolving a dispute or negotiating in a wedding. In his book, Yaj gathers together 80 one-paired rhymed proverbs and 150 two-paired rhymed ones.[26]

Two examples are given below.

Table 3.1
Examples of Proverbs

Proverbs	Translation
One-Pair Rhymed Proverbs:	
Nrog cov laus, dab tsis **hem**	Stay with elders, ghost will not scare one
Nrog cov nom, luag tsis **cem**	Stay with high officials, nobody dares scold
Two-Pair Rhymed Proverbs:	
Luj tuag tu **noob**, tsuav tug nyob qab **roob**	Mongooses all died, still one left at foothill
Tsuag tuag tu *tsav*, tshuav tug nyob qab *hav*	Mice die whole group, still one left in valley.
Lyman (2004) gives some more samples:	
Tsuas muaj tus **ntses** lawv tus *dlej*	Only the fish follows the stream
Tsis muaj tus *dlej* lawv tus **ntses**	No streams follow the fish

Note: translations by Gary Lee.

In the last proverb, *ntses* and *dlej* are half rhymes because only their vowels agree, not their tones, but in the second line of the stanza the position of the words is reversed, giving a pleasing effect. Repetition in a slightly different form is a poetic device often used in Hmong oral literature. The literal meaning here is that one should listen to, or follow, those who are more important than oneself.[27]

Anyone in Hmong society who wants to speak with authority and to be taken seriously needs to know proverbs and use them in his conversations, particularly when negotiating an issue or settling a dispute. However, one must know when it is appropriate to use a proverb so that it fits into a meaningful context; otherwise its usage does not make sense. When elders in the Hmong community speak, they always qualify their arguments with proverbs to make a point or to drive home the fact it is always better to do something based on established precedents and traditions as revealed through the proverbs. Hmong guessing puzzles have not been a subject for serious study and no published collections of these *lus txhiaj txhais* are known to exist. However, proverbs have been studied by Western and Hmong authors, and a number of collections have been published.[28]

WRITTEN LITERATURE

We have noted the importance of writing to the Hmong, even though they traditionally had none. From 1951 to 1953, the Romanized Popular Alphabet (RPA), a Latin-based script, was devised by three missionaries, Barney, Smalley (Protestant), and Bertrais (Catholic). It was successfully

introduced to the Hmong in Laos in 1955, largely through the propaga-
tion efforts of the French Catholic Mission in Laos under Fr. Yves Bertrais.[29]
When the Hmong left Laos to resettle as refugees in different countries in
the West in 1975, many books in RPA had already been published, including a primer on how to read and write Hmong together with a French-
Hmong dictionary. They took these publications with them and republished
them to use in the diaspora.[30] The RPA script has thus come to be used
worldwide today, although a number of other scripts also exist.

With the help of Hmong students in the early 1960s, Fr. Bertrais (known
in Hmong as Txiv Plig Nyiaj Pov) transcribed and published several collections of Hmong folk stories, funeral chants, traditional songs, and wedding
and funeral practices. He and his assistants continued this work after 1975
with further recording of similar materials among Hmong refugees in Thailand and in French Guyana. Visits were also made to collect information
from the Hmong in China. This life-time undertaking has seen the publication of 23 volumes in RPA on various cultural topics, including history and
memories of Hmong life in various countries. They were published between
1964 and 1998 in a collection called *Patrimoine Culturel Hmong* (Hmong
Cultural Heritage), with other volumes under preparation until the time of
his death in June 2007. Because of his devotion, the Hmong now have this
invaluable collection of transcribed oral literature preserved in RPA writing
for transmission to posterity and sharing with interested readers.

Print, Web Publications, and Video as Literature

Previous to this work by Fr. Bertrais, other missionaries and anthropologists
like Pollard, Bernatzik, Clarke Graham, de Beauclair, Hudspeth, and Savina had
published on various areas of Hmong life, history, and culture in China, Laos,
and Thailand in English, German, French, and other languages.[31] Dr. Yang
Dao was the first Hmong scholar to publish a book on Hmong economic issues
in Laos in the early 1970s.[32] Other scholars in China have also published many
books and papers in Chinese on Hmong/Miao culture and history.

During the initial years of the Hmong settlement in the United States, the
Center for Urban and Regional Affairs of the University of Minnesota published a number of monographs, ranging from Hmong language courses to
research on shamanism and the "Mother of Writing," Shong Lue Yang.
Today, there are many more researchers and writers, including younger
Hmong scholars, who publish numerous articles and books on Hmong topics.
Thanks to the meticulous work of Dr. Mark Pfeiffer, these publications are
listed in bibliographies online by the Hmong Studies Internet Resource Center
in Minnesota.[33] The Hmong Cultural Center in St. Paul, Minnesota
(www.hmongcenter.org), issues the peer-reviewed *Journal of Hmong Studies*

twice a year. This has greatly increased Hmong written literature over the years. The advent of the Internet has also seen a proliferation of online Internet information and discussion on the Hmong, and this has become an important extension of the oral traditions of the Hmong in written form. The Hmong in Australia set up one of the earliest Web sites on the Hmong with many articles on history and various aspects of Hmong life.[34] There are now hundreds of Hmong Web sites hosted by individuals and groups. The Hmong Homepage (www.hmongnet.org) has many links to the main sites, and to current events, projects, and community activities. Another excellent site has a list of all the main Hmong sites and current online publications on the Hmong.[35] The Hmong in Thailand, Laos, and China have also set up their own Web sites so that online information exchange is made possible worldwide.

Apart from such literature in print form and on the Internet, much "recomposing" of Hmong culture has been made through video and audio recordings, which are sold commercially. Let us note that many video documentaries on Hmong life in Laos, China, Burma, Vietnam, and French Guyana as well as video movies based on legendary tales and figures have been made. According to Leepreecha, these efforts to put Hmong oral literature, whether singing or folktales, on DVD provide hope for the continuance of this oral tradition.[36] The DVDs allow history and traditional oral folktales to take on a new form and be disseminated to the younger generation, reproducing and retaining the sense of a Hmong identity, rather than just dying out altogether as they might have without this electronic preservation. However, as mentioned above, much oral literature has already been lost as a result of the advent of these DVDs.

Can we call this vast undertaking in print form and Web publications, to say nothing of the video representations considered more fully in the following chapter, Hmong "literature"? The answer would be "yes" if we accept the definition by Culler, who says literature is "a speech act or textual event that elicits certain kinds of attention . . . in a context that identifies it as literature: in a book of poems or a section of a magazine, library or book store."[37] If literature is what the general reading public and literary experts define as literature ranging from essays, autobiographies to poetry and fiction, even audio books, then the Hmong can certainly be said to have an emerging body of written literature, some parts of which are now expressed on the Web and also translated into visual formats.

Prose Narratives: Novels, Plays, and Short Stories

Since the end of the civil war in Laos in 1975, about 2,000 Hmong have resettled in Australia as refugees. Most are young families, with the household heads often literate in the Hmong RPA writing system. In the early 1980s, Nyia Pao Lee (Nyiaj Pov Lis), who lives in Sydney, published a series of four novels written in the RPA script. They are *Vim Leej Twg* (*Because of Who*) published in 1985 and re-issued in 1994 and 2007; *Lub Neej Dai Taw* (*A Dependent Life*) in 1986; *Neej Kua Muag* (*A Tearful Life*) in 1989; and *Txoj Saw Hlub* (*The Love Chain*) in 1990. The two most popular are *Lub Neej Dai Taw* and *Vim Leej Twg*; readers said the latter contained much literary deep meaning and metaphorical language. It was also made into a movie by ST Universal Video in California. Many Hmong have read his novels, which all sold out with a print run of 500 copies, considered very good for a self-published author and given the small Hmong literary market.

Among known fiction books in Hmong RPA is a novel called *Ua Lub Neej Raws Txoj Hmoo* (*To Live by One's Luck*) by Xwm Xyooj (1998). Others in the online catalogue of the Hmong ABC Bookshop in St. Paul, Minnesota, include 17 novels currently being offered for sale there.[38] Apart from the titles already mentioned, they include: (1) *Hey, Hmong Girl, Whassup?*, (2) *I Love You, Zaumkawg*, (3) *Hiav Txwv Quas Txoj Kev Hlub or the Ocean Is Barrier to Our Love*, (4) *Tsis Muaj Ntxiv Lawm or There Is No Other Time Again*, (5) *Kaying and Cha: A Hmong Odyssey*, (6) *Ntuj Caus Teb Hlub: A Hmong Historical Novel*, (7) *Husi: A Clouded Future Is Still Translucent*, and (8) *Orphan Boy, the Farmer*. Most of these books are written in Hmong, and only a few are in English. Many touch on unfulfilled love and orphan life, popular themes for Hmong readers.

In addition to narratives written in Hmong, other Hmong writers also find voices by writing in English. Most have written in the form of short stories and essays that have appeared in *Paj Ntaub Voice*. Many of the best pieces have been published in a collection entitled *Bamboo among the Oaks: Contemporary Writing by Hmong Americans*, edited by Mai Neng Moua in 2002. A recent welcome addition to Hmong creative writing is Kao Kalia Yang, whose 2008 book of family memoirs, *The Late Homecomers*, has been highly praised by many of those who read or reviewed it. They are impressed with her style of writing, so much so that one of them was touched enough to say that she is without doubt the best writer in English the Hmong have ever produced. Kao Kalia is currently freelance professional writer. Another very successful book in English, which has remained on the top-selling list for the publisher since its first publication, was the 2004 *Dust of Life: A True Ban Vinai Love Story*, written by Gary Yia Lee. The novel is an attempt to write about culture through fiction; the author, who is an anthropologist, believes that his academic publications do not allow for the creative expression of feelings and the use of dialogue to discuss a topic in depth. The book has been set as a text for Hmong literature and other courses on the Hmong in the United States.

A small number of Hmong writers have chosen to express their creativity through playwriting, and it is important to note here that this is yet another aspect in which the oral literature tradition of the Hmong is finding new forms of expression, both enacted or performed, and written.

Poetry

As we have seen, the Hmong have a long tradition of performing poetry as part of their oral tradition with such texts as traditional songs, wedding chants, and funeral chants that often rhyme and show many other poetic devices. Alliteration and assonance, repetition, rhythm, simile, and metaphor are common features of all Hmong poetry, besides the complications of achieving tonal agreements and reversals or inversions. Hyperbole (poetic exaggeration) and euphony (inserting meaningless words for the sake of their sweet sounds) are also very frequent devices, and there are sophisticated techniques of irony and personification. Numbers are used to achieve particular poetic effects and often objects are doubled in gender (as in "Lady Sun, Lord Moon"). These techniques and passages are usually learned, performed, and passed down orally from performers and/or teachers to younger students. They are never performed as mere verbal recitals, perhaps because the language itself is tonal, but as songs or chants in plainsong with their distinctive melodies pertaining to their particular genre, and are always connected with a particular social event or occasion in real life. So poetry and song are a part of everyday social life, and this apart from folktales is the main means whereby the oral tradition is transmitted. Although the composition is similar, the melodies for traditional secular singing are quite different from those of the mournful *Qhuab Ke* or the *Txiv Xaiv* sung during funerals, which we have examined above. We will be able to look at traditional singing in greater detail later.

New Poetry in Hmong

Since 1975, following their second diaspora, the Hmong have introduced a new form of written poetry called *paj huam* or *lus rho* (combined words) with metrical patterns and rhymes based on Western rhyming verses. It is written usually in RPA and performed as rap, recited as poems at special events, or sold commercially as cassettes and DVDs. Although the new Hmong poetry in Hmong was born in the refugee camps in Thailand and largely inspired by Hmong messianic beliefs in a new Hmong culture, imbued with nationalism, the new poetry written in English represents the "free-spirit" nature of its practitioners—the younger Hmong educated in the West who are deeply influenced by Western ideas and literature.

The best known of the new poetry artists are Lis Txais, the former leader of the Chao Fa messianic movement in Ban Vinai refugee camp, the group Phim Nyuj Vaim, and the solo performer Bav Ntsuab, both based in the United States. They are all commercial artists and set their poetry to music on DVDs for sale. Lis Txais laments the loss of the homeland and the cruelty of forced separation by war of lovers or relatives in traditional rhyming verse, often without music. Phim Nyuj Vaim and Bav Ntsuab, on the other hand, use free verse mixed with dialogue and music, often in the style of American rappers. Their most common themes are satires on the new life in the United States, appeals for Hmong to love each other, or making fun of American Hmong women and their freedom, which usually makes their poor hapless husbands victims of American laws on sexual equality and reverse domestic violence. Because they make fun of life-problems in strange new environments, they have become very successful, each having produced five to six albums so far. Phim Nyuj Vaim even marketed a DVD of their best poetic satires in 2007.

Poetry in English

Another new breed of poets to emerge following the Hmong settlement in Western countries consists of younger men and women who received a Western education in American schools, studied and read American litera- ture, and are inspired to use American literary forms to write about Hmong themes and issues, to explore their Hmong identity and concerns in the diaspora. They write in English, using Hmong familiar metaphors. Some of their early works can be found in the 2002 book, *Bamboo among the Oaks*.

Among the most active Hmong poets writing in English is Ka Vang, the playwright. She not only publishes poems but also gives public read- ings of her poetry. Vang's poetry has strong imagery and metaphors that fuse contemporary social concerns with pop culture and literary symbols of both Western and Hmong origins. Katie Ka Vang is another poet who, like Ka Vang, also writes plays and does public readings of her poems. Her latest collection of poetry was released as a chapbook called *Never Said* in December 2008. She has been described by Bryan Thao Worra, the famous American Laotian poet, as a significant voice within the Hmong arts community. The third well-known Hmong American poet is Pacyinzs Lyfoung, whose family re-migrated from France and who started writing poetry as a way to find her own place in the United States. She is a niece of the famous Hmong leader, Touby Lyfoung. She has also published her poetry and is a popular public reader of her own works. May Lee Yang, a member of the Hmong American Institute of Learning (HAIL) in St Paul, Minnesota, has published her poems in *Paj Ntaub Voice*.

Mai Neng Moua, who edited *Bamboo among the Oaks*, has written many poems and short stories, mostly focusing on war (for example, "Along the Way to the Mekong"), family issues ("Father Died Twenty-five Years Ago"), the generation gap between traditional Hmong parents and their Americanized children ("My Mother Is a Coffee Table"), or the gulf between Hmong and White Americans ("My White Lover"). Gary Yia Lee writes poetry in a more metrical classical form, mainly about love and feelings toward family and friends, searching for a Hmong identity, and marginalization issues in modern society (for example, the "Lost Beloved"). Some of his poems have been reprinted in various other publications and most are hosted on his own Web site.[39]

The most influential of the new poets remains Bryan Thao Worra. Although he is not Hmong by birth, he has adopted a Hmong name and been accepted into the Hmong community as one of their own. He remains a major inspiration to young Hmong writers through his short stories, plays, and essays. This is further enhanced by his public poetry readings at various venues in the Twin Cities in Minnesota, and the promotion of his books on My Space or on his own Web site.[40] His works have been published in Australia, Singapore, Germany, England, and the United States. He is featured in anthologies such as *Bamboo among the Oaks, Outsiders Within*, and *Contemporary Voices from the East*. Four books of his poetry have been published: *The Tuk-Tuk Diaries: My Dinner with Cluster Bombs, Touching Detonations, On the Other Side of the Eye*, and *Barrow*.[41] He explores a wide range of social and cultural themes, and the transient nature of identity and home. He has been a recipient of many awards, including the National Endowment for the Arts fellowship in 2008, the Minnesota State Arts Board Cultural Collaboration Award in 2005 with Mali Kouan-chao, the Minnesota Playwrights Center Many Voices Artist-in-Residence in 2002, and literary awards from Otterbein College.

There are other Hmong poets who occasionally write in English, whose work can be seen in various issues of *Paj Ntaub Voice* magazine and other publications. However, those who are better known are the few poets who regularly take part in the public reading of their poetry, such as Lyfoung and Ka Vang. Their recorded poetry readings can be seen on YouTube.

Literary Organizations

Minnesota, with its 60,000 Hmong population, has been the home of many budding talents in Hmong literature and play-writing. Most have

Poetry reading night, 2007; from left to right: Ka Vang, Bryan Thao Worra, Pacyinzs Lyfoung, and David Zander, event organizer. Courtesy of the authors.

been nurtured by two organizations. The first is the Hmong American Institute of Learning (HAIL), which publishes *Paj Ntaub Voice*, the longest-running literary arts journal devoted to Hmong art and literature. Established in 1994, it supports Hmong writers and artists by providing a community forum to nurture the growth and celebration of Hmong art and writing through publication and public reading by the writers it publishes. Its magazine, *Paj Ntaub Voice,* began as a youth project of the Hmong American Partnership (which produces the teenage magazine *Hmoob Teen* in St. Paul) before coming under the Hmong American Institute for Learning (HAIL) when it was formed in 2003. Today, about 15 to 25 writers and artists are featured in each issue, and the journal is published twice a year. In 2007, HAIL adopted a new mission statement and changed its name to Hmong Arts Connection (HArC).[42] The second organization is the Center for Hmong Arts and Talents (CHAT), also in St. Paul. Its major goal is to assist playwrights and performance artists to develop their potentials and interests—whether on paper or on the stage. It held a very successful festival on August 25, 2007, at Western Sculpture Garden in St. Paul. It takes young Hmong artists as interns to help further their skills and career, and runs a weekly radio show on Hmong art and talents.

In addition to these two organizations, there is an informal Hmong Writers Group that meets occasionally under the guidance of Mai Neng Moua and May Lee Yang. Their aim is to read members' writings and offer constructive comments to help them develop their writing skills. A similar group, called the Hmong American Writers' Circle (HAWC), consisting of established and emerging Hmong creative writers, also operates in Fresno in California's Central Valley. Established in 2004, it holds bimonthly workshops where members read and critique one another's pieces, thus trying to provide social and professional support to Hmong writers. Writing about the group in *New America Media,* Mai Der Vang states that ". . . documenting how our cultural past connects to the present—as we are straddling dual identities, and rediscovering our roots—allows us to do something our ancestors long ago could not: preserve this moment in history for the next generation to read."[43]

Online Literary Magazines

There have also been online magazines that cater to the needs of Hmong artists and writers. Two well-known ones are: *Unplug/Writer's Block* (a Hmong subculture magazine)[44] and personal stories by Renee Ya. The recently inaugurated *18 Xeem*, a cultural Hmong magazine, also includes poetry and short stories in very expensive colorful layouts. Its target audience is young Hmong people.[45] Overall, there seems to be proliferation of talents, individuals, and groups whose aim is to support the development of Hmong written literature, at least in the United States. Not much literary development has taken place in Laos, Thailand, or France, probably because of the lack of institutional and personal support for artists and writers in those countries.

Fast assimilation of the younger Hmong into mainstream cultures during the last 35 years has played a big part in whether or not some of them will want to write using Hmong themes and values. Many will not have much feel for the Hmong culture, and will not miss it strongly enough to want to write and capture its loss on paper. Hmong oral literature will continue to be used well into the future so long as their traditional belief system continues to survive, especially traditional funeral texts such as the *Qhuab Ke,* the *Txiv Xaiv,* and the *Nkauj Plig,* as well as the traditional singing and reed pipe *qeej* music. Funeral chants are still mandatory for any traditional Hmong funerals where the families involved are still following Hmong religious beliefs. Strict procedures have to be followed, and every chant has to be in its proper place, or else the soul of the departed will not reach the land of the ancestors. Conversion to Christianity and other religions will erode the use of these funeral texts, and a large part of Hmong oral literature might disappear as a result.

Folktales may not be told orally anymore among the Hmong in Western countries, but they have been recorded in books and will be read from time to time. They are still being told in the more isolated areas in Laos, Vietnam, and China where television and other forms of modern entertainment do not occupy people in the evening. Even here, the movies that have been made from these myths and stories are sometimes watched on video or even DVD players if there is electricity to run them. What is likely to flourish in the next few years will be the new Hmong poetry (both oral and written), written literature such as poems, short stories, and novels, plays, and the oral-visual forms of Hmong motifs in movies and DVDs. It is worth remembering again that the majority of Hmong only learned to read and write since the 1960s during the Lao civil war, and many women only became educated after their resettlement in the West in 1975. The future of Hmong literature will depend not only on how many people write, but also on the number of readers who read their writings. Nonetheless, it is clear that a very significant start has been made and that the talents of the Hmong in oral literature are translating well into written forms of literature.

NOTES

1. A language cannot be understood by speakers of another language. Speakers of different dialects within the same language can understand each other.

2. See Vang, C.K., Yang, and Smalley 1990, and Smalley, Vang, and Yang 1990.

3. Johnson 1992, xv.

4. Bertrais 1985 and 1992; Giacchino-Baker 1995; Johnson 1992; Livo and Cha 1991; Numrich 1985; Vang and Lewis 1990.

5. Graham 1954.

6. Bender 2006.

7. Bender 2006, 159–68.

8. Ibid., 163. It is probable that Chinese censorship has deleted references to a deity here.

9. Ibid., 166.

10. Van 1993, 304–37; Lemoine 1972b; Proschan 2001.

11. Johnson 1992, 115–117.

12. Livo and Cha 1991, 43.

13. See versions in Graham 1954, Lemoine 1972b, and Geddes 1976, 23.

14. See, for example, *Tub Yug Nyuj thiab Ntxawm* (1996), *Nuj Phlaib thiab Ntxawm* (1998), *Ntxawm Qaum Ntuj* (no date), *Nkauj Nog thiab Sis Nab* (no date), *Niam Nkauj Zuag Paj thiab Txiv Ntraug Ntsuag* (2002), *Ntsuag Plis thiab Paj Tsua* (2002). Many movies were made without a date on the cover.

15. Bender 2006.

16. Hudspeth 1937, 9–10; Geddes 1976, 4.

17. Bender 2003.

18. Mareschal 1976, 91.

19. We are grateful to Tou Ger Lee, of the Hmong Culture Center in St. Paul, Minnesota, who kindly gave Gary Lee permission in 2007 to use a copy of his recording "Showing the Way" (*Qhuab Ke*) and Soul Chanting (*Nkauj Plig*), which he has been using to teach young Hmong people there.

20. Based on Gary Lee's own live recording of Mrs. Tong Yer Thao's funeral on January 21, 2007, in Plower, Wisconsin. Permission to record and use of this material from her family is hereby fully acknowledged.

21. For translations of the *Qhuab Ke*, see Lemoine 1972b, in three articles, and 1983; Symonds 2004; and Chindarsi 1976.

22. Bertrais 1986.

23. For a complete transcript of the *Txiv Xaiv*, see *Kab Ke Pam Tuag* (Funeral Rituals), Vol 2: *Cov Txheej Txheem (the Rituals)* published by the Hmong Culture Heritage, French Guyana 1986.

24. Mareschal 1976, 108.

25. Mareschal gives the musical scores and Hmong words for all these; there is also a record and CD available. The spontaneous songs sung by women to the deceased at a funeral are known as *kwv txhiaj tuag*, but this practice has virtually disappeared today.

26. Yaj 1976.

27. Lyman 2004.

28. See Yaj 1976; Mottin 1978; Heimbach 1979; Vang and Lewis 1990; Leepreecha 1994; Lyman 2004.

29. Smalley, Vang, and Yang 1990, 151–54.

30. Bertrais 2002.

31. Pollard 1919; Bernatzik 1970; Graham 1954; de Beauclair 1970; Hudspeth 1922; Savina 1924.

32. Yang Dao 1975.

33. See Pfeifer 2007, who lists 612 works mostly in English on the Hmong between 1996 and 2006, excluding masses of newspaper articles but including a growing number of MA and PhD dissertations by Hmong themselves; Olney 1983; Smith 1988 and other bibliographies listed in http://www.hmongstudies.org.

34. See http://www.hmongnet.org/hmong-au/ozintro.htm. Accessed 19 May 2010.

35. http://blog.lib.umn.edu/fangx046/ealhmong. Accessed 19 May 2010.

36. Leepreecha 2008.

37. Culler 1997, 27.

38. See www.hmongabc.com. Accessed 19 May 2010. This is the only Hmong bookshop that carries the most titles available on the Hmong, including art and crafts items.

39. http://www.garyyialee.com. Accessed 19 May 2010.

40. http://thaoworra.blogspot.com. Accessed 19 May 2010.

41. In 2003, 2003, 2007, and 2009, respectively.

42. For more information, see http://www.hmonghail.org. Accessed 19 May 2010.

43. "On the Verge of a Hmong-American Literary Movement" by Mai Der Vang 19 August 2008, available at http://news.newamericamedia.org/news/view_article. html?article_id=1d0fdf1242aa3c465b768ece052a89a9. Accessed 2 January 2009.

44. At http://www.unplugmag.com. Accessed 19 May 2010.

45. Samples of articles can be accessed at www.18xeem.com. Accessed 19 May 2010.

4

Theater, Dance, Music, and Film

CULTURE CONSISTS OF the end-products resulting from the production, regulation, representation and consumption of cultural formations in society. Among other things, theatre, dance, music and film form those components that are classified as the performing arts. Like other cultures, Hmong performing arts consist of these components but also include public poetry reading, funeral chants, wedding songs, and epic singing, with the latter being more common among the Hmong-related groups in China. In Vietnam, the Hmong are said to have a form of rhyming poetry that tells mythical history. Recently, they have adopted many kinds of solo or group dances and have given dazzling performances at New Year competitions and other special events. These dances are usually adaptations of dance styles from other cultures such as Lao, Thai, Chinese, Indian, rap, and hip hop. The rap dances in particular are very popular with Hmong young people, and always draw whistles from members of the audience. Apart from dances, other forms of modern entertainment have also been added to the Hmong cultural repertoire.

THEATRE

Traditionally, the Hmong do not have performing arts used for entertainment, except for wedding singing and funeral chants. For example, Graham states that the Chuan Miao or the Hmong in Sichuan, China, "have no theatricals."[1] This may have been true 80 years ago, but today it is very different as the Hmong have assimilated theatre ideas from neighboring groups and have started their own performances in this field.

Village and Community Performances

Unlike the Chinese, Lao, and Thai, the Hmong did not have village theatre until a few years ago. Some of those in Laos and China had probably seen folk operas performed by mainstream troupes at local festivals, playing well-known national folktales, but there had never been Hmong performers using Hmong stories. It was not until they became refugees in Thailand after 1975 that Hmong began theatre performances for the first time, thanks to the inventiveness of the Chao Fa messianic movement in Ban Vinai refugee camp. Its leader, Lis Txais, not only formed a band with an assortment of musical instruments, both modern and traditional, but also presented skits on stage during Hmong New Year celebrations.

In 1985, a health theatre project was initiated in Ban Vinai by Dwight Conquergood.[2] The project aimed to bring health education to the camp's Hmong residents. The first campaign was to get Hmong families to bring their dogs for vaccination against rabies. After communication by word of mouth failed to attract any attention, the project used two young actors dressed as a tiger and a rooster, respectively, who walked through the camp delivering the message while other members of the troupe dressed in normal clothes accompanied them with Western-style music. The next day 500 dogs with their owners turned up at the camp's health station for vaccination. Other campaigns then followed. This health theatre is a good example of how the Hmong were introduced to theatre shows, using their own culture and performers to bring attitude change and education to the people.

A similar project has been going on in Laos where national development can bring many modern benefits, but where rural people are not informed about how to make the best deal in a negotiation, how to avoid being lured into prostitution by human traffickers, or even how to get information on health issues and government services. Theatre is seen as an effective method of awareness-raising on such issues and can therefore play a key role in community education.[3] A Hill Tribe Theatre was, thus, formed in March 2004 by the Lao government with assistance from foreign donor organizations involved in development work in Laos. It has five teams representing the five main hill tribes in Northern Laos and their rich diverse cultures: the Khmu, Hmong, Yao, Lahu in Bokeo, and Akha in Luang Namtha province. Each team performs in their ethnic language in markets and villages of the same ethnic background.

Although theatre is new to rural people in Laos, it allows even those without formal education to be involved in issues relevant to them while also being entertained, especially if the stories are based on the local culture, and are told through dialogues mixed with ethnic music and dance from the actors. Since their establishment, the teams have performed in 37 villages on the subjects of drug abuse, HIV/AIDS, micro-finance, agriculture, and gender equality. The Hmong team is called Team *Tsim Kho* or "Bring Changes." Its members are from Xaichaleun village, in Nampuk area, Houei Sai district (Bokeo province). They are all farmers, and are of the White Hmong subgroup. Two members of the *Tsim Kho* team are said to be talented artists who learned to make visual aids to enliven their presentations. The team has developed a number of plays to encourage adult women to participate in short-term education programs, to promote soybean as a cash crop, or to show audiences the problems of drug abuse.

Modern Theatre and Plays

Modern theatre and plays among the Hmong in the United States are a recent new field appropriated from the mainstream culture, an area in which many young Western-educated Hmong have been most active, whether through schools or in the broader community. Some examples will be discussed to illustrate this form of Hmong performing art in various U.S. cities.

In 2005, Professor Kim Morin from the Theatre for Young Audiences at the Department of Theatre Arts, California State University, Fresno, co-wrote a play with five students called *Yer's Pa Ndau: A Hmong Tiger Tale.* It had a cast of three Hmong and an assortment of other characters like a tiger, a crow, and a monkey. The play was adapted from a Hmong folktale called "Yer and the Tiger" as a way to share the rich culture and folk arts of the Hmong people, and to present Hmong culture, as Yer gradually discovers the importance of traditions and family in the story. The play was performed by student actors in nearly 30 elementary schools around the Central Valley in California. The nine actors went through several costume changes, including puppet costumes, to interact with their young audiences, thus also giving opportunity for aspiring Hmong and other artists to showcase their talents.

In another part of the Midwest United States, another company called Creative Theatre Unlimited presents Hmong music, storytelling, and dance on stage in both Hmong and English to audiences in the Twin Cities in Minnesota with its large Hmong population. This was set up in 1983 by Charles Numrich, who later published a short book of Hmong folk stories.[4] According to its Web site, "as the Hmong become more and more a part of mainstream life in the United States . . . the stories, music, dance, and handcrafts (sic) of this ancient culture provide excellent introductions for the broader community, and for the Hmong, a means to preserve this heritage in this country."[5] The presentation includes music, dance, and stories performed by various Hmong artists, with Numrich providing background information to help the audience understand these art forms and their place in Hmong culture. Performers play the *qeej* or reed pipe music instrument, the flutes, the two-stringed *xim xos*, and the mouth harp or *ncas*. The Hmong folktales are told in English.

As with the play *Yer's Pa Ndau* in Fresno, California, Hmong students play a large part in developing and acting in plays and skits that relate to the need of maintaining their Hmong culture and the positioning of themselves in urban America. This may not seem like much for countries that are used to having a long history of professional theatre like England and the United States. However, keeping in mind that the Hmong have been exposed to this art form only since their settlement in the West, to be able to write, act in, and produce a modern play on stage for an audience is no small accomplishment. Those involved in this process show that they have adopted theatre as a means to convey important messages that are vital to themselves and their community, especially the younger generation dealing with identity issues faced by many of them in their everyday life.

An excellent example of this self-exploration is the play staged on November 22, 2008, at the University of Minnesota Student Hall, by the Hmong Minnesota Student Association. The play, called *Crossroads in Time*, was part of the *Hmong Heritage Show, Keeping Hmong Culture and Traditions Alive,* and was attended by more than 700 people. The play focuses on who the Hmong are by depicting the main protagonist as a young Hmong rebel who prefers to be known by his American name, Paul, and rejects his own ethnicity in the present. The play shows him travelling back in time in his sleep to the past in Laos in 1975, when the Vietnam War was about to end. There, he met a young Hmong girl, named Suab Nag (Sound of Rain), who saved him when he became sick. Suab Nag reintroduced Paul to the values of being Hmong. Through her he discovered who he was and learned to accept his Hmong identity. They fell in love but she died on their way back to the present because she belonged to the past. The show also included other Hmong cultural items such as Hmong *xim xos* violin playing, flute, the traditional singing of *kwv txhiaj*, Hmong dances, and Hmong songs.

An earlier Hmong theatre initiative that tried to be professional was the *Pom Siab Hmoob* Theatre (Gazing into the Heart of the Hmong). Based in

Minneapolis, in the Twin Cities, like the Creative Theatre Unlimited, it was described as the first Hmong theatre in the world. Formed in 1990, its aim was to bring Hmong culture to both Hmong and U.S. audiences through the medium of theatre arts. In 1995, the *Pom Siab Hmoob* presented its fourth play, *The Garden of the Soul,* a play that had 16 characters, and was directed by Nkauj'lis Lyfoung, who also devised the costumes and props. The writers included Jaime Meyer, Nkauj'lis Lyfoung, Cy Thao, Pang Thao, Teng Xiong, Kaola Vang, Seng Moua, Shoua Moua, Terri Thao, and Lee Vang. The play was described by the local *Star Tribune* newspaper (December 8, 1995) as "community theater in the best sense of the term," with its story of a Hmong family's struggle with male domination, assimilation, and the conflict between Christianity and shamanism in the United States described in Chapter 2. As an indication of its appeal, the third annual Hmong National Development Conference invited the *Pom Siab Hmoob* Theatre to perform *Hmong Tapestry: Voices from the Cloth* on April 10, 1997, in front of participants of the conference in Eau Claire, Wisconsin, where there was a sizable Hmong population.[6] The play was chosen because of its focus on Hmong history, beliefs, and culture, which would enrich conference attendees' knowledge of the Hmong.

By 1997, *Pom Siab Hmoob* had put on four plays, with the first being *Hmong Tapestry: Voices from the Cloth* that is available today on video. Their second play was *Peb Yog Hmoob: We Are Hmong*, about the pressures inside a Hmong family. The third play, *Tub Ntsuag Thiab Nkauj Zaaj: The Orphan Boy and the Dragon Princess* combined several famous Hmong fairy tales into one epic tale. Other plays followed, such as *Hmong! The CIA's Secret Army* by Lee Vang, *Hush Hush, The Orphan Boy*, and the 2007 *The Myth of Xee*. With financial support from the Bush Foundation, Northern States Power, the Otto Bremer Foundation, the St. Paul Companies, and the General Mills Foundation, the theatre organizers decided in 1998 to expand to include artists in other fields in the Hmong community. The group's name was thus changed to the Center for Hmong Arts and Talent (CHAT), which still continues today. Their focus now includes visual arts, literary arts, music, traditional Hmong arts, and multimedia arts-making. Today, CHAT tries to have more impact through the harnessing of the arts as a source for individual empowerment and as a means for social change. The organization offers open microphone nights, afterschool art classes, and other educational endeavors geared toward at-risk Hmong children and teens. In addition, CHAT hosts a weekly Hmong radio show, annual arts festival, and a fashion show.

In 2007, CHAT decided to go back to theatre work with its Dawning/ *DabNeeg* Theatre in a program called *Old Stories in a New Light*. The aim of the program is to encourage Hmong artists to be involved in all artistic aspects of the theatre, from actor to designer to director, so that they can have recourse to all art forms. Hmong playwright May Lee-Yang's play called *Stir Fried Pop Culture* was the first to be produced under this program. After being very well received in the Twin Cities in Minnesota, where it ran from January 11 to 13, 2008, the play went on tour to colleges in Minnesota and Wisconsin in April and May to celebrate Asian Awareness Month. Commenting on the first performance at the Mounds Theatre in St. Paul, Song Vang wrote that *"Stir-Fried Pop Culture* is an intelligent and comical play about the stereotypes and identity issues Hmong-Americans face."[7] Like other plays in the past, it examines the fluidity of culture and what it is to be Hmong in the United States with five vignettes written, directed, and performed by Hmong artists. According to Kathy Mouacheupao, CHAT executive director, "the goal of Dawning is to share the Hmong experience through theatre. . . . We have never had that before and *Stir-Fried Pop Culture* is only the beginning. We hope it will create a spark that will eventually grow into a substantial Hmong theatre arts community."[8]

No stage plays and theatre performances would see the light of day without playwrights, directors, stage managers, and actors. However, theatre and films are an area where few of those involved stay long enough to become well known, as is common in the entertainment industry. Among those who have had their plays performed or published is Katie Ka Vang, who is based in St. Paul, Minnesota.[9] She has acted in plays for CHAT, the Pangea World Theater, Theater Mu, and Exposed Brick Theatre. In 2007, she directed and co-wrote the youth play *Myth of Xee,* and is the Creative Associate for Exposed Brick Theater and a 2007 Naked Stages recipient. Vang has performed for different theaters around the Twin Cities of Minnesota. She is part of the Pangea World Theater ensemble, and performed with them in *From the Ashes* in New York City at the National Asian American Theater Festival and also performed solo performance art piece *5:1 Meaning of Freedom; 6:2 Use of Sharpening*, produced by Intermediate Arts. She has often collaborated with the Hmong writer May Lee Yang.

A second very productive playwright and community activist is Ka Vang.[10] Her first one-act play, *DISCONNECT*, was performed at the Playwrights' Center, Minneapolis, and by Theatre Mu during the 2001 New Eyes Festival. It has also appeared in the 2002 anthology, *Bamboo among the Oaks*. Another play, *Dead Calling*, was performed at Intermedia Arts in Minneapolis in 2001. It deals with the problems of inter-racial marriage in the Hmong community. A third play, *From Shadows to Light*, performed by Theater Mu in the fall of 2004, focuses on contemporary international women's issues and traditional art forms from Asia.

A third Hmong playwright is Michele Lee, based in Melbourne, Australia. Lee was born in Australia, of Hmong parents who were former refugees from Laos. She did tertiary studies in theatre and playwriting, and has written four plays, one of which was set in Canberra, the capital of Australia and her family's home. In 2008, she completed a play called *See How the Leaf People Run* that had its first public reading in December of that year in Melbourne. The play explores Hmong memories of the pre-1975 war in Laos, and how it affects their life in present-day Australia. She has received a number of playwriting awards, and has acted in mainstream stage productions. These are new forms of production for the Hmong, in English, and it is encouraging to see how their traditional gifts for expression are meeting with success in such new formats.

The success of theatre productions depends also on the talents of their actors. A well-known Hmong male actor is Ethen Xiong, who has worked with *Pom Siab Hmoob* Theater in which he acted, directed, and co-wrote such shows as *The Orphan Boy and the Dragon Princess, Hmong Cinderella*, and *Hmong Tapestry: Voices from the Cloth*, among others. Another well-known Hmong theatre personality is Nkauj'lis Lyfoung, who co-founded the *Pom Siab Hmoob* Theatre. She is an actor, director, and playwright. She co-wrote and directed the 1995 *Garden of the Soul*.

Sandy'Ci Moua is another longtime actress, also based in the Twin Cities, Minnesota. She has been acting for the last 11 years in films and on stage, not only in Hmong but also in mainstream plays. Apart from appearing as the lead in four films, she has acted on stage in *Watching Porn*; *Midsummer Night's Dream*; *1,000 Cranes*; *The Buddha Prince*; *The Laramie Project*; *In the Heart of America*; *From Shadows to Light*; *Women! Live Onstage!*; *The First Time: Three Voices*; *Orphan Boy and the Dragon Princess*; *Boy Meets Girl*; *Hush, Hush*; *The Vagina Monologues*; *History of the Hmong*; *Hmong!: The C.I.A.'s Secret Army*; and *Cinderella: Nkauj Nog*, among others. She frequently works with Theater Mu, and has had her work published in the anthology *Yell-oh Girls*. She recently branched into production and casting consultancy work and is in the process of compiling a free listserv, "The Hmong Actor's Database," where she will also announce acting opportunities for aspiring performers and subscribers. In 2008, she helped with the casting of Hmong actors in Clint Eastwood's film *Gran Torino*.

We should also mention the first Hmong solo stage performer in the United States who has emerged since the Hmong migration there. A member of the Association for Applied and Therapeutic Humor (AATH), Tou

Ger Xiong is currently a diversity consultant, comedian, storyteller, rap artist, and actor. He has been described as part Elvis, part Jim Carrey, and part Chris Rock but 100 percent Hmong. According to his online biography, he was born in Laos in 1973 and graduated valedictorian from Humboldt High School in St. Paul in 1992.[11] After graduating with a degree in political science from Carleton College in Northfield, Minnesota, he created *Project Respectism* in 1996. The project uses comedy, storytelling, and rap music as a means to bridge the gap between cultures and generations. Xiong has taken his message about respect to 44 states, and has given over 1,600 presentations to audiences of all ages and ethnic backgrounds. He has been featured on national television, radio, and newspapers. A documentary on his work, entitled *Hmong Means Free*, was also aired on public television. Xiong also starred in *Portraits from the Cloth*, a television movie about a Hmong family's escape from war. He was awarded the National Alumni Hall of Fame Award from the United Neighborhood Centers of America and the Pride of St. Paul's Spurgeon Award.

Oral and Musical Traditions as Performance Art

Before ending on Hmong theatre, it is important to note that Hmong oral and sung texts like the wedding chants and the funeral chants, as well as the reed pipe music and traditional singing we will consider in this chapter, can also be seen as a form of performance.[12]

Gifted singers and musicians will draw a large crowd or will sell many DVDs of their recorded songs. They will be admired and get paid for their performances, whether at the New Year festival or at a wedding. The *mej koob* or marriage negotiators who know many wedding chants will be asked constantly to perform at weddings. They work in pairs and if they complement each other well, their performances will be praised and remembered. They will be sought after, but they will need to be careful not to drink too many cups of rice alcohol, the drink used for weddings, to avoid being drunk and unable to perform or become sick from alcohol poisoning. In terms of story-telling, a gifted raconteur will tell a folktale with appropriate gestures and vivid physical actions, mimicking the dialogues in the story, taking on the voices of different characters, with great shouts and noises to mark dramatic happenings, and so on. When it is a genuine performance, it can draw quite a crowd. In performing the song "Showing the Way" at a funeral, the chanter's actions constitute a performance in its own right as he reaches crucial stages in his chanting, like placing a cross-bow on the dead man's chest or hemp in his hands, as he tells the dead man to stuff up the yawning jaws of the Dragon and Tiger mountains.

Many Hmong ritual performers have shown highly developed skills for dramatic performance in many traditional ceremonies. The shaman is a good example of one who provides a most dramatic and exciting performance verbally and in his actions when he is in a trance. It is perhaps not surprising that the talents of these performers have been so successfully transformed into new media for consumers today.

DANCE

Traditionally, the Hmong did not have public dances as we know them with other societies, the sort where performers make lithe bodily movements in time with the sound of enchanting music. The only public dance was for reed pipe or *qeej* players, using their feet to jump up and down and around, sometimes falling on the ground and contorting their bodies like Houdini, while continuing to play their musical instruments without hurting themselves, a feat that only young men with supple bodies can manage during New Year festivals and other occasions. In China, young women now perform the *qeej* dance with men, but they only jump around with their legs in a line or in pairs. These public dance displays seem to be for the benefit of tourists, and the reed pipes played by the dancers do not have to be in tune with each other.

The Hmong only had words to describe the qeej dance as *tawg qeej* or "making turns with the *qeej*." No other term for dance specifically existed in their vocabulary, and so what we might call dance existed only in ritual form, as a performer used his body in combination with music to express a particular meaning connected with a specific social occasion—as with the *qeej* reed pipe players who could perform at death, at the New Year, or on other festive occasions, sometimes with amazing twists and bounds. Dance was not separate from normal social life as it has become in modern society. The phrase *seev cev*, meaning "undulating the body," came to be used for dance in general after they had migrated to other parts of the world in the 1970s. Of course, those who had worked previously in Laos as public servants or military officers were used to Lao dancing at official parties, and generally learned to *lamvong* (Lao style party dancing) quite nicely with their wives. After they arrived in the United States, they continued to *lamvong* wherever there were big celebrations like the New Year festival or other community events.

Although Hmong in China have been performing dances on stage for several decades, most of the dances are Chinese folk or stage dances that involve one to several dozen performers dressed in special antiquated dance costumes and brandishing colorful fans and other paraphernalia. Dancers are organized by provincial or county-level troupes and usually are choreo-graphed by trained artists influenced by the Stanislavsky school of drama, which came to China from the former Union of Soviet Socialist Republics (USSR) around folk motifs. Stage dances were not found with the Hmong in Southeast Asia until very recently, after the Hmong from Laos migrated to the West and became exposed to dances from other cultures with live stage shows or in movies. Initially, young girls rehearsed for dances to be put on at New Year parties around the country. However, Hmong leaders in U.S. cities with large Hmong populations and major New Year festivals soon encouraged dance competitions with big prize money.

Spurred on by these competitions, many Hmong girls in high schools begin to improvise and borrow dances from other people that appeal to them such as Thai, Indian, Chinese, and American. They usually spend months practicing their dance numbers. With the help of their parents, they design expensive dazzling costumes, most with Hmong motifs but some with exotic designs of their own. The costumes depend much on what dances they have improvised or borrowed from which cultures: Indian dan-ces would need Indian costumes, Thai dances Thai-style costumes, and so on. They call their groups fancy Hmong names such as *Nkauj Hmoob Paj Nra* (Hmong Girls of the Plains), and some pay professional choreogra-phers to work with them. The music used is that of the culture from which the dance is learned; for example, Lao music is used for Lao classical dance. A most popular dance with the younger people is rap or hip-hop dance, performed by groups of young men and women, to rap music.

It would thus appear that there is no going back for the variety of visual and performing arts that the Hmong have adopted. The direction they will take is hard to predict, but more and more diversity and creative talents are being displayed each year. Many Hmong dances are featured on You-Tube.[13] Another Web site, Hmong International Television: Kaj Siab Kev Lom Zem, sells Hmong music and movies, but also has clips on Hmong movies, dances, and music. Visitors can listen to Hmong modern songs. It also lists video and film producers.

Most of the dance groups only perform locally, but some are active in competitions at Hmong New Year in various states. These very enterpris-ing groups include *Paj Yeeb Ntsha* (dressed in Hmong costumes), *Mai Ker* dance (Hmong costumes), *Nkauj Hmoob Tshias Nag, Ntxhais Nra Iab, Ntxhais Qaim Hli,* and *Nkauj Hmoob Yaj Yuam.* Many tend to use very nationalistic music and songs about the Hmong diaspora, being separated from loved ones as refugees, and appealing to the Hmong people to love one another. Many girls participate out of national pride as talented young Hmong wanting to enrich Hmong culture and be part of its ongoing

Indian-style Hmong dance at New Year, in St. Paul, Minnesota, 2007. Courtesy of the authors.

evolution.[14] These songs also go to the hearts of the audience, pulling at not only their heartstrings but also their tear ducts. Both the poignant music and the glittering dance bring out all the emotions a Hmong can muster. Culture is being re-created through these new forms.

MUSIC

Graham notes that the Hmong in Sichuan in China, whom he calls Chuan Miao, have

many ballads, which are sung by individuals, and not in concert or in groups. . . . The instrumental music is pleasing to the Western ear. Especially interesting is the *luh sen*, which is a wind instrument having six tubes. When it is played the musician performs a dance much like that of a Scotch bagpipe player.[15]

Hmong traditional music besides singing consists of performance on solo instruments such as the reed pipe (*qeej* or *luhsen*), with the drum (*lub nruas*), various kinds of flute (*raj*), and the Jew's harp (*ncas*).[16] In Vietnam, the White Hmong also used to play a Chinese oboe (*suona*) that looks similar to a bugle or trumpet (*xyu*).[17] However, it is not found among the

Hmong of Laos, although the Hmong in China still use it at weddings and on other occasions. Before 1975, most Hmong music was heard only through the live playing of these traditional musical instruments.

Reed Pipe Funeral Music: Qeej Tuag

In Hmong funerals, we find the primary examples of ceremonial music. Apart from the *Qhuab Ke* ("Showing the Way"), the *Txiv Xaiv* chants, and the soul chanting (*nkauj tuag* and *nkauj plig*) that we considered in the previous chapter, the reed pipe funeral music (*qeej tuag*) is one of the most important performances in a Hmong funeral ceremony. These seemingly wordless tunes are performed after the *Qhuab Ke*, usually by two or more performers. The songs can be verbalized as verses, but their meanings are only communicated in music through the different notes of the pipes. Since the language is tonal, notes in the tunes signify words to those who understand them. These bamboo pipes are of different sizes and lengths, and emit different musical notes. When they are blown by the performers, their sounds can be deciphered as words from the funeral songs. They can be very melodious and touching to those who can "read" them in the music of the pipes. They are very sad, and easily bring tears to the eyes of those who know what they are saying. They are played both during the funeral and when the "soul-release" ceremony (*tso plig*) is performed some time after the burial when the soul of a dead person is invited back to the house so that it can be finally "released" to be born again.

The *Qeej Tuag* played during a funeral consists of many tunes, each of which is broken down into several parts. It starts with the *Qeej Tu Siav* (Life Expiring song), the equivalent on the *qeej* to the *Qhuab Ke* chanting. This piece of music follows immediately the *Qhuab Ke* in the funeral process, and is seen as the most important.[18] Not all players of the reed pipe know this long piece of funeral music. Like the *Qhuab Ke*, it is played to guide the soul of the dead to the land of the ancestors. It has six sections, each with a number of stanzas seen as steps in the journey to the Otherworld. The first stanza is called *Mob Tuag* and explains in music what brings death to humankind. The second, *Ntxuav Muag*, is played before washing the face of the dead. This is followed by the third stanza, *Ua Dab Vaj Dab Tsev Tsaug*, thanking household spirits such as (1) *Rooj txag*, the bedroom door spirit; (2) *Ncej Cub Ncej Txos*, the central post and fire place spirits; (3) *Hauv Plag*, the central wall spirits; (4) *Hav Pag Xua*, the main floor spirits; and (5) *Rooj Tag*, the main door spirit.

The fourth stanza, *Nce Ntuj*, is the longest and depicts the ascending to the village of ancestors of the soul: Day 1, 1 Step; Day 2, 2 Steps; through

Day 13, 13 Steps. This ascension to the Afterworld has 12 chants (*zaj*) of funeral music: (1) *Mus Xyuas Ntaiv Ntuj*, inspecting the Heavenly Stairs; (2) *Noj Lauv Qaib Siab*, eating the rooster's heart so the soul of the dead will follow/obey it as a guide to the land of the ancestors; (3) *Mus Teb Sov Ntuj Nkig*, when going through the Hot Land and Brittle Sky, use your umbrella; (4) *Mus Toj Kab Ntsig Rawm Kab No*, when going through the Slope of Caterpillars, the Hills of Cold Worms, use your hemp shoes; (5) *Mus Rhau Zag Ncauj Tsov Lo*, when going past the Dragon's Mouth and the Tiger's Teeth, feed them with hemp threads to make them busy so they will not bite you; (6) *Mus Toj Tsaus Huab Rawm Tsau Nag*, when passing through Cloudy Slope and Rainy Hill with noisy insects and howling leopards, do not be afraid, they are only your living relatives making funeral music for you; (7) *Mus Chaw Ua Daj Ua Lis Luam*, when reaching the plain of play and trickery, do not spend time playing sliding or you will never get to the ancestors; (8) *Ntxwg Nyoog Hav Pas Dej Iab Pas Dej Daw*, arriving at Ntxwj Nyug's's bitter pond and salty water, scoop three handfuls of water for the dead, three for the living, and three for yourself; (9) *Ntxwg Nyoog 99 Txoj Kab 88 Txoj Kev*; when at Ntxwj Nyug's 99 trails and 88 paths, take the high path to the ancestors, the lower path only leads to the land of trading horses and selling cattle; (10) *Mus txog chaw Koj Qaib Qua Luag Qaib Teb*, when reaching where your rooster crows, their roosters reply, these are not your ancestors; (11) *Mus txog chaw Luag Qaib Qua Koj Qaib Teb*, when reaching where their roosters crow, your rooster replies, this is where your ancestors live; (12) *Mus txog poj txog yawm*, after arriving at the ancestors, they will ask how you get there and you should say grass hoppers and crickets (metaphors for reed pipe and drum players) sent me here.[19]

The fifth stanza in the Life Expiring piece is called *Qeej Zais Roj Zais Hneev* or playing the *qeej* to hide the performers' tracks as the reed pipe musicians hide their presence from the spirits of the dead so they can safely return to the world of the living. The sixth and final recital, *Qeej Tiag Hauv Ncoo*, ends the *Qeej Tu Siav* playing by asking the soul of the dead to accept its fate of having to stay in the Otherworld and not be sad.

These *Qeej Tu Siav* musical stanzas closely mirror and reflect the progress of the soul as chanted in the *Qhuab Ke*. After it is completed, the *qeej* can be played to signify the following occasions: (1) *Qeej tsa nees*, putting the dead on the funeral horse[20]; (2) *Qeej lam xab lam hmo*, music to pass the night and the day; (3) *Qeej cob tsiaj*, offering sacrificial animals; (4) *Qeej tshai*, invitation to breakfast; (5) *Qeej su*, lunch offering; (6) *Qeej hmo*, dinner; (7) *Qeej tsa rog*, making war (with Chinese) to clear the way; (8) *Qeej xyuas xaus*, ending the day; (9) *Qeej hauv qhua*, music for official guests; and (10) *Qeej laug hnub laug hmo*, passing the day and night. It can also be played just to entertain the dead (*Qeej ua si*). On the last night of the funeral, the *Qeej hais xim/txiv xaiv*, music for the chanting of the *Txiv Xaiv*, is played. This has the following steps: (1) *rub rooj*, setting up the table; (2) *muab ncej xub qeej*, firing the "*ncej xub*" or arrow; and (3) *hlawv ntawv*, burning the paper money.

The last day before the burial sees the playing of the *Qeej hnub tshwm tshav thiab sam sab*, music for the (last) "open" day that further consists of: (1) *Qeej tawm nras*, taking the body out of the house to the open air; (2) *Qeej cob nyuj*, offering bull sacrifices to the dead; (3) *Qeej muab nyuj plig*, taking bull souls; (4) *Qeej foom ntawm qhov rooj*, blessing at the door; (5) *Qeej taug nyuj hneev*, following the bull steps; (6) *Qeej nas ncuav:* music to the squirrel; (7) *Qeej sawv kev*, setting off (to the gravesite); and (8) *Qeej ntxuav muag*, cleaning the face or the feet of those who go to the burial so as to leave evil spirits from the grave behind.

The reed piper players are the busiest performers at a funeral, and have the major role in each step of the funeral process. Like other funeral experts, they have many songs to perform to progress through the mortuary rites. Some of their funeral music scores are also played during the "soul-release" ceremony that takes place 13 days or sometime after the burial of the body. Without the *qeej tuag*, no traditional Hmong funeral will be possible.

Qeej; musical instrument used by Hmong in the funeral ceremony to send the spirit of the deceased to the afterlife. Also played at the Hmong New Year and other events. Members of the *Qeej* Troupe at Hmong Culture Center are pictured in this 2003 photo after a community performance. Courtesy of the Hmong Culture Center of Minnesota (http://www.hmongcc.org).

Traditional Singing

Traditional singing, one of the most popular forms of entertainment in Hmong society, can be solo or between singers of the opposite sex engaging each other in traditional dialogue songs known as *kwv txhiaj* (or *lus txhaj* in Blue Mong) during the New Year or on special occasions like weddings, and sometimes even funerals. This singing calls for poetic improvisation of verses that are sung without music, what Johns calls "Hmong sung poetry."[21] Some of these songs can be learned from other singers, but those who are very good with words can simply compose impromptu verses to sing in reply to each other. As we have noted, improvisation is a major aspect of the oral tradition. Most songs have four to five stanzas that come in couplets, which repeat the same pattern of words with only the last word of the verse changed to rhyme with the end of the next verse. The structure of the composition is what is known as parallelism, where the words in each verse repeated with only the last one changed to rhyme with the end of the next verse. This applies to nearly all Hmong oral poetry chanting, whether it is love songs or funeral soul chants. One needs a good memory to remember the words that are being repeated in each parallelism, and this repetition functions as an *aide-mémoire*.

Singers perform without any musical accompaniment, and the aim is to see who can deliver the most touching lyrics that have the best rhymes. Novices can learn the lyrics or poetic scales that make up the songs from other experienced singers. They can be improvised or composed on the spot by more experienced people, especially in a paired competition between a male and a female singer of the kind that occurs at the New Year. There are different genres in this style of singing, although generally it is associated with young people and courtship: (1) love songs or *kwv txhiaj plees* to engage in courting; (2) widow songs or *kwv tyxhiaj poj ntsuam* to express the feelings of suffering widows; (3) orphan songs or *kwv txhiaj ntsuag* to lament the plights of being an orphan; (4) wedding songs or *kwv txhiaj ua nyab* to wish the newly married a happy marriage or to lament the plight of being a daughter-in-law; (5) funeral songs or *kwv txhiaj tuag* to send the departed and to wish those living a good life, as we have mentioned in the previous chapter; (6) competition songs or *kwv txhiaj sib lwv* to express love and to outwit the opponent in a competition match with impromptu replies; (7) loss of home and country or *kwv txhiaj poob teb chaws* to express longing for people and places left behind; and (8) parting songs or *kwv txhiaj sib ncaim* to express sadness of having to go away from loved ones. *Kwv txhiaj* of most types are characterized by protracted long-drawn notes marking the end of verses or pauses in the song, with quite frequent yodelling to change up to a falsetto register and then back down again, always in a pentatonic scale.

Mottin, in his collection of 55 Hmong love-songs in Thailand, added a few other themes such as war songs and drinking songs that appear to be unknown to many Hmong today.[22] Among the Hmong of Laos, the most popular songs at present are about love, loss of country, and being orphans. However, a type of often moralizing song that he calls *lus taum* is very common to the Hmong of Vietnam, Laos, and Thailand, and is different from the *kwv txhiaj*. This has its own characteristic type of recitative rhythm and tune and always starts with the words *ua ciav* at the beginning of a verse. These are more serious than the other *kwv txhiaj*; they can be ballads or stories and tales of the past with a moral twist, and although they are sung, they sound more like spoken language than the courtship songs, with an urgent or compelling tone about them. They can also be used for love purposes, however. There also used to be a category of "scolding" or "lament" songs that a wife could publicly sing outside the house to shame a bad husband, one of the few devices a wife in traditional society could use to escape an unhappy marriage, short of actual suicide or divorce. Mareschal describes yet another genre known as *seev lus rov* or singing by using words in their reverse order, with its own particular tune. It may be used where a young man may wish to make a public announcement about his love for a girl of his choice without shaming her. The word you want to say is hidden between two others, so if one wants to say *lees*, one sings *leeb lus xu*. The notes are repeated in the same order each time.[23] However, this form of singing is now obsolete, and few Hmong know how to sing in this way.

Traditional singing exists among the Hmong in both China and Southeast Asia. Graham notes that the Hmong in Sichuan, China, have "many ballads, which are sung by individuals, and not in concert or in groups," although the tune varies from group to group, and especially from one region to another.[24] The variation in the scale or tune or *seev suab* depends on what subgroup of Hmong (White, Blue, or Striped) and which geographical locations are involved. The Hmong in China tend to sing in one scale, and without verses that repeat themselves or rhyme like the songs found in Laos. The Hmong in Vietnam near the Chinese border also sing in the same manner, and this is often difficult to understand for the Hmong in other areas. The further south we move toward Vietnam, Laos, and Thailand, the greater are the differences of scale and melody.

In the northwest of Vietnam near the Lao border, 12 main melodies can be found, typically in pentatonic scales, many of which share almost the same style of intonation as with the Hmong in Laos, because the people in this region speak the same Blue Mong and White Hmong dialects. A number of singers, both male and female, have recorded songs in the various registers.[25] The most famous proponents of these many styles are Shoua Yang, Mai Vue, and Pob Tsuas Lis, whose DVDs are readily available from Hmong video shops.

As in many indigenous art forms like jazz, improvisation is a most important part of Hmong traditional singing, as it also is in the folktales considered in the previous chapter. Often *kwv txhiaj* are made up on the spot by a couple singing to each other, which can be a test of their skillfulness and quickness of thought. The spontaneous funeral laments or *nyiav*, too, can be very moving as they are often sung straight from the heart.

During the civil war in Laos in the 1960s, much traditional Hmong music was played on radio broadcasts for propaganda purposes, thus making this style of singing well known to the general public. Many traditional songs have also been compiled into books in the Hmong RPA writing system. During the past 15 years, local and U.S.-based producers have created videos for international commercial release of Hmong village singers in Thailand and Laos, dressed in Hmong costumes, singing traditional songs. Often, a man and woman are seen singing in reply to each other—usually with songs composed impromptu on the spot about any subject, usually love (*kwv txhiaj plees*). These producers may pay the singers only a few hundred dollars each, and take any profits they can make from the sale of the videos. About a dozen of these videos are made each year. They are bought mainly by elderly consumers rather than younger Hmong in the diaspora because the poetic language used in these traditional songs is better understood and appreciated by them.

There have been major changes to Hmong traditional singing, not so much in its composition or style that has remained much the same, but in its delivery and use. In the past before there was electronic recording, only live performance was available so that it was not possible to listen to such singing when or where you wanted. Today, it is only a matter of putting an audio cassette or a compact disc with such music in a cassette or CD player, or downloading a music file from the Internet, and you can listen anywhere, for however long you want. The delivery may be "cold" but it is accessible any time, any place. The second most important change is in the use of the variety of scales and melodies that used to be specific to each region (northern or southern White Hmong) or a subgroup of Hmong such as Blue Mong or Striped Hmong. Formerly, these singing tunes or *seev suab* were markers of where the performer came from. Today, however, many singers have learned to sing in many melodic styles and White Hmong can sing in Blue Mong or vice versa. The result is that it is now difficult to distinguish the subgroup or regional origin of singers on the basis of their singing style alone unless we come to know them through other characteristics as well. Like their traditional costumes, traditional singing is now all mixed—making the Hmong even more like one single people with one global identity.

Modern Music

Hmong modern music developed mostly after 1975. Although some early compositions with modern lyrics and band music were attempted by Yang Dao in 1968 and Ly Pheng in 1972 in Laos, they were not widely known. When the first Hmong asylum seekers escaped from Laos to Thailand and were confined to Ban Vinai camp in 1976, many young men did not have much to do and also suffered from homesickness. Some began to use old guitars, cans, and tins as musical instruments to start a band. They imitated the Lao and Thai modern style of music by composing nationalistic or romantic tunes, recording them on portable cassette recorders and selling them as a way of making ends meet in the camp where handouts from the Office of the UN High Commissioner for Refugees were the only means of survival. At the same time, Lis Txais, the camp's messianic leader, also used band music and modern songs in a completely new style of singing to spread his message on the new world order for the Hmong.

From this early beginning in Laos and Thailand, a new form of musical entertainment slowly developed and has become a major part of Hmong culture today. The trauma of exile, the guilt of leaving loved ones behind in the homeland, and access to modern musical instruments or recording facilities contributed to accelerate this change. At the beginning, there were only a handful of singers who recorded their own songs on cassettes and sold them themselves. Some of these early recordings were well received by the Hmong public, especially younger Hmong Americans who preferred Western-style music. Notable among these early singers were Es Lis, Lis Pos, Tub Lis Vam Khwb, Toj Lis, and Mas Lis Vwj, the latter even making a few concert tours around the United States and France.

The success of U.S.-based singers has made other young Hmong with artistic ambitions in Laos and Thailand try their luck on the new music scene. One of the most successful Hmong singers in Laos in the 1980s was Koob Lisnhiajvws, while in Thailand, Luj Yaj and Tsab Mim Xyooj became the favorites. All three made a number of tours to the United States in the late 1980s, and later also acted as the leads in a few movies produced by ST Video International, the first video production company set up in Fresno, California, by Xub Thoj, a Hmong refugee from Laos.

Luj Yaj has remained in Thailand, but Tsab Mim later married an American Hmong and now lives in the United States. Other famous female singers include Ntxhee Yees Xyooj (Thailand), Paj Muas (Thailand), Ntxhais Yaj (United States), Dawb Thoj (Laos), Lis Vaj (United States), Maiv Muas (Laos), Mim Haam (China), and Npaub Vaj (United States). For male singers, some recent notables include Zeb Vwj (Laos), Yujpheej Muas (Laos), Pov Thoj (Thailand), Ntsaim Thoj (Thailand), Lis Ntaj (France), and Maim Lis (Laos).

With improvement in the quality of recording and singing, the market has seen many new singers coming on the scene, as older ones fade away. All are amateurs, few have any professional training. To appeal to a global audience, many singers have appropriated lyrics from other cultures such as Thai, Lao, Chinese, Japanese, Korean, Indian, and the West. Younger and more Westernized Hmong artists in Thailand and the United States also do rock, rap, and pop music. They also write lyrics mixed with English, forming their own bands and doing their own recording. This experiment in musical hybridity and simulation is not unusual, given that many Hmong artists and consumers have long been exposed to a vast variety of Asian and Western music. The field is very fluid. Even Hmong singers in China have had their songs recorded on videos and marketed.

Today, modern Hmong music has overtaken traditional singing in its appeal to listeners, and many radio stations now play fewer and fewer Hmong traditional songs. The new music is popular mainly with younger listeners, as older Hmong continue to prefer listening to traditional singing. Although many of the modern songs are about love, a theme popular with younger listeners, some singers also try to appeal to the older people by singing about the loss of the homeland and their separation from relatives in other places.

During the last 15 years, Hmong modern music has also been made popular on the Internet through online radio stations, music Web sites and YouTube with their many uploaded Hmong songs. Among the Web sites where modern Hmong songs are available for listening are: (1) http://www.music-zoosiab.com, which has instructions on how to open files to listen to music, but not to download; (2) http://www.hmongmusic.org, one of the oldest with a very comprehensive collection of modern Hmong, Thai, and Lao songs; and (3) http://www.ehmongmusic.com, which has a forum where readers can voice opinions on Hmong issues, not just Hmong music (all accessed 20 May 2010). A recent Web site lists a staggering 7,439 recorded modern songs from 123 Hmong artists and 14 music bands on 147 of its pages for people to listen to online.[26] There are many other personal and entertainment Web sites that offer Hmong music to download

Luj Yaj and Maiv Rwg Xyooj, two renowned Hmong singers from Thailand, on U.S. concert tour, 2007. Courtesy of the authors.

or simply to listen and enjoy online, depending on one's taste and preparedness to surf the Internet. Often, online Hmong radio stations such as the Suabhmoobradio and Hmong Minnesota Radio have many songs and even traditional music in their archived files for listeners to click and listen.

FILM AND VIDEO

The Hmong have also gone into film and video productions after they migrated to the West. Apart from making video and CD recordings of Hmong modern music and traditional singing, some producers also make documentaries on life in the old country of Laos and feature films. Many of these media productions have become big commercial successes among Hmong consumers in the diaspora. Traditional folk-tales have been used in movies as an important part of oral literature, and traditional singing has been put on video.

Documentaries

The earliest known documentary on the Hmong was made in 1936 by David C. Graham, a missionary who worked among the Ch'uan Miao in

Western China. It was a 14-minute, silent, black-and-white film that showed various aspects of village life and shamanic practice. In 1971, professor W. R. Geddes, of the Anthropology Department of Sydney University, made the film *Miao Year* about the Blue Mong in Meto, Chiangmai, Thailand. At the same time the ethno-documentary *The Meo* was made for Granada TV and shown in the BBC *Disappearing World* series by Brian Moser and Jacques Lemoine; it showed the daily life in Hmong villages in Laos, including a short shamanic session, and examined the impact of war on the Hmong of Laos. Other documentaries followed, by NBC (news reports) and the Central Intelligence Agency (CIA) (*Journey from Pha Dong*). Others were made about Hmong refugees after their arrival in the United States with such titles as *Becoming American* and *The Best Place to Live.*

The Hmong only began to produce documentaries in their own language in the early 1990s when some of the U.S. Hmong began to pay visits to China in search of the distant homeland of their social memories. This was followed by other documentaries on the Hmong in Burma, Vietnam, and Laos. These documentaries were first started by Xu Thao of All-Pro Productions, and ST Universal Video, Fresno, California, and became popular among the elderly Hmong who cannot read books or use the Internet. The early videos deal with the traditional life and exotic culture of Hmong communities in Asia. Some of them show American Hmong visiting the Hmong in China and engaging in cultural exchanges through singing and playing music, to see what they have in common or in what aspects they are different from each other. The video reconstructions of Hmong history in Laos and China by Yuepheng Xiong of Hmongland Publishing, Minnesota, have also been well received. Examples of his titles include *Taug Txoj Lwv Tshav* (*Follow the Blood Trail*) in two parts on the history of the Hmong and Miao in China; and *The Hmong and General Vang Pao: Secret War in Laos 1960– 1975*, also in two parts. This series of videos on Hmong history is an attempt to educate Hmong viewers about their national history in Laos and China. They inform the Hmong in the diaspora about the first legendary Hmong/Miao king, Chiyou, and other major figures of their past.

Since 2002, a political lobby group, the Fact Finding Commission (FCC), based in Oroville, California, has issued short videos made by Hmong guides with Western journalists who went secretly to areas occupied by remnants of the Hmong CIA "secret army" from the days of the Lao civil war in the 1970s. These were the Hmong on the Royal Lao government side who could not escape to Thailand as refugees after 1975, or who remained deep in the jungles of northern Laos to put up resistance against the new communist regime. Through the documentaries, we see these Hmong rebels living in bunkers under the cover of tree foliage, surviving on eating roots and leaves, with young men maimed by years of fighting against Lao government troops, children suffering from malnutrition and alleged chemical poisoning, and old soldiers pleading to be saved from the atrocities of the Lao authorities.

The 2006 documentary, *Hunted Like Animals*, was made by UN lobbyist Rebecca Summer on the plight of the Hmong at Huai Nam Khao (White Water), Petchaboon, Thailand. A third of the 8,000 asylum seekers there escaped from the jungles of Laos after many years of resisting the new Lao authorities. The video depicts young Hmong raped, killed, and disemboweled by Lao government troops in the most graphic details. It has interviews of Hmong women who used to be in the resistance movement but who surrendered to government troops with their families and were allegedly made sex slaves for Lao soldiers, being passed from one barracks to another. One woman, who even claimed to have become pregnant as a result, is seen pleading to be accepted for resettlement in a Western country.

Hmong video documentaries are thus a very powerful medium and have been used effectively by them for education, entertainment, and political purposes. They have been very powerful in terms of their impact on Hmong identity, nostalgia, longings, and on transnational homeland politics. Through the colorful images of the documentaries, Hmong traditional life, the sense of being dispossessed, and being victims of a more powerful and ruthless enemy continue to be passed on within the community and to the younger generation across the diaspora.

Feature Movies

Since their settlement in Western countries, the Hmong have made hundreds of feature films in America, Thailand, China, and Laos, although they are mostly amateur productions. A few of the younger directors have studied film production in American universities, but most have gone into the industry with only a lot of passion and the desire to use films as a way to transmit culture, feelings, and ideas in the Hmong diaspora. The process often involves a producer or director travelling from the United States to Laos or Thailand. With a movie camera or two in hand, he or she will try to get together a cast from Hmong villages to act for a few hundred dollars. He or she may already have a script or at least enough of a story line to improvise dialogue with the cast as they progress. As he or she usually travels on a tourist visa, the filming needs to be completed within two to three months, so the story has to be simple with only a small cast. The finished product is then taken back to the United States for editing and releasing to the market world wide within six to eight months.

Most of these Hmong movies try to make a hurried presentation of Hmong culture in celluloid form. A favorite theme is love and its many tribulations. However, the most common theme is the Lao civil war and its impact on the Hmong, how they fought in the jungles of Laos, and how they escaped to Thailand and to the West. Some movies show middle-aged men going back to Thailand or Laos to look for the families they left behind in their rush to seek asylum in a distant country. More recently, many directors seem to focus on the mid-life crisis suffered by Hmong males in the United States who go back to Laos and Thailand as *nyuj nrhiav zaub mo* (old bulls pining for tender grass) in search of younger wives before or after divorcing their older first spouses in the new country. Comedies have been well received, as evident in the very successful series *Dr. Tom* from the talent of Nkaj Muas, who is based in California. This is a parody of a Hmong conman in the United States who returns to Laos and tricks money-hungry young girls into marrying him or succumbing to his conniving, often with the help of his domineering wife back home. Hmong movies have thus covered a wide range of subjects and genres, from serious drama and melodrama to comedies aimed at Hmong consumers but not viewers outside the Hmong community.

This has somewhat changed in 2008 when the famous Hollywood actor-director Clint Eastwood made a film, *Gran Torino*, in Detroit, Michigan, where there is a large Hmong population. It featured a Hmong American cast, with a story involving a Hmong family who lives next door to a grumpy old white man played by Eastwood. One day, a boy named Tao from the Hmong family tries to steal the elderly man's vintage car, a Gran Torino, and this starts off a chain of events that makes him confront the Hmong family with violence. But the family reacts to his anger with benevolence and he eventually comes to make great friends with them and the local Hmong community, even sacrificing himself to protect Tao and his family at the end of the film.

The film provided mainstream American society with exposure to the Hmong for the first time since their settlement in the USA. After holding open casting calls attended by hundreds of Hmong in St. Paul, Fresno, and Detroit, Eastwood selected 10 Hmong leads and supporting players. Only one had acted before. Also hired were Hmong crew, cultural consultants, and dozens of extras for the film.[27] This was the first time that Hmong had gone Hollywood in such numbers. In the past, only two actors of Hmong background had had roles in Hollywood productions: Wa Yang in a small part in *Letters from Iwo Jima*, and teen actress Brenda Song, who has a recurring role on *The Suite Life of Zack and Cody*. Song had a starring role in the Disney TV movie *Wendy Wu: Homecoming Warrior*, about a Chinese-American prom queen turned woman warrior.

Films and videos are difficult and costly to produce, and the financial returns are often minimal, especially where no cinema release is available, as is the case with Hmong productions. Their financial success depends almost entirely on DVD sales in shops and at video outlets. It is no wonder that few production companies stay long on the scene. The consumers benefit the most. The current high demand for these film and video products has made them an integral part of the Hmong diaspora, a part closely tied to the imagined homeland and the traditional life left behind in the past. Few viewers can return in person to these places of their heart, but they can share the journey of those who can from their living rooms, and they can experience a mythic Hmong past in the form of fiction dramas or enjoy scenes of traditional singing contests. The migration from China was more than a century ago and many ties with China had already gone, but many Hmong in the diaspora still have fresh memories of Laos. Many connections with that part of the world remain, so they make and buy these films to satisfy their longings for it.

TRANSLATION AND THE QUESTION OF HYBRIDITY

Hmong theatre, dance, music, and film are mostly new inventions following recent exposure by the Hmong to other cultures such as Lao, Thai, Chinese, and American. Ideas for much of these different forms of entertainment are learned while living in the cities in Laos or in Thai refugee camps and later in Western countries. Whether they are imitations or appropriations from Chinese, Thai, Indian, and Western hip-hop dance styles, can the new Hmong dances, for example, be said to be part of a cultural hybridity process, or are they a new cultural formation altogether?

Something is hybrid if it is a mixture of different varieties or species, or if it is heterogeneous in origin or composition. Hybridity, when applied to a culture, is a process by which a culture borrows cultural elements from neighboring cultures to incorporate into elements of its own. It also means borrowing within a culture from different subgroups of the culture that traditionally have their own distinctive dialects, costumes, or styles of music, some of which are brought together to make new cultural forms. Another related concept is that of translation. Translation means "to carry or to bear across. . . . A migration colony begins as a translation, a copy of the original located elsewhere on the map . . . a far-away reproduction that will, inevitably, always turn out differently."[28] To translate a culture is similar to translating a text from one language to another, with the end result being rarely the same as the original.

For the Hmong, the most obvious examples of cultural hybridity and translation during the past 30 years include: (1) within their own community, they have greatly changed Hmong women's costumes by borrowing the rich colors and patterns from different Hmong geographic and dialect subgroups to mix into new designs, new costumes; and (2) from outside their own group, they have adopted forms of modern music, theatre, painting, and literature that have been heavily influenced by the many cultures the Hmong have come into contact with in recent years. Through the process of cultural appropriation and assimilation, the Hmong, like other groups in a similar situation, have been able to bring their culture up-to-date to be on par with the rest of the people they live with. Moreover, they have been able to enjoy a modern identity, pride, acceptance, and appreciation based on what Ziff and Rao call "borrowed power," the ability to enrich themselves culturally by imitating or borrowing ideas from people around them.[29] We shall see some more examples of this in the new forms of painting, sculpture, and story-cloths the Hmong have developed in the next chapter; we shall also see how the Hmong have been able build on their traditional gifts for design and performance in creating these new hybrid forms of creative activity.

NOTES

1. Graham 1926, 304.

2. Conquergood 2005, 82–83.

3. From the Web site at http://www.theatrefordevelopment.com/index.html. Accessed 17 May 2008.

4. Numrich 1985.

5. http://www.mnfolkarts.org/creative/creative.html.

6. "Hmong Theatre Performance Set for April 10," News Bureau, University of Washington-Eau Claire Web site, www.uwec.edu/newsbureau/release/past/1997/97-04/41hmong.html. Accessed 18 June 2008.

7. "Stir-Fried Pop Culture" by Song Vang, TC Daily Planet, 11/01/08, at http://www.tcdailyplanet.net/article/2008/01/11/stir-fried-pop-culture.html. Accessed 22 June 2008.

8. From www.aboutchat.org. Further information is also available at www.myspace.com/aboutchat. Accessed 22 May 2008.

9. For more information on Kathie Ka Vang and other Asian American artists, visit the Web site of the National Asian American Theater Festival at http://www.naatf.org/index.php?page_id=168. Accessed 22 June 2008.

10. Not to be confused with Kathie Ka Vang.

11. For Tou Ger Xiong's biography and other information on this unique Hmong performer, see http://www.loe.org/images/081219/TOU%20GER%20XIONG%20BIOGRAPHY%20Feb%202008.doc. Accessed 25 June 2008.

12. The Hmong Culture Centre in St. Paul, Minnesota, is one of the few formal organizations that promote the learning and maintenance of Hmong culture in its various forms. For more information, see http://www.hmongcc.org.

13. www.youtube.com/watch?v=9zV3DW0ZDIM. Accessed 19 May 2010. Many styles of Hmong dancing are uploaded here.

14. See "ViewFinder: Dance Group Shows Pride in Hmong culture" by Sharon Cekada, Post-Crescent photojournalist, December 7, 2007, in www.post crescent.com. Accessed 25 June 2008.

15. Graham 1926, 2003.

16. For more information, see http://hmongstudies.org/HmongFolkArtsPresentation/pdf. Accessed 27 June 2008.

17. Mareschal 1976, 159.

18. We are again grateful to Tou Ger Lee for his kind assistance with information and freely giving Gary Lee his own recording of the *Qeej Tu Siav* from the archives of the Hmong Culture Centre, St Paul, Minnesota.

19. The funeral music performers should not be mentioned directly, as their souls may be kept in the Otherworld, and they will become sick or die after the funeral.

20. This refers to the funeral bier or stretcher used to hold the body.

21. Johns 1986.

22. Mottin 1980b.

23. Mareschal 1976, 65.

24. Graham 1926, 303.

25. For example: (1) *Traditional Singing in 12 Variations* by Pob Tsuas Lis (2007), and (2) *Kwv Txhiaj Ntau Lub Suab (Songs in Many Tunes)* from Hmong-Inter Productions (no date).

26. www.music-zoosiab.com. Accessed 19 May 2010.

27. Schein, Louisa. "Eastwood's Next Film Features Hmong American Cast," *Asian Week*, 3 October 2008, available at http://www.asianweek.com/2008/10/03/eastwoods-next-film-features-hmong-american-cast-exclusive-interviews-from-the-set-of-gran-torino/. Accessed 19 July 2008.

28. Young 2003, 138–39.

29. Ziff and Rao 1997.

5

Art

TRADITIONALLY, HMONG ART (like drama, music, or poetry) is not a separate sphere as in Western societies. It is intricately linked to everyday human activities, because it is involved with tool-making, textile art, and handicrafts that are used to fulfill various functions in life. The farmer goes to his field with the basket, which he wove himself, to bring back his produce at the end of the day. His wife wears clothes adorned with colorful embroideries that she made herself a few months before. The baby on her back may be carried in an apron with cross-stitches her own mother gave her as a gift after the birth, and the baby may also have a handmade embroidered hat on its small head.

If art is the production of objects that provide a sense—and an appreciation—of beauty, meanings, and good taste, then the Hmong possess art in a variety of forms. Hmong art, however, does not comprise works that hang on walls or are displayed in art galleries. Hmong traditional art is not the fine arts of cosmopolitan society like paintings and sculptures, nor are they performing arts like operas, dances, and ballets—although talented members of the Hmong community now living in Western countries have launched themselves into these artistic areas. These forms of art are what Lyteck Lynhiavu had in mind when he was asked why there were so few Hmong artists in the 1970s in Laos. In his view, "the Hmong dream only at night. An artist must dream all day, and we don't have time."[1]

HMONG FUNCTIONAL ART

Traditional Art

At a practical level, the Hmong have what is known as functional art or crafts such as textile art works and other handicrafts. These enable the Hmong to function in their everyday life, and to lighten the burden of menial tasks that are necessary for subsistence hill farmers in relatively isolated primitive environments. Like art in other cultures, these functional art forms help to embellish the ordinary, and to elevate common things to a plane that inspire admiration and wonder. This applies in particular to Hmong textile art—elaborate embroidery patterns made by hand in different colors of threads and materials as separate pieces to wear as headgear or on top of the normal costumes, or to add color and variety to the clothing by being sewn directly onto them, particularly on the front and sleeves of blouses and shirts. Hmong textile art include techniques like embroidery, appliqué, reverse appliqué, batik, cross-stitch and other kinds of stitch; recently some of these methods have been used to make representational "story-cloths." Hmong hemp-making, batik, and embroidery are prime examples of traditional art.

Batik

Batik is a dyeing technique where wax is first applied to a piece of cloth in a particular pattern, contrasting with the unmarked parts before the material is dyed. After the garment is dried, the wax is taken off, and the garment is dyed several times in a big vat, leaving the design on the fabric. To achieve the desired design on the cloth requires meticulous attention to detail, precise tools, and skill. It is not a form of art work found with the White Hmong, whose women's skirts are made out of plain white material. However, it is popular with Blue Mong women whose colorful skirts are the result of careful batik work. Among all the minorities in Southeast Asia only the Mong knew the technique of batik. This method was used to put colors and design on white hemp fabric that was usually made by the women themselves, although today not many of them grow hemp or cotton plants and harvest them to make cloth. Batik cloth is now mass-produced in factories in China and elsewhere, and computer designs are beginning to be used for the patterns. However, Blue Mong women still buy ready-made hemp cloth from the market and batik the fabric to make their skirts. The dye they use is indigo, so the skirt ends up looking blue from a distance. It is this color on the women's dresses that is often thought to explain why the group is called Blue Mong, in contrast to the White Hmong, who do not dye their women's skirts.

Hmong batik work. Courtesy of the authors.

Today, Hmong women can readily find lighter fabrics that are dyed by machine and more colorful, so the heavy hemp materials are often not used, although those handmade from hemp are still seen as the more genuine articles for Blue Mong skirts. Batik skills have thus become scarce. Batik is not an art every woman has to learn like embroidery. The result is that only a few women in a village have the artistic skills necessary for batik work. Furthermore, making the skirt after it has been batiked is also a very time-consuming task. A skirt, which is pleated, requires many yards of materials and the pleats are carefully stitched together by hand. Most Hmong women now prefer to buy ready-made and machine-stitched nylon skirts from shops where they can choose not only the materials but also the assorted colors they want. However, because some people will always want the authentic hemp articles, batik will remain a required art form for some time to come.

Embroidery

The Hmong call this form of art *paj ntaub* (Padau or flower cloth). It is the most praised item of the Hmong's material culture in Asia. As such, young girls learn the art of *paj ntaub* from a very early age. Like other forms of art, many may try to do it, but only a few have the talent to become very good at it. In the words of Lewis, a "tiny needle, strands of bright threads, lengths of varicolored cloth, and the genius of a Hmong woman—these are the ingredients of some of the most exquisite needle-work to be found anywhere."[2] Hmong embroidery, involving various kinds of stitch (such as chain-stitches, cross-stitch, running stitch, or satin stitch) and often embellished with appliqué and reverse appliqué, is a painstaking undertaking, requiring what Paterson calls "a cool heart and a watchful mind."[3] This is because the most rigorous standards are applied, and artists compete to see who will be able to meet the criteria for the finest work such as "even, tiny or invisible stitching, intricacy of design, precise patterning, straight borders and smooth surfaces."[4] Anyone who has perfected these skills inspires awe, respect, and pride among other women, as we also show in Chapter 7.

Embroidery is usually done in the evenings after all the household chores of the day have been completed, or during slack farming times by women to decorate traditional Hmong costumes for both men and women. It is also used to make ornate head-pieces that look very "flowery" to be worn by babies and young women with their Hmong costumes. All colors of threads and lining materials are used, but the borders are often red. Designs vary according to the preference of the artist and the materials available, but often reflect the close relationship between the Hmong and natural objects in the hill environment of Asia where they live. The John Michael Kohler Arts Centre says that motifs used in Hmong textile designs are modeled on: the *paj zaub* or vegetable blossom, *noob dib* or cucumber seed, pumpkin seed, squash seed, peach blossom, centipede, tick, fern leaf, eye of the peacock, fish scales, chicken eye, chicken foot, and chicken tail.[5] Other motifs may reflect the spiraling snail shell or *qwj*, crosses, circles, half-circles, and steps.

Embroideries can be used on many parts of the Hmong costume, especially the head dress or *phuam*, the back of women's shirt collars called *dab tshos*, and on the long red-and-green sashes (*hlab se*) used to tie around men's and women's waists over the front of their pants or skirts. Embroidery is also used to decorate the edges of the openings of the blouse (*ntiag tsho*), and the long piece of apron on the front of women's skirts, called the *sev*. The men may have embroidery on the front of their Hmong shirts, and on the red sashes they use as a belt to tie their pants around their waists. Apart from their practical use, embroideries (like other adornments) are believed to have sacred meanings and magical power, according to Seexeng Lee, a famous Hmong artist and teacher in Minneapolis.[6] They protect the wearer from harm or give him or her a clear Hmong identity. Thus, a newborn baby is given an embroidered cap, a three-metal necklace

Hmong textiles and jewelry designs. Courtesy of John Michael Kohler Arts Center, Sheboygan, WI.

made of twisted steel, silver, and copper (*lub xauv hlau*), or lucky silver neck platelet (*daim phiaj xauv*) to wear to protect it against evil spirits who will mistake the baby for a flower and prevent it from harming its soul. The beauty of such adornments also keeps its soul from wandering away from the body and making it sick. Embroidery on a funeral costume allows the dead person to be recognized and accepted by the ancestors on its journey to the Otherworld. Mountains in the shape of triangles on embroideries on a person's clothes are believed to safeguard him or her from danger as if he or she were surrounded by a protective fence or a range of natural barriers.

Embroideries are a source of pride for the wearer and artist, because they indicate the level of wealth in the family. More importantly, they show that the wearer or her mother has adept fingers to achieve such fine and colorful handiworks. Nowadays, of course, many embroideries are made by other people for mass marketing, and the pride in them as the fruit of one's own talent is gone. Some patterns are even made by factories in China, and are thus no longer considered works of art but only commodities. Hmong women in Laos and Thailand continue to do their own embroidery, but this handicrafts skill is now largely lost to the Hmong in the diaspora where they tend to prefer to buy commercial items that are

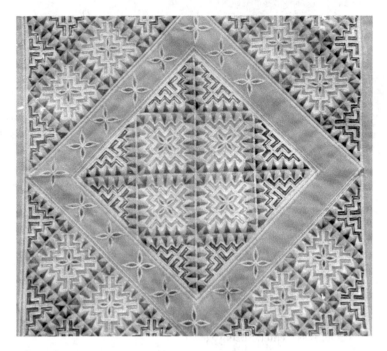

Embroidery close-up. Courtesy of the authors.

made in large quantities and sold in shops or through personal contacts. These items still perform their traditional function, but have lost their aura as fine pieces of art that are personally made by their wearers.

Thirty years ago, before the Hmong moved to the West or started going to school, virtually every young Hmong woman had to learn embroidery, know how to sew and how to cross-stitch, and how to make her own clothes. Some might even learn how to make materials from hemp plants that the family grew as a normal part of their farming practices. Some (among the Blue Mong) might even learn to do batik work. This is because the traditional role expected of a woman was to get married and to "patch and wash" (*ntxiv ntxhua*) for her husband and children. If anything, she had to at least know how to patch up a hole on a torn pair of pants or shirt. In general, then, most Hmong girls followed the steps of their mothers and grandmothers by learning embroidery in addition to sewing and making clothes. Their abilities to fulfill their roles as women were judged on the quality of what they could make. A family's fortune is reflected in the costumes and jewelry their daughters wear at the New Year festival. There is a saying that "what you wear is what you're worth."[7] Thus, in the old days, rich Hmong families were those that could access

Embroidered women's costume, Guizhou, China. Courtesy of the authors.

the most colorful threads and the best materials for their women to make multicolored embroideries and costumes for their members. Those with the most skills in embroidery made the brightest costumes by hand.

Today, however, the rich are those who can buy the best machine-made costumes in the latest style and embroideries that can be found in fashion shops. So, needlework has become a lost art for many Hmong women, particularly those in the diaspora, where few girls want or need to learn embroidery, being more concerned with going to school or working for wages. Having so many other things to do, few even know how to thread a needle, let alone how to use it. Materials are plentiful in shops and ready-made clothes saturate the market, in Hmong and other styles. Instead of longing to get hold of needles and colorful threads, many young women would rather go after the latest music CDs, touch the computer keyboard to surf the Internet, or engage in chats with distant cyber-friends. This is the price the Hmong and others like them pay for the power of Western capitalism, consumerism, and modern education.

Young Hmong girls, Fresno, California. Courtesy of the authors.

Handicrafts

Crafts can be anything fashioned for use in everyday life, such as jewelry and tools, that require special skills or craftsmanship to make. As a subsistence people, the Hmong possess important traditional handicraft skills that include weaving, basket-making, and blacksmithing.

Making Hemp Cloth

Before either batiking or embroidering, which we discuss above as forms of art, the fabric itself must be made. In the past, as we have mentioned, the Hmong used to make their own hemp fabric when growing hemp (a species of marijuana) was still allowed by many governments. A quarter-acre of densely sown hemp seeds would yield enough plants to harvest for a year's need of cloth. When the hemp plants grow to two or three feet high, they are cut and the hemp fibers separated from the stems and twisted together often by hand. After soaking and drying, the thread is wound around sticks and spun around a framework of four spindles into long threads that are rolled into balls of yarn for weaving. The process involves many stages, including boiling the coarse material in hot water, washing it, and flattening it down to a finer piece of fabric.[8] It is then often dyed by the batik process, to be used for making garments or dresses. Again, only a few women in a village know how to make cloth, but the process has fallen out of favor because hemp clothes are coarse and their colors do not last. People prefer to buy modern nylon and synthetic fabrics that are better quality. Making a skirt from hemp can take up to a year to complete, as it is done only when women have some spare time from other work. For this reason, it is easier for Hmong in Western countries to order ready-made costumes from Laos, Thailand, or China.[9] Crucial in the weaving process is the Hmong loom, a unique tool that is worked by pressure from the back, since the woman sits attached to the spindle by a back-strap loop similar to those used by the Zhuang people in China or the peasant Japanese looms. Treadle-worked looms were also used. A Hmong loom (*lub ntos*) is made up of over 100 different wooden parts.

Basket Weaving

Bamboo and rattan splices are used to weave a carrying basket known in Hmong as *kawm*, as well as the scuttles or dustpans found in most Hmong homes. The shape and form of the baskets are very similar, but each weaver may be able to achieve different levels of skills. The baskets are used to carry produce from the farms on the back, or as containers. Apart from carrying baskets, the Hmong also weave stools or *kwv teeb* used for sitting, and circular trays (*vab*) to winnow, separating the chaff from the rice grains. Basketry can be of either simple cross-cutting squares, diagonal combinations of three splices crossing over alternately, or a more complex (and stronger) method of combining cross diagonal squares. Again, not everyone can do basket-weaving, and the few men with the skills are often in great demand for their handicrafts that are widely used by all.

Blacksmithing

In the traditional setting of Southeast Asia, each village often had its blacksmith artisans who made knives, machetes, axes, and other steel tools for sale or use by other villagers. The steel was often obtained from scrap metals or bought from city steel dealers. The anvil and tools used were simple but perfectly designed, using charcoal and a bellows (made of a tubular wooden cylinder with a metal piston softened by feathers passing through a sheet of paper, attached to the forge by bamboo pipe) to heat up the metal on the forge before fashioning it into the shape of a tool. It was heavy work in conditions of intense heat, and only men could do this kind of handicraft work. Those who could make the best tools in term of looks and durability were lauded with praise and their products were always sought after.

Due to the spread of commercial products, however, blacksmithing has become victim of the globalized mass market. Hmong knives, axes and machetes are still made locally, but other tools are now easily obtained from urban shops. It is not unusual nowadays to find Chinese chopping knives in a Hmong household. Hmong steel tools are virtually absent in families living in the diaspora, because of the lack of access to them.

Silversmithing

Like blacksmithing, making jewelry such as the Hmong necklace, earrings, and bracelets is still practiced as a way to bring in additional money into the families of those men who are skilled at this form of functional art work. In the past, Hmong silversmiths were famous. They often learned from the Chinese, but were much sought after for their own skills. Although the Hmong continue to fashion jewelry, some are now using aluminium and not silver as they used to do, because the latter is seen as being too heavy to wear and expensive to obtain. Although aluminium products are preferred by young girls for their lightness, they are seen as cheap imitations, not reflecting the true wealth of a family as silver jewelry does. These traditional ornaments continue to be bought by Hmong in Western countries to meet their nostalgic and identity assertion needs. They are mostly imported from Southeast Asia where some village silversmiths can still be found. Few Hmong in Western countries have the skills or the tools and facilities to make their own Hmong jewelry anymore. Yet the traditional designs of Hmong necklaces and other adornments are still valued while new designs and models are created or searched out.

Making Musical Instruments

Hmong musical instruments include the *qeej* (reed pipe), the flute (*raj*), a bamboo pipe with a reed, and the *ncas* (mouth organ or Jew's harp), made out of wood with a brass tongue. Music is also made, very skillfully, by blowing on leaves, but these require no special skills of construction. The *qeej* is a Hmong national icon, made up of six long bamboo pipes of different sizes and lengths equipped with copper reeds made by a blacksmith so as to give different musical notes, and we have seen how important it is to Hmong culture, especially in funerals. The pipes are attached to a wooden

Hmong silver necklace. Courtesy of the authors.

base known as the "gourd" with a mouthpiece (also finished in brass). Playing the *qeej* requires many years of practice, as the musical notes denote words of poetry and each note has to be carefully played. The instrument can be used for enjoyment, but it is more commonly for playing funeral music, so its playing tends to be reserved for these sad occasions. Because of this major cultural function, the *qeej* is still made by fine craftsmen in Laos and Thailand for consumption by the Hmong worldwide. A good reed pipe can cost up to $500 and may last three to four years as the bamboo pipes may split or come loose from the sleeve and lose their tones.

The flutes and the mouth organ are musical instruments used for general entertainment and courting. The mouth harp and the long flute are favorites among young men who use them to let girls they are courting know about their love messages and their presence in the dark at night outside the girls' houses. The messages are in the musical notes played. The musical instruments of a gifted maker will emit particularly melodious notes that make people seek them out, especially the long flute (there are four kinds of flute) and the Jew's harp that require very precise incisions of the blade or *nplaim* for it to make the needed musical sound and to last a number of years.[10] The Hmong also make copper gongs for the shaman and drums for the funeral out of wood and cowhide.

A wooden carrier. Courtesy of the authors.

Woodwork

Carpentry is also a Hmong skill. Around a Hmong house there is much evidence of their skills in wood—the frame which bears the back-basket, the saddle for the pack-horses made entirely out of wood, and the hand-mill made out of a combination of wood with two grindstones. Wood is also used for making ladders, tables, and stools, for instance. Hmong craftsmen would also make the famous Hmong crossbow (*rab hneev*), and in the past, their own muskets; they also produce pipes such as the bamboo hubble-bubble (*lub yeeb thooj*).

Functional Art—Conclusion

These textile products, tools, and cultural artifacts constitute the Hmong's main functional art and craft objects. They continue to survive, some in small quantities, produced and used by their makers. Others, like the embroidery and jewelry, are made in large numbers, because they have become commercial products in demand by the Hmong in the diaspora. A visit to Hmong shops and flea markets in the United States will reveal many of these craft items, utensils, and musical instruments, thus making the Hmong culture come alive through its silversmith artisans, music instrument makers, and needlecraft workers. Without them, Hmong culture would not be able to survive, even if their mass production has somewhat reduced their values and authenticity.

MODERN AESTHETIC ART

Do the Hmong have aesthetic art? This is a new area for them after their settlement in Western countries and exposure to modern art studies and exhibitions. Modern art tends to be acquired and learned formally at schools and colleges, although natural talents may also play a large part in its development in a young artist. This is similar to Hmong functional arts where a mother teaches her daughter embroideries from a young age, or a reed pipe player has to apply himself to his art by learning and practicing nearly every day. Living in the West has allowed many young Hmong to become exposed to Western visual arts at school and some began to experiment with video production and photography as part of their school activities. Some began to paint or draw for school projects or as hobby. However, the gap between modern and traditional Hmong arts remains huge, with modern artists still searching for direction, originality, and identity. Many modern Hmong painters remain focused on Hmong themes, but some have branched out to abstract and other modern (for the West) art forms, without always aiming for the mass market that Hmong traditional art objects such as embroideries now often supply.

Hmong Art Organizations

Hmong modern artists may have developed their talents through their own skills and efforts, but many have also benefited from nonprofit organizations that have been established in American cities with a sizable Hmong population. They not only help by providing speakers and facilitators in informal meetings to guide budding writers and artists, but also run exhibitions of Hmong art works three or four times a year in art display venues in various locations, and ensure the most exposure to the local media. In this way, many Hmong artists come to be known within the local Hmong population and the public at large, gain support from grants bodies and government agencies, and know where to put their works on show.

Some of the better-known groups involved in these activities in the United States include the producers of *Eye.D Magazine*. This is an online publication that carries in-depth articles on established and successful individuals, with spotlights on emerging artists, writers, educators, and those who offer unique perspectives, by publishing features on their works. A second influential group is the Hmong artists' collective with the motto

"Creativity for Hmongs," based in Sacramento, California. Formed in 2003, it aims to unite Hmong artists in the cyber world. It not only promotes the artistic works of members but also involves them in voicing their concerns about human rights issues experienced by the Hmong in Laos and other parts of the world.

The third and very influential organization is the Hmong American Institute of Learning (HAIL), now renamed Hmong Arts Connection (HArC). As the publisher of the journal, *Paj Ntaub Voice*, this organization has been most active in promoting Hmong arts and writing. To this end, *Paj Ntaub Voice* publishes the works of emerging Hmong writers and artists, as well as promotes them through exhibitions in various art venues. In its 2007 issue called *Humor (less)*, for example, it published 23 pieces of writing and the work of 3 artists. From 2007 to 2008, it organized two exhibitions and a series of art education talks for members of the local Hmong community in St. Paul, Minnesota, where it is based. Its mission is to promote and inspire artistic expressions of Hmong culture, with the vision for an international professional community of Hmong artists and writers living in communities where art is valued and appreciated as a necessary part of life.

The final organization that supports Hmong modern art is the Center for Hmong Arts and Talents (CHAT), also based in St. Paul, Minnesota. It organizes an annual two-day Hmong arts and music festival in August to publicize Hmong art events and activities. The festival showcases the experiences of the U.S. Hmong community as seen through the dreams of its visual and performing artists, with a selection of juried visual artwork, hosting of traditional and contemporary musicians and performers, showing pillowcases from its Dreamcatcher Clothesline Community Art Project, and organizing a cake-decorating competition, games, food vendors, and displays of community resources.

Outcomes of Hmong Art Promotion

With the active support of the above organizations and through the personal initiatives of individual Hmong artists, much progress has been made in Hmong modern aesthetic art in the United States. The Hmong have been living there only since 1975, but already a big impact has been made in local art scenes in the Twin Cities in Minnesota and other urban centers with large Hmong populations.

Painting

Modern painting has been taken up by many young Hmong artists in the United States, with frequent exhibitions of their art works held in various galleries in major American cities where the Hmong live. Some artists also promote their works through their own Web sites. The best known is Seexeng Lee, who markets his art collection through his Web site at www.seexeng.com. Others promote their works through a shared Web site.[11] Many also do it through exhibitions, art festivals, and exposures in Hmong literary and art magazines in print like *Paj Ntaub Voice* or online such as *Eye.D Magazine*. A Hmong refugee from Laos, Seexeng Lee is currently an art teacher at South High School, Minneapolis, Minnesota. He has been painting and making sculptures for some time, and has had a few solo exhibitions in small galleries and coffee shops in and around the Twin Cities. In May and June 2006, he held a major show at Concordia University, St. Paul, to exhibit a new work titled "The New Hmong Paj Ntaub," which was inspired by what he perceived as the "core elements" of what it means to be Hmong, and issues faced by Hmong Americans such as the loss of culture, the problem of assimilation, and the need to find an identity. He also displays his works at the Hmong New Year in St. Paul in November each year, and is a frequent speaker on Hmong arts at meetings and tertiary educational institutions.

An earlier edition of Seexeng's Website mentions the granting of an art award to Leurseng Chang at Ordway, Minnesota, on May 19, 2006, although no other details are available of this young Hmong artist. Others

Regeneration, a painting by Hmong artist Seexeng Lee. Courtesy of Seexeng Lee.

who have recently had their works put on show include: Mai C. Vang, Pao Hour Her, and Sai Vang, whose works were featured in the *Intergenerational Exhibit REmixes Hmong Traditions* in July 2008 at the Homewood Studios gallery in Minneapolis. REmix is an art display that aims to forge links between the Hmong in the Twin Cities and the more established local groups, as well as among different generations within the Hmong community, by featuring the works of 12 Hmong artists from around the world. Although most of the exhibits consist of paintings, there are also photographic collages and portraits of Hmong—all of which reflect different aspects of what it is to be Hmong, to try to find one's place in the world through the medium of art.[12]

Sculpture

Not many Hmong have attempted sculpture. Most have been happy to try painting and other forms of visual art. Again, Seexeng is the only Hmong artist known to have molded a number of well-known sculptures. He has four of them featured in the Permanent Collections on his Web site. They are "Self-Portrait," "Sadness, Part 1," "Sadness, Part 2," and "Fine Details: Hmong *Paj Ntaub* and Story Cloth." The latter were relief rather than full 3D sculptures consisting of a 24K gold *qeej* and a 24K gold *Paj Ntaub*.

Personal Collection: *Sadness Part 1*, a sculpture by Hmong artist Seexeng Lee. Courtesy of Seexeng Lee.

Seexeng's most striking and most prominently featured sculptures were completed in 2007. They were commissioned by North Point Health and Wellness Center for its atrium in Minneapolis. They hang from the ceiling in the public gallery and are entitled "Convergence." Made up of five spherical elements, each represents a healing element: Concern, Family, Culture, Science, and Wisdom—his most ambitious work to date.

Story-Cloths

Hmong functional art was traditionally abstract art in the sense that it did not represent nature in an easily identifiable way, although the embroidery designs with their geometrical patterns such as circles and squares can be seen as having abstract meanings such as the family and the clan, gardens, rivers, fields and other natural objects found in the highland environment of China and Southeast Asia, the traditional home of the Hmong. Although the designs used may be the same from one artist to another, their interpretations may vary, depending on the metaphorical meanings put on them by each artist. However, since the refugee experience, using traditional art forms to graphically represent events in real life has become very common, especially in the well-known tapestry "story-cloths," which refugees made and which have now become a much sought-after commodity.

These Hmong story-cloths are a new form of art, and are discussed here as modern aesthetic art because they do not fall into the category of traditional Hmong functional art. They are used for hanging on walls or as bedspreads to look at, although they use sewn-on patches and embroidery. They range in size from three square feet to a queen-size bed spread. Their prices range from $10 for a pillowcase to $400 for a bed cover. The story-cloths, also known as wall-hanging narrative textiles or pictorial embroideries, are a unique invention by the Hmong of Laos after they became refugees in Thailand after 1975.[13] Three factors played a large part in their development in the refugee camps: (1) economic needs in the deprived refugee environment camps; (2) the desire to make political statements about their sufferings at the hands of the Lao communists; and (3) nostalgia for a traditional life left behind in the hills of Laos. Using Hmong traditional textile traditions to create marketable items that could be sold in the West through relatives and formal marketing outlets was a response to conditions of scarcity. Working closely with Western refugee workers in the camp, Hmong women devised the new representational textile creations that contrasted with their finer and more brightly colored traditional embroideries to suit the tastes of buyers in Western countries where the cloths were sold.

The images used in the story-cloths depend on market demand and the political messages their makers wish to pass on. The motifs may include Hmong traditional social events such as weddings and farming activities, wild animals, and flora around Hmong villages. War traumas are depicted with communist

Lao soldiers shooting at women and children or chasing Hmong escapees on their way to Thailand, people dying along jungle trails and survivors swimming across the Mekong River. Some motifs also include life in the refugee camps and refugees being welcomed by Thai and UN officials. The Hmong in Laos never had this representational art before 1975, although other Miao groups in China already had embroideries of butterflies and dragons and other natural symbols. This sudden turn to representational art was to satisfy not only the artistic tastes of foreign tourists or because of the refugee weaving projects in the camps, but also corresponded to a genuine need of the Hmong to express their horrid war experiences in a new graphic form for the world to see, for foreign buyers to know, and for museums to display. There was a need to make some additional money, but the political statements were equally as strong. These cloths are now seen in museums and galleries around the world.[14]

Although the refugee camps are now closed, story-cloths continue to be made by Hmong women in Laos and Thailand for the tourist market. To make a story-cloth requires money to buy the cloth and colorful threads, a lot of time, dedication, and skills. The motifs are drawn in pencil on the blank cloth before threads are used to embroider them in. This may take two persons, one to draw and the other to do the embroidery. As most Hmong women did not go to school and learn to use a pencil, they usually ask a male relative to help. The process is painstaking and slow, not unlike doing a landscape painting. Thus, at a personal level, this time-consuming task can be said to help to heal the broken hearts of the refugees over the loss of their homeland, their family members, and their social organization. Committing their social memories to a cloth, just like painting on a canvas, helps overcome the traumatic suffering experienced, the racism, the political killings, and the persecution by their enemies.

Instead of remembering their past life as geometric lines, they now keep their past as alive scenes that constitute their history. Hence, these tapestries are called "story cloths." The growth of this new art is in fact due to economic and financial needs . . . but all traditional or new forms of art help to preserve memory, history, and an oral tradition of the ethnic group.[15]

The quality of a story-cloth is judged by such criteria as style, technique, attention to detail, "and above all they must represent the truth, must have evocative power of history events . . . they must act as the moral imagination of social history. They must capture a collective vision. A good story cloth must elicit a complex mixture of pride, excitement, sadness and pain, a flicker or more of anger."[16] It must convey to the younger generation what the older one has gone through and help them remember. As political statements and romantic evocations of a by-gone Hmong lifestyle, these story-cloths act as the social construction of Hmong collective memories, and as a deconstruction of human suffering. They are declarations of what life used to be for their makers, and what it should be for all, without political persecution. Furthermore, their presentation of traditional Hmong life and political experience also serves as a bridge between Hmong and U.S. consumers of the product by placing "the artists in the reflexive position of looking at us looking at them; they must decide what is appropriate for us to see, and in what form we should see it."[17]

This is the first time the Hmong have used their traditional art as a political tool, as assimilated representational art that shows

the resourcefulness of a culture to translate its principles and experiences into new creative endeavors, to pluralize its aesthetic system rather than relinquish control of them . . . another way of showing Hmong expression of self and society through medium of needle and thread . . . [of using] textile art as a badge of ethnicity, each [cloth] a complete text for examination. They are art, craft and industry; export, history and rhetoric, but more especially they are willed communications. . . . The embroidered images do more than reflect concepts of truth, value and experience; they shape the reflections of those who view them.[18]

Hmong story-cloth: Farming. Courtesy of the authors.

Story-cloth: Scene of traditional village life. Courtesy of the authors.

The Hmong in Western countries now no longer have only functional art in which art objects are fashioned for their usefulness in everyday life such as embroideries or basket-weaving, musical instruments, or tools. While many Hmong in Asia still carry on these functional art forms, others in Western countries have adopted both visual and performing arts by learning to paint on canvas, to sculpt, to dance on stage, to perform plays, and make movies. Even the Hmong's traditional functional art has undergone many transformations, especially embroideries that are traditionally used to adorn Hmong costumes but have now come to be framed to hang as decorations in homes. The bigger pieces of story-cloths now are used as tablecloths, bedspreads, and museum wall hangings. This diversification raises some questions about whether the new forms are authentic Hmong art.

Authenticity implies genuineness or the quality of being true to the original, not corrupted or altered. An authentic art object is thus seen as "one created by an artist for his own people and used for traditional purposes."[19] An object is no longer authentic when it loses its traditional usage, as when a piece of Hmong embroidery is made and sold to tourists for use as a tablecloth instead of its traditional role as décor for costumes. Thus, if we take this a step further, an authentic object is one that is of high quality, produced by a native artist with traditional design, and made by hand for traditional purposes.[20] If these criteria are applied to the

Hmong in Western countries, most of the traditional embroideries sold in Hmong shops would cease to be authentic, because many of them are made by Lao women in Laos who are not Hmong or by machines in factories in China. However, it is people who make their culture, not their culture that makes them. If the Hmong choose to make new art objects and transform their old artistic forms to convey new meanings, and they express a Hmong sense of identity and a Hmong viewpoint on the world, then they can also be seen as genuine for the Hmong.

This chapter has discussed both Hmong functional and modern arts in their various forms. Since migrating to the West, the Hmong have adopted new artistic practices such as painting, sculpture, dance and music, poetry composition and public reading, writing and movie-making. They have adapted their traditional skills in design and crafting to new ends. Some of these artistic activities may not be seen as strictly Hmong, in the sense that they are borrowed from other cultures. However, so long as they meet the daily and artistic needs of the Hmong, so long as their performance or production is undertaken by Hmong people or involves Hmong subjects and a Hmong point of view, then they can be seen as authentically Hmong. Moreover, new cultural elements, artistic or otherwise, have to be seen as stemming from original forms and meanings that are familiar to the people for them to be accepted. The story-cloths, where traditional needlework and embroidery skills are being used in quite new ways, are a very good example of this, and so also is the adaptation of traditional dramatic skills used in ceremony and ritual in new forms of performance art, as we saw in the previous chapter. As Seexeng Lee states, "Hmong culture today is in a very brittle state. It is beautiful and worth preserving, but our arts are evolving and changing at such a rate that if we are not careful we will eventually lose them. Extending the meanings and functions to our arts is a good thing, but not to totally disregard its origin and intended purposes."[21]

NOTES

1. Garrett 1974, 111. For an online brief discussion on Hmong art with many illustrations, see Dr. Kaoly Yang's website at http://www.hmongcontemporary issues.com/. Accessed 15 May 2010.

2. Lewis 1984, 104.

3. Peterson 1988a.

4. John Michael Kohler Arts Centre 1986, 21.

5. Ibid., 21–22.

6. Gallego 2008, 2.

7. Garrett 1974, 86.

8. See Kirk, "Hmong Textiles and Costume of North Vietnam" in www. garyyialee.com.

9. Gallego 2008, 4.

10. On flutes, Mareschal 1976, 155 describes and draws the common *raj nplaim*, the *raj ntsaws* or *ntsia*, the *raj ntse hau* or *hlav ncauj* (in Blue Mong), and the very rare *raj nplooj*.

11. At www.hmongartists.net. Accessed 13 August 2008.

12. On the Remix exhibition, see Schell 2008.

13. MacDowell 1989.

14. See Cohen 2000.

15. Kaoly Yang, no date, "Traditional Hmong Art" page on her Web site: http://www.hmongcontemporaryissues.com.

16. Peterson 1988b, 11.

17. Ibid., 13.

18. Ibid., 14–20.

19. Rubin 1984, 76, note 41.

20. Errington 1998, 142.

21. Gallego 2008, 4.

6

Space and Housing

SPACE AND PLACE

IN THIS CHAPTER, we will move from a discussion of Hmong senses of space generally, particularly regarding the use of geomancy for locating grave-sites, villages, and houses, toward considering the importance of the traditional house as the center of the Hmong world and the universe. Vernacular architecture—designing spaces for living that are appropriate both for the human world and the natural environment, using locally available materials, resources and traditions—has recently become very fashionable. Many kinds of traditional architecture, like the Hmong house, are vernacular in this sense (but not all, if you think about some of the grand temples and palaces of the past). Hmong traditional methods, plans of construction, and ways of thinking about space have a lot to teach the modern designers and sophisticated architects of today.

We can think of Hmong space as physical/geographical, personal/social, or ethno-cultural. There is also another dimension of imaginary or cyber-space that partially overlaps with the ritual space of the ethno-cultural dimension. Traditionally Hmong physical or geographical space was bounded by a conceptual distinction between the wilderness of the *hav zoov*, or valleys and forest, and the security of the *vaj tsev*, or the house and its surrounding gardens. At varying distances from the household were the fields cultivated, mostly not on a permanent basis and usually scattered among different plots and patches; the *teb*, referring to upland fields.

The Hmong have always visualized themselves as living on the forested high mountains, *toj siab* or *roob*, where most of them lived, and have contrasted the dry uplands of their habitual cultivation, the *teb*, with the *liaj* or irrigated rice fields of other peoples they could see stretched out in the valleys beneath them. The association of Hmong with mountain dwelling is a strong and historically constant one. Like many mountain-dwelling people in other parts of the world they have preferred their high-altitude dwelling places to the low altitudes of the river valleys inhabited by lowland dominant majority people such as the Thai, Lao, Kinh (Vietnamese), or Han Chinese. Early nineteenth-century reports often recorded the discomfort and fear of Hmong taken to lowland dwellings that they saw as hot, uncomfortable, noisy, dirty, and disease-ridden.[1] Many of them became ill when transported to lower altitudes or fell victim to parasitic illnesses such as malaria, which did not exist higher up, or other infectious diseases like tuberculosis and diphtheria that were very uncommon in the cooler and sparsely inhabited highlands. Even today, Hmong in Thailand, such as those in Doi Pui, say they prefer to stay in their upland villages rather than move to lowland cities.

The village, or *zos*, has never been a very strong concept in the Hmong imagination, and there is some debate as to whether the notion of a village traditionally existed at all.[2] It seems that most settlements in the past were formed by a group of four or five closely related patrilineal families and that this sub-lineage, or *ib tug dab qhuas*, was the functional group more than the village. In other words, the traditional village tended to be composed of the members of only one lineage or surname. Such villages, or the more common cluster villages with two or more clans represented, would be formed generally at altitudes of above 5,000 feet, near a source of water and protected wherever possible by a belt of forest. Beyond the Hmong villages the upland market formed the main arena marking the boundaries of a purely Hmong world, where the members of other cultures, such as the Thai or Chinese, Yao or Lisu, would be encountered. The concept of the market, or *kiab khw*, has been an important spatial notion for the Hmong, and it seems that they may have always enjoyed relations of some kinds with markets. In these areas of southern China and the foothills of northern Indochina, markets were arranged in a hierarchical regional system of standard, intermediate, and central markets, which operated on a periodic basis.[3] Within a given 10-day period of the lunar cycle, markets would take place in certain set locations not every day, but on certain days of the period, often the first, fourth, and seventh days, or the second, fifth, and eighth days. This meant that traveling peddlers could go from one market to the next selling their wares, and periodic markets made it easy for one to attend more than one market if one needed to. Traditionally the political states the Hmong lived in and the notional borders that separated them were not of great account to the Hmong.

Life and spatial concepts have immeasurably changed today. Many Hmong are living not only outside Asia but also in modern towns and cities within Asia. There has been the adoption of irrigated rice techniques (flooded flat-level rice paddy fields) by groups of Hmong and their recognition of the reality of modern states and their borders. There has also been the movement over the past 100 years toward larger and larger well-established settlements. Moreover, there have been overwhelming social and physical pressures to change their traditional agricultural systems, and the forest cover has rapidly disappeared. However, these distinctions between the household and the forest, cultivated fields and the wild, rivers and mountains, uplands and lowlands, are strongly marked in the Hmong language and sayings, and continue to influence spatial thinking about the world. This is because, like most traditional people, the Hmong view of space was not merely limited to physical or geographical realities, but also importantly expressed in supernatural terms, and in a host of ritual and everyday practices, habits, customs, and beliefs supporting them. We have seen how the Hmong divide spirits into the wild ones of the forest and the domestic ones associated with the household, besides those special categories of spirits associated with particular activities like shamanism, hunting, or blacksmithing. These conceptual divisions reflected real physical and ecological distinctions that were important in the past. The practical importance of the market, for example, is shown in the fact that it is often used as a metaphor for the passage between this life and the next, since the market was seen as a place where change and transformation, of one good into another, could occur. So it became an apt metaphor for the place between the worlds of *yaj* and *yeej*, or the material and the spiritual; a place where men could meet and communicate with spirits and spirits with men, and you would not know which men were men and which were spirits.

It is this religious cosmology that has largely formed Hmong views and visions of the space around them. At the heart of this cosmology is the Hmong house—its inhabitants, its domestic animals, tools, and the vegetables and fruits grown around it; the house posts inhabited by different kinds of spirits; and the roof with its rafters, conceived of as the vault of Heaven. Indeed, the house is a microcosm of the universe, with its floor standing for the Earth and the social life of men and women occurring between the two. The main pillar of the house was the Axis Mundi (world pillar or cosmic axis) of the universe, and in the following sections, therefore, we shall focus on the Hmong house and its centrality to Hmong ideas of place and space, and the importance of the Hmong sense of home and place despite their traditional lives as shifting cultivators. We shall also see how a system of geomancy was resorted to for the siting of villages and graves—the residences of the living and the dead—that has always spoken of a deep understanding and appreciation of the need for harmony between humans and their natural environments.

TSHAIS TSEV: "MOVING HOUSE" AND MOBILITY

The traditional Hmong lifestyle is usually described as semi-nomadic because dry shifting agriculture means that when the soil fertility is exhausted, usually after about 12 years, the village moves to a new location where forest will be cleared by burning and rice planted in the earth fertilized by the ashes. There are different types of shifting cultivation, or fallow management system, and the Hmong used to practice the most radical form, known as pioneer shifting cultivation. In this form, a village would sometimes move 100 miles or more to find virgin forest to clear. When this happened, new houses would be built, but the family would bring main posts and pillars, doors, and anything they could carry, with them. Over the past 50 years, virgin forest in the Asian homelands has become increasingly scarce owing to the many people besides the Hmong now making a claim to it. Increasing national restrictions on deforestation have also led to many alterations in the system. In China, such movement is impossible, and it is now very difficult in all the neighboring countries where Hmong live except to some extent in parts of Burma. Today, the cultivations will move around the village; this means that sometimes fields are at great distances from where people live. So field huts, which the Hmong have always built in the fields for times when labor on the fields needed to be intensive, have become more important. Families may spend more time in them than in the past, and they can come to resemble almost permanent habitations. The Hmong still move village and house for a variety of reasons, some personal or for reasons of health, usually to join other members of their family or lineage living elsewhere; however, now it is usually just sections of the village that will move, sometimes just a few related households, to join other families in other semi-permanent settlements.

Lowland population pressure, protected forest reserve areas, wildlife sanctuary and national park land legislations, land tenure law, and competition for and ownership by more powerful members of the broader community all mean that the Hmong in Asia now confine themselves to restricted areas allocated to them by government officials or acquired through purchase by the more wealthy Hmong. The need for education for their

children and health care also means that they have to live close to or in settlements where these facilities are available. Many Hmong in Thailand have
adopted commercial cash cropping, and the market gardening of flowers
and fruits, which makes it necessary for them to live closer to markets and
means of transport such as roads than they did in the past. Electrification of
much of the countryside in Laos and Thailand also makes it more difficult
to move to areas where electricity and the use of modern electronic technologies become impossible. This enforced process of sedentarization has led
to the growth of much larger settlements than in the past, and quite frequently a Hmong village in Asia today will contain a minority of members
of other groups, Thai, Khmu, Chinese, or Karen, for example, also living
in the same village. Although in the not-so-distant past Blue Mong and
White Hmong villages were always separately established, modern development has led more and more toward mixed villages of this type containing
a variety of different surnames/clans. As the Hmong see it, it is good to
have access and reduce spatial distance to the members of different surnames because it makes marriage, which can only take place between the
members of different surnames, possible. If it is true that in the past only
single-lineage hamlets were the norm, which slowly changed to larger settlements for purposes of defense and solidarity, today it is very rare to find a
Hmong village without at least two or three surnames living together in it.

The Hmong occupied the areas of Asia where they now live for a long
time before modern national boundaries were imposed following nineteenth-
century colonization, and they have been used to crossing the borders
between Burma, China, Laos, Thailand, and Vietnam without much regard
for national frontiers or immigration restrictions. Yet even today the Hmong,
like many other ethnic groups in these regions, often live across borders and
may be seen (like the Kurds, Basques, or Inuit peoples) as "cross-border," or
"border-crossing" peoples. Now that Hmong have emigrated to countries
like Canada, France, Australia, and the United States, they have become
transnational, but this is different from their traditional border-crossing characteristics, and the two should not be confused. The Hmong are, and always
have been, a very mobile people simply because of the shifting nature of their
system of agriculture that has led to extensive movements across national borders and within nations in Asia. There is also a new form of transnational
mobility in which Hmong from the United States, for example, may visit
their relatives in Thailand or Laos or even search out groups of Hmong in
China. Yet all this characteristic mobility does *not* mean that the Hmong do
not have a sense of home or an attachment to place, as it is often incorrectly
believed. Indeed, the Hmong generally have a very strong attachment to their
native lands and the places where they were born and grew up. The Hmong

have particular rituals to ask for the protection of the spirits of the locality and to worship the spirits believed to inhabit certain boulders or trees, which are becoming more important today under the influence of a new awareness of the importance of ecological practices. One might almost say that, as traditional frequent movers, the Hmong are experts in making new homes in new places and have a particular gift for forming an attachment to a particular place, precisely as a result of this need to make new homes in new places so often.

LOOJMEM: "SIGHTING THE VEINS OF THE DRAGON"

This very strong sense of the importance of place is often expressed by the Hmong in a particular system, shared with the Chinese and some other minority people of the region, known as *feng-shui* (or *kanyu*) to the Chinese, or "winds and waters." The Hmong, however, generally refer to it as *saib loojmem*, "sighting the veins of the dragon," or *saib memtoj*, "sighting the veins in the hills." This system of geomancy, or divining the future from the shapes of the landscape, is very important in the traditional places where the Hmong people live, and is based on a unique vision of the reality of, and need for, harmony between humans and their natural environment. *Feng-shui* has recently been applied to urban settings in Asia and has become very popular in the West for interior decoration, but the traditional system is a very complex one closely related to the natural landscape, in which natural symbols are used to express particular meanings that are associated with health, good fortune, and prosperity. In this way the natural and human (or social) worlds are aligned, and correspondences traced between them.[4]

For example the symbol of the Green (Azure) Dragon marks the direction of the East, or as the Hmong say, the direction where the sun rises, while the White Tiger marks the direction of the West, or the direction of sunset. In the traditional Chinese *feng-shui,* the dragon is a symbol of natural energy and the mountainous landscape is often thought of in terms of the shape of a dragon's body. The system evolved in the south of China, which is characterized by a series of valley basins and mountains marked by rivers and waterways, and has always been closely associated with mountains and waters. Particular formations may be said to look like a tortoise or a fish, for instance, and carry particular meanings. It is a system particularly used for deciding where to locate graves that are seen as the residences of the dead, or for houses and villages that are the residences of the living. It is very generally believed that the future fortune of the person and his family will depend on the location chosen. For the landscape, the "veins of the dragon" are marked by strong and weak spots, places of energy, which affect the living. The descendants of an ancestor will therefore benefit by having his grave located in a favorable place, just as the fortunes of the living may be affected by where their houses or villages are situated.

Often the fact that one family is successful, while another is not, will be explained by pointing out that the grave of their grandfather, or a more distant ancestor, was located in a good place, geomantically speaking. Indeed, the historical conflict between the Lis and Lauj clans in Laos has been explained by some Hmong in geomantic terms. The grave of Touby Lyfoung's father was believed to be in a geomantically favorable location while Lo Bliayao, who was his father-in-law and political rival, was buried in an insignificant spot. Touby later did well in his personal life and political career with the former pro-American Lao Administration, while Lo Bliayao's descendants did not gain any meaningful positions in the current Lao communist government.

The ideal place for a burial, according to older Hmong who have specialized in this knowledge, is located halfway down a central spur of three mountain ridges separated by rivers, overlooking a grand and spacious valley basin.[5] The mountain on the left should be longer and curl round the one on the right. The opposite would be extremely inauspicious. In the system, the left is always the honored side associated with the male line of descent, and the right is the inauspicious side associated with daughters in the descent line. The Hmong believe that if the right side (female) has hills that are higher than those of the left (male), then the female descendants will be in a more dominant or auspicious position than the sons, and a good grave site should not allow for this. Daughters will marry out of the family and therefore should not benefit at the expense of sons. Like the Chinese, the Hmong envy the one who succeeds in burying his paternal ancestor in the best place since he will also succeed in life. The same belief applies to great leaders who are said to have become so because of the favorable location of the family graves of their ancestors.

The system of geomancy is not entirely superstitious because it incorporates many practical recommendations for ensuring fresh ventilation and drainage, and in its widest sense, means that people must take care to locate themselves in harmony with the environment where they live. Indeed, *feng-shui* has been described as a kind of traditional town planning system. Often a belt of trees is preserved above a Hmong village for geomantic reasons, for example, which has the practical effect of preventing soil erosion and preserving the forest, while houses are generally built facing uphill with granaries beneath them so that household waste is carried away from the places where people live. The best place, geomantically speaking, is usually also the most practical and aesthetically pleasing place in which to locate a village.

In a Hmong village, houses should not directly face each other since in geomancy it is believed that malign influences, which are sometimes conceptualized as spirits, travel in straight lines. Hmong houses are thus not aligned north-south or east-west in order to avoid what is seen as "building on top of each other" (*ua tsev sib tsuam*), which would take away the good fortune of the houses below. The houses may look higgledy-piggledy, but actually, this has sound practical effects in ensuring a measure of privacy and lessening the likelihood of neighborly disputes. Also for geomantic reasons, the houses are usually arranged in a horseshoe shape, in a shaded valley, out of the direct blast of the wind or storms; well arranged for defense and protection; and not right on top of a mountain, where they would be too exposed to the elements and to attack and would lead to serious soil erosion, but generally somewhat below the summit.

This important *sense of appropriateness to a particular locality*, not only at a social but at a personal level, can be materially expressed in other ways besides ideas about illness, ritual, and location of villages and houses. It is also expressed in terms of the physical structures of vernacular, or popular, architecture.

A "House-Based Society"

The traditional Hmong house in most of Southeast Asia is built out of upright wooden planks placed directly into grooves in a square wooden base

A Hmong village in China. Courtesy of the authors.

course on the flat earth, which is soaked with water and tamped by foot into a smooth, even texture over a period of several days. The floor is generally swept every day several times by the woman of the house so that most Hmong houses are spotless within, and the house is covered with wooden shingles, or thatch made out of long sturdy grass. Since the 1960s, zinc or corrugated iron roofs have become more and more common for those who can afford them, although they tend to be much hotter than the traditional thatch roof that allowed ventilation and the escape of smoke from the cooking fire under the eaves. Today it is mostly only the poorest who still maintain thatch roofs in a village. The house is built around a structure of wooden house posts that must be erected according to a particular pattern, because they are inhabited by and are the residential sites of spirits associated with the household and its family. House building is a collective activity that requires as many hands as possible, like transplanting wet rice. Usually a family will call on its close male relatives and brothers-in-law to help with the house building, and reward them with meals and help in the future with their own houses. So a family would need only to get all the building materials together. Neighbors and relatives will then help to put up the new house in one or two days through co-operative labor.

Houses are built when a village moves or when a family from a village moves to another house, but also after an elder son has married and the couple has had a few children and decide to move out to a new home, often nearby. If a house is inherited, it is generally by the youngest son who is expected to remain at home and care for his parents. Women are expected to move out of the family when they marry to join their husbands elsewhere, so that they cannot normally inherit a parental house. The knowledge of house building is a matter of informal expertise; most older men will know something about it, but like many other skills in Hmong society (geomancy and wedding songs, for example), there may be one or two men in the village or lineage who are particularly knowledgeable about how a house should be built, so they may be consulted for their advice when a house is erected. Constructing a new house is an exercise that requires a lot of skill, since traditionally no nails were used at all in the building of a Hmong house; it was all done by a series of mortise and tenon joints cunningly held together by clever workmanship.

HOUSE PLAN AND CONSTRUCTION

The house is basically one room, with sleeping quarters partitioned off, often quite roughly by a sheet of timber or bamboo, toward the back of the house opposite the altar. In the main room of the house, the most important feature is the household altar. This is a piece of rice-paper adorned with gold and silver leaf smeared with chicken's blood and feathers that is stuck on the front wall of the house. To its right there may be other altars. If a shaman lives in the family, there may be an altar for the auxiliary spirits of the shaman known as the *thaj neeb*, a standing tiered wooden structure adorned with strips of white spirit paper and ritual objects. There may be a smaller altar for the spirits of herbal medicine if there is a practitioner of herbal medicine in the home. There are two fires: a central hearth (*lub qhov cub*) in the middle of the floor where the family's meals are cooked and where the family will gather for warmth and conversation with guests, and a much larger oven (*lub qhov txos*) to the left of the household altar where food is cooked in a huge wok for the pigs. For banquets and major meals, this oven can also be used for cooking food for guests. Each fire has its associated guardian spirit. There is also usually a raised bed for guests (*lub txaj qhuas*) to the right of the front door, and a special place—in a corner or sometimes under the guest's bed—may be reserved to store the rice. There is no need for any window in the house; light and air penetrate under the eaves or through an opened door, while watchdogs act as good sentinels to warn of the approach of any strangers.

The central house posts, or pillars to a house, are odd in number—often five—supporting the ridgepole, which runs laterally the length of the whole house, and from which the roof descends toward the walls. Such pillars or posts are usually made of a strong local wood. White Hmong and

Exterior of a traditional Hmong house in Laos. Courtesy of the authors.

Blue Mong houses differ slightly in their design; in a White Hmong house there are two entrance doors, the main ceremonial entrance (*qhov rooj tag*) that is often not used, and a side or back door (*qhov rooj txuas*) that often functions as the door for daily use. Some houses may be L-shaped. In either case, the altar faces the front or main door, above which will hang, in non-Christian households, a strip of red cloth with five coins over a strip of white cloth or paper, honored at the New Year and renewed in a special ritual sometimes performed (if it is prescribed to have "fallen" by a shaman) in honor of the spirits of wealth and richness (*dab txhiaj meej*), who guard the fortunes and prosperity of the family. Although somewhat old-fashioned now, because a Hmong family may suffer from various taboos (*caiv*) in case of sickness or after a childbirth, it is customary for any guest to pause on reaching the front door and call out loudly to ask if there is a taboo in progress (*nej caiv los tsis caiv?*). If there is not, he or she will be invited to enter, although he or she may be expected to leave his or her shoes and bag behind in case of a not-too-serious prohibition. And if there is only a woman in the house, a man would not be expected to enter. Someone who entered during a taboo period would break the taboo and bring misfortune to the family, so it would be the height of bad manners to enter a house at such a time, although, of course, those unfamiliar with Hmong customs often do so. The Hmong are generally too polite to point this out to them. Before entering the house, there may be a small porch (*taw rooj*) between the mainframe of the house and the door.

There must be three rows of pillars, the highest down the center of the house supporting the high roof, and the other two parallel with these but half their length or less to form the side walls. In the central row, apart from the two pillars standing at each end of the house, the three others are not evenly distributed along the ridgepole; the ones immediately following the end pillars will be evenly spread out; the central pillar, the most important in the house and the first to be erected, is placed about two-thirds along the length of the house, to the left of the altar. This is the *ncej tas*, the center of the Hmong cosmos, which is the site of the main ancestral spirits of the household.

Although there is no altar there, the central post is believed to have its own spirit, the *dab ncej tas* that is honored in various rituals, funerals, and other occasions. It is also the site of taboos associated with particular clans or sub-clans. For example, in a sub-section of the Vang (*Vaj*) clan in northern Thailand only men of the household may sit behind it, near to the fire; guests and women are expected to sit in front of it. It is under this pillar that the placenta of a newly born boy child will be buried, as a symbol that he will uphold the household ceremonies and line of descent. All

Hmong, whether male or female, must come back to collect their placenta or "coat" of birth where it was buried before beginning their journey to the Otherworld after death. The placenta of a girl may be disposed of fairly unceremoniously, usually buried in the floor of the master bedroom (*niam txiv txaj*) of the house where the head of the family with his spouse (or spouses if he has more than one) sleep. Young children will sleep with them, until puberty when boys and girls are separated. Near the door of this bedroom a dry calabash is hung up with a small dead tree branch, where the paraphernalia used for the *dab roog* ceremony are kept.

Today, many Hmong live in modern houses with a variety of designs and constructions using different kinds of building materials. In a traditional Hmong house, however, the five central pillars (*ncej ru*) are intersected by crossbeams (*nqaj nthab*) about halfway up their length, which are themselves simply supported by the four corner pillars (*ncej kaum*) that go to form the walls on each side of the house. These four wall pillars on each side of the house in turn support lateral tie-beams running along all side walls of the house. If there is a shaman in the house, a special crossbar is suspended down from the ridgepole of the house parallel with it but shorter, across the *ncej tas* and the pillar to the right side of the house, known as the *nqaj neeb* or support for the shamanic spirits. Above the ridgepole two cross-sticks at either end support an additional hanging frame made of four pieces of cross timber in a hanging loft (*nthab*) where household dry crops and rice may be kept, with a rough ladder leading up to it. Again different sub-clans may have different taboos over who may ascend this ladder to the loft; often the daughters-in-law living in the house are forbidden access to the loft. The roof itself is finished off with intricately placed cross-running and diagonal pieces of wood and bamboo running directly up to rest against the ridgepole, tied together with strips of rattan or bamboo. They may be repaired with rattan leaves or bark.

Outside the house and around, in the enclosure known as a *vaj* or household garden, there are usually various lean-to temporary wooden structures including pigsties, chicken coops, and perhaps an outside toilet. Formerly, pigs used to run loose, but in Thailand today they are mostly penned as a result of education and health campaigns.

Within the house is a large open space arranged around the hearth and central pillar, and this would be the main living and eating space for all members of the family. Personal space is very limited; privacy is a concept not over-valued in Hmong culture and there is no single Hmong word that can be literally translated as "privacy." Yet people will make their own ways within this space, arranging the low wooden stools common in southern Chinese homes to suit their needs at varying distances from a source of light or heat according to individual need. So a student might be learning from a book in a corner while dishes are washed just outside the back door, a young woman might be doing some embroidery or sewing near the open door, and a conversation may be in process around the fire. The rough bedrooms are normally only used for sleeping and often conversations will take place between the people in different bedrooms through the night.

Space within the house is also constrained and ordered by social considerations, since as we have seen customary taboos and prohibitions are applied to many parts of the house, although these differ between surnames and sometimes within sub-groups of surnames. In many clans, a father-in-law and a daughter-in-law are expressly forbidden to enter each other's bedroom. In many sub-clans daughters-in-law are not allowed to climb to the roof of a house, or to get up to the drying platform or *nthab* above the fireplace. In time of sickness, as noted, a household and its members may go through a *caiv* or prohibition period from one to three days as part of the healing process and according to instructions from the shaman. During this time, they are not allowed to go outside the house, and visitors, particularly strangers, are also forbidden to enter the house. Depending on the severity with which the prohibition is applied, a known visitor reluctantly may be permitted to enter, but must leave his or her bags and shoes outside. After childbirth, too, for a month the household undergoes a taboo period. A newly delivered mother is not allowed to go outside her house for 30 days, and all visitors must leave their shoes outside to prevent her milk from drying up. The household, then, forms a ritual as well as a domestic and kinship unity.

Following some catastrophic event such as an epidemic or natural disaster, a whole village may be closed off to outsiders, normally with a prohibition sign posted at the entrances to the settlement. The sign is usually represented as a panel of cross-hatched bamboo lattice mounted on a stick. It is also called a *phiaj caiv*, similar to that applied to a household. There may be certain spiritual objects or sacred places such as rocks, caves, or large trees, particularly those with aerial roots known as *ntoo xeeb*, which people avoid. Under the importance of a new ecological awareness, some of these avoidance practices have now become a useful means of ensuring the preservation of particular areas of the forest, as we described in Chapter 2.[6]

The Hmong do not build with stone or concrete, because they often move, at least in the past, although they now have adopted more permanent houses and build with modern materials where they can afford to. Hmong houses are not based on elaborate architectural plans or drawings because they do not need to be; there is an enormously rich store of popular knowledge and wisdom about how and where to build a house, which must conform with Hmong religious practices and geomantic principles. A Hmong's house is his temple and his place of worship; everything should be in its proper place within it.

VARIATIONS OF STRUCTURE

We can see how closely the vernacular architecture and spatial concepts of the Hmong are associated with their daily and ritual life, and with oppositions between the inside and the outside.[7] Yet while this may be the most traditional structure of the Hmong house, which has survived to the present day in remote parts of Southeast Asia such as Laos and Thailand, in many parts of Vietnam and China, the Hmong live in quite different types of houses. Walls there are often made of adobe, or even of stone, rather than wooden struts, for instance, and there seems to be considerable variation within the house, too. In Hoa Binh province of Vietnam, the Hmong live in huge long houses with vast spacious loft areas that are quite unlike the structures found in Laos or Thailand. In Sapa, northern Vietnam, the Hmong live in huddled stone houses quite like Chinese village houses; in Sichuan, China, large whitewashed courtyard houses are common in keeping with the house designs of other people around them. These are situated at great distances from each other, spread out across the mountainside, rather than in the compact villages found in Laos or Thailand. Yet this variation in house structure does not seem to affect Hmong beliefs in household spirits and the rituals associated with them, which are the same everywhere.

Enormous changes have taken place in the traditional imagination of space, not only because of the removal of a large proportion of Hmong society to countries quite unlike the traditional lands of Asia, but also because of processes of modernization and the ever-increasing impact with other ethnic groups in Thailand, Laos, Vietnam, and China. Although there are young Hmong in the Sichuan province of China who are not aware there are any Hmong in the neighboring provinces, in general radio, news, visits, and the widespread marital links—over great distances sometimes—of Hmong families have led to a very general awareness in almost all Hmong communities that the Hmong are now global citizens. The impact of returning American, French, Canadian, and Australian Hmong visitors on Hmong communities in Thailand, Laos, even China and Vietnam, has been considerable, too. In some ways this has forced a realization that being Hmong is not an exclusive definition of humanity, as it used to be thought of in the past. Traditionally, and to some extent still today, spatial proximity between Hmong and Hmong was dictated by blood ties, clan affiliation, and affinal relationships through marriage, while those with non-Hmong were dictated by economic exchanges, educational needs, official dealings, and ties of friendship. The more social and cultural components the two parties shared, the closer their spatial relations would tend to be. Social and physical space were very closely integrated, so that different kinds of behavior were expected toward those closest to you, the members of your surname, and toward the members of other surnames to whom you were related through marriage (that is, all other Hmong at the widest reaches), and then toward those beyond the pale of Hmong society. This sense of social space and distance is changing and contracting. There is a new tolerance of other ethnic groups and recognition that they may contain good people among them, just as there is unfortunately a new awareness that not all Hmong are the same and that there may be good and bad people among the Hmong, too.

The adoption of Christianity and membership in a global community of believers has brought about this shift of moral and spatial perceptions, and so, too, have been new forms of travel and media communication. In Laos and Thailand, the impact of Hmong radio broadcasts has been fundamental in bringing about a new awareness of space and of other Hmong communities inhabiting spaces wider than any traditionally envisaged. In Vietnam and China, Hmong-language radio broadcasts have been received and been important in altering the traditional consciousness of a more locally bounded space. Although few Hmong in Vietnam, China, or even Laos have much access to the Internet, for Hmong communities outside Asia and to some extent within Thailand, cyberspace has provided a new domain or realm in which a Hmong cultural identity can be built and communicated across huge distances of time and physical space. As we will see later, through art, new forms of customs, design, and communication through chat rooms, blogs, and Web sites, new notions of globalized space intersect with those more narrowly bounded by local, social, and moral contexts.

NOTES

1. Savina 1924.
2. Cooper 1984.
3. Skinner 1964–1965.
4. See Freedman 1979, 313–34.
5. Feuchtwang 1974.
6. See also Tomforde 2006.
7. See also Symonds 2004.

7

Traditional Dress and Cuisine

HMONG COSTUMES AND DRESS

HMONG COSTUME IS rich and varied. Costume is a sign of identity, and in the East Asian and Southeast Asian context, it has been most important for expressing the differences between cultural groups. As people of different ethnic groups move from place to place, or village to village, the differences between such ethnic groups even today are often signaled by the differences of the costumes they wear. Moreover, differences within those groups can be signaled by different customary styles of dress. Since the early twentieth century, there has been widespread adoption of modern dress by the men in these groups, so that often it is only the women who retain their customary apparel. This is associated with the general impact of the cash economy on traditional economies. In a traditional economy, the men are most usually the first to take up new cash-paying occupations, while their wives are generally left to support the more traditional economy. Eventually, ethnic costumes come to be worn only on special ritual or festival occasions, or as parts of regional or national display. In the multicultural societies of the United States and Australia, for example, where many Hmong now live, costume takes on a new significance as a sign of traditional Hmong identity, and is particularly worn as part of displays and performances on such occasions as Hmong New Year, which we discuss in more detail in Chapter 9.

In Southeast Asia, there have always been very strong distinctions of dress, as of dialect and some other customs, between the White Hmong (Hmoob Dawb) and the Blue Mong (Moob Ntsuab). In northern Vietnam, there is a separate group, the Mong Leng, who have now largely assimilated to the Blue Mong of Laos, so that these terms are sometimes used interchangeably. A further cultural division in Laos and Thailand is the Hmoob Quas Npab (Striped or Arm-band Hmong), who speak White Hmong but are distinguished by the women wearing tunics with sleeves decorated in alternate strips of blue and black cloth, and an embroidered Tai-style headdress rather than a turban. Traditionally, the women of the White Hmong wore white or undyed pleated skirts, while those of the Blue Mong women are dyed with indigo and decorated through the technique of batik. It has been said that these cultural divisions were so named because of the color of their women's skirts, although there may be other explanations for the names of these subgroups. Moreover, since passing through northern Vietnam, the White Hmong women have given up wearing their skirts on a daily basis and have adopted the trousers of the Vietnamese women, which they wear with a long apron in front. Today, white skirts alone are not often found outside some parts of Vietnam, except on special occasions such as the New Year or weddings.

The White Hmong and Blue Mong are not the only cultural divisions of the Hmong, and in parts of northern Vietnam and southern China there were a number of other Hmong cultural sub-groups, such as the Hmoob Sua, Puas, Pe (Pw), Xau, and Si. Although these cultural divisions, unlike the White Hmong and Blue Mong, have practically disappeared today, from old photographs and the writing of some Chinese Hmong themselves, we know that these divisions were also clearly marked by differences of dress.[1] Despite these differences, the colors used have no relationship at all with the names of these groups. In Sapa, Lao Cai province, in northern Vietnam, the Hmong wear a distinctive dark purple costume that is quite unlike that of either the Blue Mong or White Hmong, the women there wearing something similar to culottes. Some of the Hmong groups in Bac Ha, also in Lao Cai, wear a costume very similar to that of the Blue Mong, but far redder and with wider bands of embroidery at the base of the skirt and on the sleeves. This is very similar to the costume of the Hmong Pe in Wenshan, China, and is similarly worn with a wide reddish turban. In different regions of Laos, Vietnam, and China, there were also regional differences, often of hairstyle or headdress, which marked a Hmong as coming from a particular region, such as that between the Hmong of Luang Prabang and those of Sam Neua or Xieng Khouang, all in Laos. However, with the new hybridity of costumes adopted and mixed from all over the world, these functions of costume signifying a particular place or cultural identity are rapidly becoming lost.

In China, some entrepreneurial Hmong, particularly in the Wenshan region that borders Vietnam, have designed imaginative Hmong-style clothes based on their own traditional styles, but with the additions of motifs and patterns from the costumes of the Chinese and some other neighboring ethnic minority groups like the Dai. These have proved wildly popular with the Hmong in the United States and France for use at weddings and at the New Year. For festive occasions, costumes may be decorated with bright beads, coins, glass sequins, and tassels of colored thread and such decoration is common with these Chinese-imported costumes, which are now often assembled in a number of different countries around the world as they circulate among the relatives of a family.[2]

In a traditional village, girls and women spend a large part of their time weaving or stitching and embroidering clothes for the family. The techniques are usually taught to daughters by their mothers. To have a new costume by the New Year is a most important thing since that is often the time when suitors may be met and weddings arranged. The techniques of making fabric, weaving, spinning, stitching, and embroidering are primary forms of Hmong arts and crafts, as shown in Chapter 5. In intermarriages between the cultural divisions, a woman will usually adapt to the dress habits of her husband's group, though she may pass on some of her group's skills and techniques to her own daughters. In this way there is some movement of styles and fashions between the divisions, as indeed there is between the different localities between which intermarriages occur. A girl needs a trousseau for her marriage and a great deal of time and effort by mother and daughters goes into preparing this. Traditionally, her eligibility as a wife would depend not only on her looks and appearance, but particularly on her needlework skills, so it was well worth practicing these at every opportunity if she wished to attract a particular boy. As night falls and after the day's work is done, you can often see girls and women sitting by the door to catch the fading light or squinting at their embroidery by the light of a candle or storm-lamp or even the fire. Whenever there is a spare minute a girl will pick up her embroidery and do a little more work on it. At death the corpse should be dressed in a special suit of new clothes and hemp shoes, which are often prepared some months or even years in advance. These are among the finest clothes of the Hmong, and quite a few museums in the West such as the Smithsonian Institution in Washington and the Museum of Mankind in London display such funeral suits bought from the Hmong at different times over the past century. Another popular item of costume is the women's baby-carrier known as *nyias*, used by adults to carry young babies on their back. It, too, is often a labor of love and very carefully embroidered.

When Hmong from Laos started fleeing to Thai refugee camps from 1975 onward, they were a sad and dispirited people, having felt they had lost the war in Laos and been deserted by the Americans they were trying to help and their own leaders. Traditional life had been completely disrupted over several decades and the men found little worthwhile work to do in the camps. Many of them became ill or suffered nervous complaints. The women, however, still had their traditional household duties and children to feed and look after, and their traditional skills at weaving and embroidery did not desert them. Traditional Hmong design is entirely abstract, unlike the Chinese-style butterfly and dragon patterns of the Hmu people in Guizhou. However, with the encouragement of some Western women working in Non-Governmental Organizations (NGOs) in Ban Vinai and Nam Yao refugee camps, the Hmong women began for the first time stitching in cloth a representational account of the devastations they had been through in Laos.[3]

These large stitched embroideries, also discussed in Chapter 5, became the famous Hmong story-cloths depicting the dropping of "Yellow Rain" chemical warfare on Hmong villages, Hmong fleeing through rice fields and villages into the machine guns of war, and crossing the Mekong River between Laos and Thailand. They proved a popular item to sell to tourists and soon new clothes designed with patches of Hmong embroidery were on sale to tourists all over Thailand, bringing in a comfortable income not only for some of the refugee Hmong, but also for their cousins living in Thailand who soon entered this new market. Today Hmong costumes, clothes, and embroideries can be found all over the world in ethnic markets and exotic boutiques, while Hmong women have started their own needlework cooperatives, as documented by Nancy Donnelly in Seattle.[4] We may say, too, that in this new representative art some of the Hmong refugees found a kind of therapy and solace for some of their sufferings in war-torn Laos after so many losses and bereavements.

The Hmong are well known in particular for their batik, as noted earlier, a technique known to them alone among the ethnic minorities of Southeast Asia, and for their skilled embroidery (*paj ntaub*), in which they use chain stitch and cross-stitch techniques, often in combination with cotton appliqué or reverse appliqué, which may form several layers. Indigo paste is obtained from the dried leaves of the indigo plant. The dye is prepared with various additives such as lime in a vat and the cloth dipped in it twice a day for a week or more to obtain a deep darkening effect.

Beeswax is applied to the dyed cloth with a special small instrument called a *cab*, and is then boiled off in a vat leaving triangular and rectangular cross patterns behind.

In remote areas in China and Southeast Asia, the Hmong have always made their own cloth and clothes; although as early as in the 1930s, the Hmong in Sichuan, China, were reported buying cloth from the market place and giving up the use of traditional dyes for synthetic ones.[5] Hemp, and sometimes cotton, is cultivated by families near the village and it is dried, stripped, and then joined together into long lengths to be spun and woven into hemp cloth by the women of the household, as mentioned in Chapter 5. In Wenshan prefecture of Yunnan province in south China, Hmong women can still be seen walking to the fields carrying a bunch of hemp sticks attached to their front belts that they are slowly peeling and binding as they walk. The skin of the hemp they peel is used as threads to be woven into materials. This may be supplemented by printed factory-batiked cloth and wool bought from the market to make skirts and costumes.

The traditional costumes of White Hmong and Blue Mong men differ in that the Chinese-style pantaloons of the White Hmong are widely flared at the bottom, while those of the Blue Mong are very baggy, with the seat reaching down almost to the ankles. Leggings or puttees are worn that protect their calves and ankles while working in the fields. Above the pantaloons is

Blue Mong costumes. Courtesy of the authors.

Young girls at market, Sapa, Vietnam.
Courtesy of Shutterstock.

worn a sash of red cloth known as a *sev*, embroidered at both ends; a turban that might vary from region to region, or a skullcap, is worn on the head. The long-sleeved tunic is parted behind and to each side, and lined with a shade of blue that is different for White Hmong and Blue Mong and is turned back up at the cuff of the sleeve so it can be seen, with a small collar buttoned up and pocket to each side. This tunic may also be made of satin. Silver is an essential accompaniment to the dark costume of the Hmong men, and this may be worn in the form of neck-rings (*xauv*) with a platelet or *daim phiaj* hanging from the neck. They may also wear thick silver bracelets, either Hmong-made or purchased from local Chinese traders As mentioned, with the coming of modernity it is usually the men who adopt modern clothes while the women retain their traditional costumes and this has been the case, too, with the Hmong. Today men only rarely wear their traditional costume, except for festivals or ritual occasions, while it is still quite common for women to dress traditionally.

Women's bodices, which may also be of satin, are in three pieces with the arms separated from the main body, and open at the front that is seamed, usually by sewing machine, the two pieces crossing over. There is a small square collar folded over at the back of the neck that is embroidered and stitched at the hems with multicolored threads and is of ritual importance. The bodices are lined like those of the men, and they too wear

Mixed subgroup and regional costumes, Australia. Courtesy of the authors.

leggings. The knee-length skirts are always pleated, and can be more than three yards in length without the pleating. They are made of three bands of cloth stitched together the whole way along; the top piece is undyed, the hems of the bottom are embroidered and the ways they are embroidered and their colors may still reveal regional or sub-cultural differentiations, as with the Bac Ha Hmong women in Vietnam mentioned above. The skirt is not joined up, but opens at the front, and is attached to the waist by two sashes that cross over the opening and are knotted at the back. One of these is green/blue or black while the other is of red calico and from them is suspended a long, thin, black satin apron reaching (for the White Hmong women) almost to the ground. As with the men, silver is essential to complete the dress, and is worn as bracelets, neck-rings, and also in the form of a variety of special designs of earrings, which have proved popular on the tourist market.

There are various embroidery and stitch work designs that are particular to the Hmong, although they may be copied by other people. One of the best known of these is the spiral snail pattern; crosses are also very common. Triangle motifs may be referred to as mountain patterns, and wavy lines as river patterns, but these are all abstract, geometrical designs and people differ in the names they call them. Sometimes particular patterns are said to

Hmong/Miao girls in Zunyi, Guizhou, China, and their embroidered costumes, 2009. Courtesy of the authors.

be seed patterns, or the tracks of various beasts, or spider web, heart, or shell patterns, as illustrated in Chapter 5f. While the Hmong have many legends about how they lost their form of writing, the story (like that of butterfly origins) that they hid it in the patterns of their costume is probably originally from another Miao group in China, the Hmu. However, it has been widely circulated through Chinese translations among the Hmong, and is sometimes repeated by them today. Certainly it is true, in a wider and more metaphorical sense, that in the designs and patterns of the Hmong dress and costume are hidden important clues to their identity as a people with a unique tradition and a special way of living.

HMONG CUISINE

Hmong food is strongly rice-based, although there is some evidence that in the past when the Hmong lived at even higher altitudes than they do now in most of Laos and Thailand, in particular in the northern parts of Vietnam and southern China, maize was more commonly eaten than rice. The normal words for "eating" are *noj* or *noj mov*, which means "eat" or "eat rice/food" because almost everywhere today rice forms the staple diet and it is often taken to refer to food in general. Maize is regarded as food for the pigs, which also eat other household waste items like corn cobs and bamboo parts. The rice is husked before eating so that like most Asian people only white rice is used, not brown rice. The hill rice the Hmong usually eat is of a semi-glutinous variety, said to be more protein-rich and delicious than the irrigated rice grown at lower altitudes. The Hmong consume sticky rice, but not as often as the lowland Lao and northern Thai people. However, in many places the Hmong today use the lowland varieties of irrigated rice as they have settled at lower altitudes or constructed irrigated terraced rice fields for themselves in the hills. At festivals, particularly during the New Year, the Hmong enjoy a particular delicacy known as *ncuav*, a kind of plain rice cake made from mashed sticky rice. Some Hmong may also make *ncuav qab zib* out of maize or buckwheat dough and sweetened with sugar. Children are particularly fond of these because traditionally there would be no other sweet foods in a Hmong village.

Meals are eaten three times a day: breakfast, lunch, and supper. The wife or older daughters usually get up very early in the morning to sweep the floors, feed the pigs and poultry, and put on the pot of water to boil rice for the morning meal. Lunch is often eaten cold in the fields where the family is working, so they may take it with them, wrapped in banana leaves. The family will gather again for the evening meal. Very early it was reported that the Hmong used large wooden spoons for eating, unlike the chopsticks of the Chinese or the fingers of the Lao and Thai. Today, the small Chinese spoon is still a very common item of cutlery at a Hmong meal.

Etiquette is very important at Hmong meals, and indeed in the whole of Hmong social life, as we will emphasize in Chapter 10. In their relations with one another, the Hmong have retained many traces of a Confucian morality that have been lost in China. If someone is passing by, it would be the height of rudeness not to summon him to join in the meal, it is polite to refuse for a while to join the meal when invited, and sometimes a visitor may have to be forcibly dragged to the dining table, protesting politely all the while. One should not begin before one's host and should not appear too greedy. It would be rude for a host to finish eating or leave the table before his guests. One should not hog the best dishes, and Hmong say you can judge a person's character by whether they help themselves to the burnt pieces of rice or not. At ritual feasts there is even more etiquette, and a particular way of toasting one's neighbor before one drinks one's own cup. The children are usually fed first, since they are small and hungry, and quite unceremoniously, may wander about while they are eating. Generally, the men are served before the women sit down to eat, particularly if company is present. More informally, the family will sit down to eat together. Men sometimes cook or lend a hand with the cooking, so there is no hard-and-fast rule about this, just as men may cradle children and walk about with small infants, but generally it is the women who are responsible for the family cooking and the diet, so they may often still be cooking while the men are eating.

To accompany the rice, there are usually some vegetables, often gathered by the women on their return from working in the fields, and these may be served with the boiled cooking water to make a slightly bitter soup, without salt. Various cucumbers and gourds or pumpkins may also be prepared in this way, particularly cucumbers known as *dib*. Vegetables commonly used include green beans and peas, soya, mustard, Chinese cabbage, and aubergines. Extensive use is also made of root crops such as cassava, taro, yams, sweet potatoes, and red potatoes, and the Hmong are particularly fond of a bitter vegetable known as *zaub iab* that grows in the wild. This is hankered after by many of the older Hmong refugees from Laos; many people take medicinal herbs and vegetables back from Laos on visits to plant around their new homes in the West. Sometimes chicken or duck eggs may be used in the cooking, or eaten whole, but these tend to be rare since the chickens in many Hmong villages do not lay well, perhaps because of the poverty of the soil. Medicinal and other herbs may be placed in the cooking or soups for health and for taste. The water used for cooking the rice is carefully preserved for cooking purposes. Bamboo shoots and mushrooms can also be prepared to make, or add to, a dish.

Meat of any sort is traditionally very rare. It is generally roasted or boiled or stir-fried with vegetables. Young men and boys shoot birds with crossbows or rifles, but mainly for fun, and game has become very scarce in all the areas the Hmong live owing to the scarcity of forest. Sixty or more years ago there would have been an abundance of wild cat and field mouse, large lizard, rabbit, pheasant, monkeys, squirrels, deer, hedgehog, wild boar, and even the occasional bear or tiger, but none of these has ever formed a regular part of the Hmong diet, although fish are enjoyed when they are occasionally caught or bought. The main meat available is that of the chickens, ducks, and pigs that every household of any means keeps. Unlike the Chinese and Iu Mien, dog is never eaten. Traditionally, a chicken or pig was only killed for a particular occasion, such as the New Year or after the new rice harvest, or for a funeral or a wedding, or during the sickness of a member of a family when the sacrifice of a chicken or even a pig might be decreed as necessary for health by the shaman. In a reasonably well-off household, such an event might take place once a month, given the frequency of illnesses, particularly among young children, so there would be meat on the table for a few days at least once a month. Of course, a well-to-do family might decide to kill a chicken or a pig more often than this, but still meat eating is by no means an inevitable accompaniment to every Hmong meal. Chicken may be stewed in a broth, or boiled so that pieces of meat can accompany a few mouthfuls of rice and vegetable and soups. Pork is generally roasted, and parts of the beast will be saved as crackling, salted and partially smoked for consumption later in the year. Tripe and intestines can be minced and fried with onions and garlic and herbs. The blood is cooked, too, with salted water, and eaten as in Chinese cuisine. The pork fat is favored to cook with and used, like tallow, to make oil lamps.

Hmong food is not usually spicy and no chili is used in the cooking. Even salt is used very sparingly because traditionally it was hard to come by. However, small green or red chilies may be eaten with a meal, and the Hmong are familiar with such spices as lemongrass, basil, ginger, dill, and coriander that are sometimes added to a dish for flavor, while tiny pieces of burnt fat can be used like croutons to lend taste to a soup. Often a small bowl of salt with ground red pepper is placed on the table as a condiment to be added while eating. Corn on the cob is eaten as a snack, and sugar cane sucked for thirst and sweetness in the fields. Sweet potatoes can be baked in the ashes of a fire and taken to the fields wrapped in banana leaves as a snack for lunch. Bananas are another frequent snack.

That is the traditional Hmong diet, and still today there are many Hmong families eating like this, but it should be noted that the Hmong in both Laos and Thailand, particularly those living in towns or lowland settlements, have adopted many Lao and Thai dishes and tastes and elaborated their own cuisine with the addition of a good many more. Both Lao and Thai dishes tend to be extremely spicy, and many Hmong from Laos and in Thailand have developed a taste for such spicy foods and cook these for themselves. The Laotian *lap* (minced rare pork with chilies and spices) is quite commonly made after a pig is killed. Hmong cuisine itself, though, tends to be simple, healthy, and very nourishing. Around the villages and in the forest grow a variety of fruits such as pears, peaches, apricots, apples, bananas, guavas, figs, and various kinds of wild grapes, cherries, and berries, which all go to form a part of the Hmong diet.

Hmong food outside Asia is now evolving into a separate cuisine enriched by borrowings from Lao, Thai, Chinese, and Vietnamese food. Not only the *lap* and sticky rice favored by many Hmong from Laos, but noodle soups such as the *pho* from Vietnam and red or green curries are now quite common and liked. Hmong restaurants have been established, especially in the United States where there are more than 120 of these in Detroit, Michigan, alone! Many younger people may prefer fast food or burgers, at least on occasions, and breakfasts are becoming particularly minimal as is common in Western societies. Breads, pastries, and cereals are enjoyed by many in their new lives outside Asia.

Two typical recipes may serve to give some idea of the varieties of Hmong food:[6]

Traditional: Unsalted Pumpkin Soup or *Taub Tsuag*

1/4 pumpkin, skin and clean off all seeds.

Chop into small pieces 1" in size, and put in water in a pot.

Boil for 10 minutes until soft.

Serves 4 persons, hot or cold.

New: Chicken Wings in Black Mushroom Soy Sauce or *Kooj Tis Qaib Dub*

2 cloves of mashed garlic

4 boiled eggs

3–4 tablespoons of mushroom soy sauce

(Do not add salt as soy sauce is salty already)

1 tablespoon brown sugar

1 cup of water

3 tablespoons of sliced shallots and coriander

2 lb chicken wings

Put 1 tablespoon olive oil in pot and heat under low heat until hot.

Put garlic in, stir until golden, then add sugar until it melts.

Put in chicken wings and whole boiled eggs.

Pour mushroom soy sauce in, then stir until mixed well.

Cover with lid for 1 minute, then stir again.

Continue covering with lid and stirring until dark.

Add water and simmer, covered, for 10 minutes or until juice is thick.

Temper saltiness by adding a small amount of water to taste while simmering.

Turn off heat; sprinkle coriander and sliced shallots on top.

Serves 4–6 persons; serve hot on a plate covered with lettuce leaves.

Again, unlike the Iu Mien or Chinese, tea is not traditionally drunk, only hot water sometimes, but as with the Chinese nothing is usually drunk with the meal. Alcohol is made from fermented rice or maize and is drunk on ceremonial or ritual occasions. Drinking is not very common in Hmong villages in Southeast Asia, although until quite recently opium consumption was fairly common. Opium was generally smoked only for medical reasons because of its anti-tussive and analgesic properties. It reduces fever and pain, prevents dysentery and diarrhea, and also alleviates coughing in the absence of other medicines. It was sometimes used socially, and addicts were not uncommon. In China and Vietnam, drinking is an everyday activity among most farmers and many officials. A farmer will often have three thimble cups of rice wine to accompany his evening meal, so the Hmong in those countries, particularly if they are local village officials, tend to be more familiar with drinking than those in Thailand or Laos. Traditionally, alcohol was not much consumed except at weddings or at funerals or on some great occasion to welcome an honored guest.

Hmong Christian houses may not consume alcohol at all, while smoking is increasingly becoming a thing of the past or of the older refugees, in common with the prevailing trends outside Asia. When Hmong first arrived in the West as refugees from Laos, enormous changes of diet led to many health problems, in particular the greatly increased consumption of meat, especially pork, and greater salt intake. It was far easier to obtain meat than in the past, and to store it in refrigerators, so there was a lot of over-consumption by people who did not realize how healthy their traditional vegetarian diet was. Some cases of SUNDS (Sudden Unexpected Sleeping Death Syndrome) were reported among the Hmong during the initial years of their settlement in the United States, as among some other groups of Southeast Asian immigrants. Research has linked some of these nocturnal deaths to changes in diet and general lifestyle, or argued it should be seen as a combination of psychological, cultural, and environmental factors.[7]

A number of studies have reported greatly increased rates of hypertension, stroke, cancer, and diabetes, besides upper respiratory tract infections, allergies, and depression among Hmong populations in the United States compared to those in Thailand, or in relation to U.S. averages.[8] In particular, increases in meat consumption may be responsible for increased rates of hypertension, certain cancers, and diabetes.[9] Traditional Hmong cuisine, then, is a healthy and well-balanced rice-based one, and meat played a much smaller part in it than it does in most areas today. However, Hmong cuisine is rapidly evolving into new forms through the incorporation of many other Asian dishes and new foodstuffs, in the same way that Hmong costume and other traditional arts are evolving and transforming.

NOTES

1. Zhang, Yang, and Shen 1988.
2. Wronska-Friend 2004.
3. Cohen 2000.

4. Donnelly 1994.

5. Feng and Kilborn 1937.

6. We would like to thank Maylee Lee for her kind assistance with these recipes. See also Finkle 2003.

7. See Lemoine and Mougne 1983; Bliatout 1982.

8. See Kunstadter (1992); Culhane-Pera et al. 2004.

9. See also Culhane-Pera, Vawter, Xiong, Babbitt, and Solberg 2003; Cha 2003.

8

Gender, Courtship, and Marriage

LIKE PEOPLE IN other cultures, Hmong parents love their children regardless of whether they are boys or girls. Because of their religious beliefs in animism and ancestor worship, however, there may be a tendency to prefer boys, or at least to want to have a number of boys in the family. This chapter will explore the reasons for this preference, and will also look at courtship, marriage, and the family system in Hmong society. Although Hmong families exist in the nuclear form with only the parents and their offspring, this single family unit is always embedded in a bigger network of extended relatives, on both the father's and mother's sides, with spiritual ties more strongly maintained with kinspeople of the father.

In most of China and Southeast Asia, as we have seen, the Hmong are subsistence farmers who produce their own crops for consumption in the family, or they are commercial cash croppers of products like vegetables and flowers as in Thailand. They usually work without the help of machinery and draught animals, and depend on family human resources: the larger the pool of human labor, the more productive the family. Because of this, the Hmong often have many children, and some men may also have more than one wife so as to increase the number of able-bodied members of their families and to meet their labor demands.[1] Although family planning is available in most countries today, few Hmong practice it or have access to it. Their attitude is that the number of children a couple has and their gender are pre-ordained and they have to be born and raised as best as can be. Thus, family planning is seen as a defiance of the natural order.

BIRTH AND NAMES

As a rule, the Hmong do not approve of childbirth outside marriage, although premarital sex is allowed and pregnancies may occur before marriage. Young girls have tried to get rid of babies conceived before marriage by swallowing pills and drinking herbs, or by jumping up and down in the belief that the fetus will fall off. However, this may be done to avoid being discovered by parents or bringing shame to the family, rather than any personal desire to exterminate an unborn child. The Hmong do not have surgical abortion, and see such intervention as against the laws of nature and the will of Heaven (*Ntuj*). In general, if a child is conceived out of wedlock, the girl's family will usually ask the man responsible to marry her and take care of her and her child. If no man can be identified or if the man refuses to marry the girl for whatever reason, then she will be encouraged to bring her pregnancy to its full term and keep the child with the support of her parents. Children born out of wedlock are rarely abandoned or adopted out in Hmong society. There is, however, some stigma against an illegitimate child, who will have to take the surname of his mother or of his mother's later husband, and people may treat such a child with some degree of derision, referring to him or her as *menyuam tsaub* (fatherless child) or *menyuam hav zoov* (child from the wilderness).

In the village setting, Hmong birth takes place at home in the bedroom of the parents. The birthing mother is made to kneel on the floor with her hands holding onto the bed platform for support. An elderly woman relative may assist if the birth becomes difficult, but it is the husband who sits by the side of the woman in labor and may be kept occupied boiling water to wash the newborn, or doing other necessary chores. After birth, if it is a boy, the placenta is buried near the central post next to the fireplace to symbolize the fact that a son will act as the spiritual carrier and performer of rituals, the main strength for the household like the central post of the house. The burial place of a girl's placenta is under the parents' bed, as this is the most convenient and nearest to where the birth takes place. It has no symbolic role.

The Hmong in the United States and other Western countries no longer live in the kind of houses that are built on a dirt floor in their own villages with house posts clearly identified. They only have apartments and modern buildings next door to other people with few posts inside, and many do not even have a fireplace as in traditional Hmong dwellings.

Thus, the symbolic burial of the placenta no longer takes place today, both because of the new house designs and the fact that all births now take place in hospitals that do not make placentas available for burial by parents. However, girls still continue to be seen as "other people's women" and are expected to get married into other Hmong families, other clans. Boys are still seen as the true descendants/progeny of the family line. Only they and their wives, their descendants, and the unmarried female members of the lineage are remembered in ritual offerings as in the old days.

After birth, the baby is washed in warm water, then wrapped in baby blankets and given to the mother to breast-feed. Nearly all Hmong mothers breast-feed their children, except those living in Western countries who have the option of bottle-feeding. Breast-feeding may continue until the child is two or three years of age, some even continue until after the birth of another child. In Hmong villages in Southeast Asia, there are no separate cots for the new baby to sleep in, so they sleep in the parents' bed until they are old enough to be moved to the beds of their older siblings. Baby cots have been adopted by those in Western countries, but some parents may still allow toddlers to sleep in their beds until they reach three or four years of age.

A new baby is not considered as embedded into the human world until it is given a naming or *hu plig* ceremony. This ceremony is carried out on the third day after birth. A brace of young male and female chickens, together with some eggs and incense, are used in a soul-calling ritual, where the soul of the newborn is called to join the body on earth and to give it protection so that it can mature without the threats of evil spirits or discontented ancestors who might make the child sick and even die. The purpose of the ceremony is also to give the baby a name, and this is done simply by calling the baby by its given name during the soul-calling ritual. In the case of the Hmong of Laos and Thailand, the soul-calling ceremony is followed by a wrist-stringing ceremony (*khi tes*) where threads of cotton are tied around the wrist of the child as a symbol to tie the soul to the body along with all the good fortune that should come to the child. If this *khi tes* is also carried out, then the ceremony usually becomes a community affair where all close relatives and friends are invited to take part, and bigger animals like a pig or a cow will be used not only to welcome the soul of the baby into the family but also to provide food for all the guests. The richer the family, the more likely they will choose a bigger naming ceremony.

In the old days, names were often very simple one-syllable words for boys and one-or two-syllable names for girls. Examples of simple names for boys are: Bi, Beu, Long, Pao, Teng, Thai, Tou, Toua, Va, Xang, and Yang. Names for girls include Ai, Bao or Bo, Bee, Chi, Ia, Kia, Ka, May,

Mee, Pa, Xi, and Yi. Names for boys may be compounded with the name Tou (*tub*, meaning boy or son) such as Tou Bee. Girls' names may be preceded by the name May (Maiv) to denote their feminine gender such as May Kia. Some names are used for both boys and girls such as Lia, Lau, Chue, Ka, Shua, Tong, Ying, and Yeng. Today, however, the Hmong are more inventive and often give fancy names to their children based on natural objects such as Pa Fua (Flower of the Clouds) or historical figures as in Yi Leng (Eight Brothers), Kong Meng (Reputed), or Peng Xue (Valiant). Hmong movie stars and singers have also come up with very poetic stage names such as Sua Na (Sound of Rain) or Pa Nyia (Silvery Flowers). The Hmong who live in cities in Laos or in Western countries have also adopted names from mainstream groups, so a Hmong child usually has two given names: one in Hmong and one from the majority society. Thus, a boy may be known as Peter Pao, followed by his clan name on paper. Often, the Hmong name may be used unofficially and does not appear in the birth certificate. This is also the case in Thailand, China, and Vietnam. In Thailand, many Hmong now have Thai names, which they use in Thai society, while using a Hmong name with the Hmong; in China the Hmong have everywhere adopted Chinese names, and only use Hmong names in the villages or as the nicknames for children.

In Hmong society, as in traditional Chinese society, it is possible for a person to change names due to certain traumatic events in life, prolonged or severe sickness, or reaching a certain stage in life such as being a husband and father. In Australia, for example, when three young men drowned in a boating accident in 1992, the twin sister of one of them had her name changed by the family in the belief that, if she continued to be called by her old name, her dead twin brother might be able to find her and claim her life so she could be with him. A baby who suffers from chronic illness over a long period of time may have a name change, as the shaman may diagnose that it did not like the first name that was given by the parents after birth. A married man who has two or three children may be given a honorific name through a renaming ceremony or *tis npe laus* to indicate that he has reached an elder married status. The ceremony is organized by his family, but the parents of his wife are invited to join and to give the new name. Thus, name change is common throughout the life of a Hmong person, although women are not given these elder names.

Moreover, in traditional society one would not much use a personal name or a clan name. People were generally referred to and addressed by kinship terms, such as older brother or paternal auntie, and a woman even more so, was known as the daughter of someone, or the wife or mother of someone else.

Until the 1960s, Hmong births in the remote highlands of Southeast Asia were not registered as no such facilities were available or required. For this reason, many Hmong do not know their real birth dates and most had to make them up when they later obtained their birth certificates. Their ages are often reckoned on the basis of the season of the year (rice planting or harvest time), and some historical event such as so many years after the departure of the Japanese after WWII (April 1945). This affects women no less than men. Hmong of the older generation, thus, do not know their exact age but they do not consider this to be a major problem, as it allows them to be flexible. Still, it can lead to some problems. When many of them arrived in the United States, for example, some claimed to be much older than their real age and could obtain the old-age pension more quickly while others reduced their age down by many years to get education and work, but then had to wait for a long time before they were able to obtain their pensions. The same problem occurs in regard to other government benefits that are based on age eligibility.

GENDER

Having lived for many centuries under Chinese domination, the Hmong have often been influenced by the Chinese in terms of their material culture, social values, and religious beliefs. Until 30 years ago, for example, the Hmong's traditional costumes for men were fashioned after those of the Chinese during the pre-1911 Qing dynasty with large black trousers, a black shirt with blue arm band, and a shaven head with a long queue, or pigtail. Hmong men (like men in other societies) seem to be more prone to change and to adopt ideas and clothing from the mainstream society and the trappings of modernity. Today, they are more likely to be seen wearing Western clothes and prefer suits to Hmong attire on any formal occasion. Only Hmong women seem to remain faithful to their Hmong traditions, continuing to maintain their traditional costumes, and are often seen as keepers of the Hmong cultural heritage.

Children of both genders may be adopted into Hmong families. In most cases, if the couple involved has only daughters, they will resort to adopting a male child so that they will have a son to make offerings of food and money to them after their deaths (*npws laig niam txiv*). The Hmong believe that the souls of the dead still need food and money to use in the world of the ancestors, and descendants need to provide offerings of these requirements on special occasions such as the New Year and weddings. Such spiritual offerings are only made by men, as women or daughters are expected to marry out of the family into other clans. Even if they never marry, they have no role in performing rituals, so they cannot make offerings to their dead parents.

This is what Hmong parents are most afraid of—that they will have no male descendants to take care of their needs in the Afterworld. Thus, couples with no sons often adopt baby boys and raise them as their own. Because boys are valued by the Hmong for their spiritual roles, they are not always available to be adopted. So adopted children tend to come from other local ethnic groups like the Karen or even mainstream societies such as the Chinese, Lao, or Thai where there are many babies in need of care. Adoptions often take place when the baby is only a few months old or straight after birth, and are privately arranged without going through the authorities as adoption authorities do not exist in many Asian countries. Once adopted, the baby goes through the normal rituals of soul-calling (*hu plig*) and naming (*tis npe*) to become part of the family.

With regard to children with disabilities, the Hmong believe in the reincarnation of the soul from a previous life. Those who come to this world with any form of disability are believed to be the result of some misdeeds they carried out in their previous life such as inflicting bodily injuries on a person or animal or inflicting cruelty and injustice and receiving the wrath of Heaven or the curse of the victim. This applies to both physical and mental disabilities. Sometimes, a disabled child may be said to result directly from the sins or misdeeds of its own parents, as in the case of a Hmong soldier in Laos during the Vietnam War who executed a prisoner of war, and later had a severely disabled son. The child's condition was explained as a curse from the executed man who is said to have asked for mercy and to be released, but the soldier had to follow orders and carried out the execution. The victim then swore to come back and be born as a disabled child for his executioner to take care of. Other cases may have less specific explanations, but all are attributed to similar causes. There are some cases, however, where a severely deformed baby is seen as a divine gift, and may be the subject of worship for a time from local villagers. In 1977, a Hmong refugee woman gave birth to such a boy in Ban Vinai refugee camp in Thailand, and people brought gifts and incense to the couple, believing that the disabled baby was going to have superhuman powers. When they later resettled in California and the boy was about six years of age, his spine unfortunately curved so much that his lungs became depressed and he could not breathe properly. The parents refused to have him operated on, as they believed that it might affect the potential for him to develop the supernatural power allegedly bestowed by Saub, the Supreme Heavenly Guardian.

Like members of other cultures, the Hmong make gender differentiations on the basis of both tangible and intangible markers. Some intangible factors have already been mentioned such as the role differences in rituals when women cook while men eat and perform ceremonies. Women usually do household chores while men sit around and chat or look after the more complicated family and community affairs such as dispute settlement and general decision making. Apart from their names, the Hmong also have more visible markers of gender differences such as hair length, clothing, and jewelry. Thirty years ago, as mentioned above, and in some Thai villages until quite recently, the Hmong kept the hair of the men and boys long and plaited into a queue with the hair on the front and both sides of the head shaved, as seen in many Chinese kung fu movies. Although this was originally a practice enforced by the Manchu government of China (1644-1911), the Hmong belief was that the hair should be kept long to protect against evil spirits taking away the soul of the person and making him sick. The pigtail symbolized an instrument to scare such ill-intent enemies away. This explains why a Hmong shaman in Thailand was in the Guinness Book of Records as having the longest hair in the world in 1998. He stopped cutting his hair in his late teens after an illness and a dream that "warned him against further snips."[2] Today, maintaining long hair for boys and men is no longer practiced. Nearly all Hmong males now follow the same custom of other people of cutting their hair short. A round black skullcap without any brim used to be worn by men, but it, too, has become obsolete.

Women's hair, however, remains long in line with women in other cultures, mainly as decoration and a mark of their gender. Hmong women, however, do not use their hair-dos as symbols of status in life. Married women among the Black Tai of Vietnam and Laos, for example, put their hair up in a bun on top of their heads to show the fact that they are married, while young and single women wear their hair loose around their shoulders. Hmong women all have long hair but usually they tie their hair up in buns and wrap an embroidered head-sash (or, formerly, a turban or other headgear) around their heads. These hairstyles and types of headgear used to vary from one region to another and from sub-group to sub-group, but they have now lost this role and are today used in combination by Hmong women, as noted in Chapter 7. A Miao/Hmong group in the Xinshi Lake area in Western Guizhou, China, still uses hairstyle as a marker of women's status. When dressed in their colorful orange embroidered costumes, unmarried girls tie their hair into a bun on the top of their head with an embroidered band wrapped around it, while married women have no such decoration. This use of hairstyle in combination with headgear is common. In the Hmong "Chensi" style of Gongxian county of Sichuan province, China, turbans are made of hair pinned up around a round basketware cone over which cloth is draped.

As with other groups, the Hmong use elaborate costumes and differentiate between women and men through the use of embroidery on the costumes, especially those of women who also wear intricate silver jewelry. Like the head ornaments, the costumes used to represent different subgroups such as the White Hmong, Blue Mong, or Arm-Band Hmong. In the past, White Hmong women wore white hempen skirts tied around the waist by green and red sashes, topped by a black blouse and a black turban around their heads. They also put on silver necklaces with pendants covering the front of the blouse, and silver earrings. The men, however, used to wear long black pants and a black tunic with a single plain silver necklace. Today, the women still wear their Hmong costumes on special occasions, but the men have virtually given up their traditional clothes and have adopted Western casual wear. The same is true of Blue Mong men, although the women still wear batiked blue skirts and a black blouse. These are important markers of gender differences, but less so in modern life, as also discussed in Chapter 7.

Given the Hmong's expectations of their children, boys are trained from early in life to fulfill their roles of being the men of the house, performing rituals and carrying on the family line by marrying early and having children, while girls are groomed to be skilled in housework so that they can be married to men outside their own clans. The difference in the social roles attributed to boys and girls and men and women in Hmong society means that members of the fairer sex are often at a disadvantage. Many Hmong girls in Laos and Thailand, for example, are allowed to go to school at the primary level, but are not encouraged to pursue high school or college education in the cities as this involves a lot of expense for their parents, especially if they also have brothers who want to further their education. Girls are needed at home on the farm or in the house, and are seen by most parents to be of potential benefit mainly to the families of the men they will eventually marry. Because of poverty and this social attitude, many girls only finish a few years of primary schooling, barely allowing them to become literate. This situation applies in particular in countries where education is not compulsory.

Another issue of much recent concern is the division of labor and household chores between men and women. In general, married women are responsible for cooking, cleaning, childcare, helping with farm work, entertaining female visitors, providing advice to daughters, and ensuring their proper behavior. Women's roles in the care of young children are often alleviated with the help of older children who are taught to look after younger siblings, especially if the older ones are girls. Although boys may be tolerated for challenging their parents, girls are often not encouraged to have any voice at all. In village settings, boys are given the tasks of tending to the needs of domestic animals like cattle, horses, and buffaloes, while girls learn to cook, get firewood and water, clean the house, and wash the clothes. This division of household tasks, although it is not as rigid as in some societies (men do some childcare, for instance, and both women and men become shamans), means that boys and men have more free time, compared to women and girls. When there is an important ceremony or celebration, the men may slaughter pigs and cattle for meat but the women do all the cooking and put up with the heat and smoke from the wood fire while the men spend their time chatting. Once the food is cooked, the men always eat first, due to the lack of sufficient tables and chairs for both men and women to sit down and eat at the same time. Sometimes, there is little food left after the men have had their fill, but the women rarely complain.

These practices and attitudes relating to women have drawn many recent complaints from young educated Hmong, especially women who have grown up in Western countries and who have assimilated mainstream values that promote equality between the sexes. Many women now want to claim their rights to education, security, health care, and equal status shown by, for example, eating at the same time as men at family and community events. Some of the more vocal women in the United States are now engaged in education and political actions aimed at the removal of inequality. There are many issues associated with: domestic violence, unfair division of household labor, polygamy, dowry payments, child abuse, limited access to education, few employment opportunities, arranged marriages, and lack of political representation. The new Hmong women want to face these issues and to challenge this inequality that is shared by women in other cultures, an inequality perpetuated by "everyday patriarchy, typically supported by its institutional and legal discrimination."[3]

Among those organizations that have been set up to meet these challenges is the Hmong women's organization Hnub Tshiab (New Day), based in Minnesota, with its motto "Hmong Women Achieving Together." Established in 2000, its mission is "to be a catalyst for lasting cultural, institutional, and social change to improve the lives of Hmong women." The group hopes to see: (1) "a world where Hmong women and girls are valued and supported to achieve their highest potential in all of their roles"; and (2) "a society that honors the choices that Hmong women make and celebrates their ability to direct their own destinies."[4] Among the factors it has identified as contributing "to sexism and subsequent violence against women and girls in the Hmong community" are: (1) parents treating sons and daughters differently; (2) educated wives and women and their contributions not being valued; (3) marriage valued as more important than physical and emotional safety in an abusive relationship; (4) valuing having many children above the reproductive health or rights of women; (5) the belief that males are born with more power than females; and (6) supporting marriage structures that set the stage for violence. The organization has initiated a number of projects to address "these root causes" to bring about change and improvement to the status of Hmong women.

In the United States, where freedom of expression is much more permissible and where education opportunities exist equally for girls and boys, a few individual Hmong women have also emerged as the new voices of Hmong feminism. Ilen Her, a lawyer based in St. Paul, Minnesota, for example, was instrumental in 2006 in lobbying state politicians to introduce a Hmong marriage bill that would make it mandatory for the marriage negotiators known in Hmong as *mej koob*, who represent the bride's and groom's families, to report underage marriages.[5] Mee Moua, another lawyer, was elected as a Minnesota state senator in 2001 and again in 2005. Mai Moua, who has a PhD in leadership studies, has been involved in training Hmong women to become more vocal and assume leadership roles through the Hmong Women Professionals Association that runs regular seminars and meetings for members in St. Paul and Minneapolis. These role models and initiatives will contribute to Hmong women becoming more confident and skilled in achieving better conditions for themselves.

Today, the way in which Hmong parents favor sons over daughters seems to have turned against them in the diaspora. By being less strict with boys and allowing them more freedom than girls, many parents have encouraged their male offspring to become lazy and slack off, with the result that their more controlled daughters study more and work harder, so that more young women than young men now succeed in education and gain better employment over young men. A visit to any college classroom in U.S. cities inhabited by the Hmong will show that Hmong girl students outnumber their counterparts by two-thirds, and they also do better in their studies. Although traditionally in the villages in Southeast Asia boys were seen as the carriers of the family traditions, those in the diaspora have shown little interest in learning and maintaining Hmong rituals and other cultural traditions. Thus, they not only lag behind girls in modern education and the workplace, but many have failed to fulfill their parents' traditional expectations to carry on the family line and to meet male ceremonial obligations. This is, indeed, a worrying trend.

Hmong religious beliefs prescribe practices and values that often impact women negatively, because gender roles for sons and daughters, or for husbands and wives, are often based on these beliefs. Only males carry out ancestral rituals and make offerings of food and money to the spirits of their dead relatives, especially when the killing of domestic animals is required. Because of this, men's social roles are often seen as more important than those of women, while women strive to meet the material needs of the family but without the added political or religious responsibilities of the men.

However, gender role differences are likely to change in the years ahead, as Hmong religion becomes less practiced among the younger generation of Hmong living in Western societies, where fewer now want to learn Hmong rituals. Like mainstream families, Hmong parents in the diaspora are more likely to be put in nursing homes when they become too frail to look after themselves than to be cared for by their married sons, as they traditionally were. In such a situation, daughters as well as sons may share equal responsibility if they live close to the elderly parent, unlike in the old countries where daughters married and went off to live with their husbands far away from their families of origin. Therefore, the preference to have sons so they can care for elderly parents and carry out ancestral rituals may lose some of its importance.

COURTSHIP

Traditionally, young Hmong people start courtship when they reach puberty or around the age of 16. The most common form of courtship is through the ball game that is played during the New Year celebrations. On the first day of the New Year, after all the rituals have been performed on the last day of the old year, families would dress their young people of both genders in their bright and brand-new costumes and silver ornaments. This is not only to show off the family wealth but also to provide young people with the opportunity to have fun and to get to know each other in a public and socially sanctioned forum. The ball-tossing game, described in the context of the New Year in Chapter 9, consists of groups of boys and girls aged 14 to 18 or older throwing a rag ball the size of a tennis ball to each other, with the boys on one side and the girls on the other. Sometimes, it can be between one girl and a few boys, depending on who and how many choose to play with whom. While the ball is tossed, the players engage in courting conversation with each other. Some may even compete in the traditional singing of love songs that have been learned quickly a few days before, or are improvised by those who are good at composing love poetry and putting it into the Hmong style of singing.

Those couples who are good at singing, whether at the New Year or at other events, usually attract spectators around them, as the courting words exchanged are contained in the singing. The singers, while continuing to toss the ball, carry on a sort of musical conversation, with each song exchanged containing three to five couplets or verses. They try to outwit each other, to see who can devise the sharpest replies in sung poetry to their partners. In the meantime, some couples may also engage in a kind of wager game where the one who drops the ball has to give up a personal item to the other. These items can be a handkerchief, a piece of jewelry, an umbrella (often carried to protect against the hot sun). The lost item will be recovered at the end of the day at the cost of a song extracted from its owner or some other forms of mutually agreed-upon exchange such as the return of an item lost by the other party. These courting games can provide much entertainment for the village older people, and may last up to two weeks if there are many young people involved, and the courting is full of spirit. The New Year ball-tossing thus provides the beginning of a relationship for many Hmong young couples who may continue their courtship well after the celebrations.

Aside from the New Year, courtship usually takes place at night when families have finished their evening chores such as dinner and washing up, and after everyone retires to their separate bed compartments to sleep for the night. If a young man wishes to court a particular girl of another clan in the same village, he will make his intentions known by flirting with her and getting to know her. She will respond positively by being friendly and chatting with him. If he does not appeal to her, she will reject him by telling him off or not responding to his advances. After dark, traditionally, he will go and crouch outside the wall of her bedroom and try to communicate with her through a crack in the timber wall, as Hmong houses often use rough timber boards as walls with openings between the uneven planks. If he is gifted in playing music, he may use the Hmong long flute or the Jew's harp to communicate his love messages to the girl of his dream. These messages are contained in the musical notes of these instruments that most Hmong can decipher. If nothing else, the music at least indicates to the girl and her family that a suitor is present in the dark outside the house.

After this initial indication through one of these musical instruments, the young man will whisper to the girl through the small opening in the wall of her bedroom. She will initially respond by whispering back to ask who he is. If it is someone she knows and likes, they will carry on a whispering conversation long into the night. This night conversation through the bedroom wall will continue for a time until they become familiar with each other, and this can vary from a few weeks to many months. Following this stage of the courtship, several things can happen next and may vary from one region to another. In northeastern Laos, the young man may be allowed to join the girl in her bedroom and carry on the courtship game there, but often with strict rules about touching and being intimate. How far the young man can go will depend on how far the girl allows him. After a few months, if the courtship has progressed to the level where sexual relations occur, the girl's parents have the right to force the young man to marry her on the ground that having sex before marriage in her house violates the house spirits and it is not supposed to occur. If the young man refuses to marry the girl, he may have to pay a large inter-clan fine to make amends for the loss of face of her parents and to appease her ancestral spirits.

Courtship may take place during farm work when families from different clans exchange labor and young people have the opportunity to work together. Some may take the time off from their own farm work to work in a girl's field with her, especially if she is working by herself. In general, most young Hmong are shy in front of their families and do not always engage in this form of courtship. The occasion may be used as a way to get to know each other, but labor exchanges in farm work often last only a few days at a time, and this is not long enough for ongoing courting. In the old days when most Hmong villages were not linked by roads, a young man would have to travel on foot for a few hours each evening alone or with some friends before reaching the girl's hamlet to engage in courtship with her. These days, however, they may travel by motorcycles or cars, making the trip short and fast.

In some parts of Thailand, once a young courting Hmong couple begin to know each other well, the young woman may choose to go outside her house after dark and join her suitor to chat long into the night in the nearby bush, both warmly wrapped in the blanket brought for the purpose by the young man, since intimate courting is not permitted within the house. This allows for a lot of privacy and sexual intimacy, although not many premarital pregnancies obviously take place since a marriage is usually arranged at the first signs of pregnancy. A common practice today is for a young man to go inside a girl's house after she has become friendly with him, and they may chat around the family fireplace or the dining table after the parents have gone to bed. This may go on for one or two hours, and then the young man will leave so the family can get some sleep. This practice is more common among young modern urban Hmong, who have adopted modern styles of courtship and do not practice the old anonymous courting in the dark of their more traditional village peers. Many of these urban dwellers may also date by going to movies and dances, or chat with each other at school or at work in the fashion of young people in Western countries. Most Hmong parents, however, are very strict with their daughters and do not always allow them to go out with young men for fear that such freedom may lead to the tarnishing of a girl's reputation, and hence that of the family, as well as other problems.

MARRIAGE

As a rule, the Hmong always marry a member of another clan. After marriage, the woman must move out of her home to live with her husbands and the latter's kin group.[6] However, some groups related to the Hmong in China have adopted the practice of delayed marriage where a wife returns to her family home after the wedding to wait for the birth of her first child before joining her husband permanently. On the whole, daughters are expected to marry and to belong to men from outside their clan of birth. Through the ritual of *lwm qaib* (chicken blessing), a woman is adopted into the spiritual world of her husband and is cut off from her parents' ritual system as soon as she arrives at his village and the new couple is given the ritual before entering his house.[7] The ceremony symbolizes her transference from her own clan of birth to that of her husband, and three days later there will be a special soul-calling ceremony for her to confirm this. Some clans, however, make exception to this rule of exogamy so long as "the partners do not descend from the same ancestor."[8] Examples include sub-sections of the Vang clan in certain parts of Laos, of the Xiong clan in Thailand, and of the Yang clan in West and Central Guizhou, China. In general, it is unusual to find violations of the prescription against marriages within the same surname. Most Hmong follow the practice reported by Mickey for the Cowrie Shell Miao that marriage between people "of exactly the same surname" is forbidden.[9] The Chuan Miao (Sichuan Hmong) in southwest China, for instance, consider it "a crime for two persons having the same family name to marry."[10]

Chen and Wu state that some Hmong groups in China used to practice cross-cousin marriage on the father's side; that is, a boy was ideally expected to marry the daughter of his father's sister.[11] The Magpie Miao (Hmong Ntsw) of southern Sichuan, for example, favored this form of marriage, although it was not "obligatory, and sex relations between unmarried cross-cousins are freely permitted."[12] In the old days, it is said, a young man could marry his father's sister's daughter as a matter of course; and if this right was not exercised, the girl's father had to pay the boy's parents compensation for the right to marry her to another man. This practice is now illegal in China. Cross-cousin marriages, where a boy can marry his father's sister's daughter or his mother's brother's daughter, were quite common in the past. They are now relatively unknown among the Hmong of Southeast Asia. However, in some Miao parts of Guizhou the custom of offering a payment to a girl's maternal uncle by her husband still exists, and the father's sister, or *phauj*, still plays a very important part in Hmong society and inter-clan relations, showing the importance that even women who marry out of the clan still have for the members of their original families. The betrothal of small children by parents who are friends or relatives by marriage also used to exist in the distant past, especially between a brother's son and his sister's daughter. Today, there is no such arrangement and sons and daughters are free to choose their own spouses so long as the latter are of acceptable character.

There are three main types of marriage in Hmong society. The first, and most popular, is monogamy when a man marries only one woman. The second type is polygamy (or polygyny), where a man marries more than one wife at any one time, with or without the consent of the first wife. Although this is still allowed, it is usually frowned on as it is often riddled with conflicts between the wives. Men who practice polygamy are seen as greedy and taking advantage of women for their own selfish gains. The Hmong seem to be ambiguous about polygamy. On the one hand, they approve of it if the husband is rich and in a position of power. In the case of poor men, however, it is often looked on with disapproval. On the whole, it is tolerated if it is done as a result of family obligations as in the case of the levirate (see below) or in cases where the first wife cannot bear children or is sickly and unable to perform her marital duties effectively. It is more common among the Blue Mong than the White Hmong, and more common among well-off families than among the poorer ones.

The third type of Hmong marriage is the "levirate." This is where a younger male relative marries the widow of a deceased older brother or male cousin. In traditional village settings, there is no social welfare to support a widow and her children as is the situation in industrialized Western countries. The levirate is used as a form of social support when a younger male relative is willing and able to marry an older widow so as to help take care of her and her children. This tradition also ensures that the widow's young children, especially sons, will be kept within the clan or lineage group and will not be lost to it, as would be the case if she remarries into a different clan and her children become adopted by the new husband. If the younger male relative and husband-to-be is already married, permission to take the widow as a second wife will have to be obtained from his first wife. Today, the levirate is rare, as polygamy is not accepted by the younger generation and young men prefer to marry single women of a similar age range. This is all the more true in Western countries where there is no need to support a new widow through such a marriage.

Ages of marriages range from as young as 14 in the traditional village context to the late twenties for those living in Western countries. In Asia, too, later marriages are becoming more common. In a community survey in Thailand conducted in 1987–1989 among 224 Hmong settlements, for example, it was revealed that the median age of marriage was nineteen for men and seventeen for women. Today it is difficult to find many Hmong marrying young, as they have to go to school and college. Some under age marriages, however, have caused great concern in the Hmong community and beyond it. In some cases these children may be seeking to escape over-strict parents who insist on Hmong gender constraints on behavior that their children feel are no longer valid in the Western context. Certainly, however, the substantial bridewealth and other related costs often mean that marriage has to be delayed until enough money has been saved toward these outlays, for example in Western countries where it is not possible to save when one is young and only earns low wages. In the Hmong traditional settings in Asia, this saving may take even longer for the families of the prospective grooms in times of economic decline.[13] Most young men in the United States have also adopted new social values that permit them to seek a good time with girls for as long as they can. Some even experiment with living together before marriage rather than rushing off to have a wife and children whom they cannot always support or even see as a priority in life, now that they no longer need more hands for the family farm and no longer depend on farming as their parents in the highlands of Asia did.

There are different ways in which a marriage takes place. The Hmong accounts collected by Bertrais describe five of them: (1) arranged marriages between families for cross-cousin marriages; (2) mutual consent where the couple request permission from their parents and negotiations with a go-between ensue; (3) elopement, where the couple run away together; (4) "bride capture" where the groom with friends "grab" or "drag" (zij) the girl; and (5) forced marriage when a girl becomes pregnant, besides marriages for widows and divorcees.[14] Bertrais emphasizes that methods (2) to (4) (negotiation, elopement, or capture) are the most common.[15] In general, most Hmong marriages are the result of courtship and the mutual attraction between the couple concerned, usually with the support of their parents. This is the primary and most common path taken.

However, other circumstances may legitimize a marriage or make it possible for a man to trap a woman into marriage. One of the most common of these situations is when the girl has accepted a gift or item of personal belongings from the man. This is referred to in Hmong as *tau khoom* ("having accepted gifts"), as in the case of wagers during New Year ball games, or when the man gives the girl a gift of any kind on other occasions, be it money or goods. If she has no intention of accepting him as a prospective husband, she must return the wager or gift within one to two days through an intermediary. Failure to do so will mean that she is happy with him; he can use the gift acceptance as a scoring point to negotiate her hand in marriage with her parents and the latter will have to agree to his request for marriage with her.

A second common way in which a marriage can occur is through *tshoob zawj* or *tshoob nqis tsev* ("descending into the house to engage in negotiations"). This is resorted to in the case of a man who sets his sight on a girl he meets for the first time and decides to marry her without giving her time to get to know him through courtship. This may be because he does not have the time, he knows that she will reject him through such gentle approach, or he knows that her parents approve of him and will help to persuade her during the negotiations. He thus engages two very able marriage negotiators (*mej koob*) and some quick-witted elders to go to the young woman's house, and start the marriage negotiations. The negotiators will chant one wedding song (*zaj tshoob*) after another at each step, and the woman's parents are obliged to get their own equally skilled pair of negotiators to defend their daughter and themselves. They cannot just ignore the man and his party; his action puts them in a bind in case in the future they may have a male relative who wishes to do the same thing with a young woman from the other clan group. It may take both parties as long as needed, but if in the end, the girl and her family cannot find any plausible objections to the prospective groom, she will have to accept the marriage proposal. After she agrees to it, the parties then set a wedding date for the nuptial celebrations and she is now regarded as engaged to the man. This method imposes a lot of obligations on the girl and is not usually favored by Hmong parents who see it as a means to force them to push their daughters into marriage to someone who is in a better position of wealth and authority. Regardless, it is still used, sometimes even by the Hmong in the diaspora.

A third method of marriage is to force the man to marry the girl because he has made her pregnant before marriage. He is seen as having dishonored her and her family, and needs to make amends for the transgression. Although premarital sex is allowed, a premarital pregnancy that is not legitimated through marriage is seen as a great source of shame. The man has to take responsibility for it by marrying the girl. If he refuses, after the girl has accused him, he will have to pay a large fine to "clean her face" (*ntxuav tsej muag*) or restore her honor.

A fourth but again usually disapproved method of marriage is by capture or *zij* (grabbing or pulling). It is also called "bride capture" or kidnapping in the eyes of modern young Hmong girls. The capture may be real or only a pretense. Where it is real, it can lead to much distress and tragedy, for it usually means that there is little or no prior relationship between the man and the girl involved, and it means that the man has simply seen the girl and taken a fancy to making her his wife. In most cases, it involves a married man who wants to take a second or "small wife" (*niam yau*) as the Hmong call it. There may be a few previous attempts at conversation with the girl by the man, but this often leads nowhere. The man thus uses force to take her. Once she is safely inside his house and the *lwm qaib* or chicken blessing ceremony is performed to accept her into his family's spiritual domain, her family can no longer accept her back. Any rescue of the girl has to occur before this ceremony takes place. Where parents do not learn about the event until it is too late, the girl will have to go through the wedding ceremony but afterward, such girls often kill themselves or try to obtain a divorce. Some may reluctantly stay with the husband and accept their fate, and it may even lead to a happy married life if the couple is monogamous.

In the old days, marriage by capture was almost always only a pretense, a game played by the man and woman concerned to gain respect or "obtain face" (*tau ntsej muag*), particularly where the boy was poor and could not pay the bridewealth, or where the couple feared one of their families might disapprove of the match. A mutual arrangement might be made between them for the man and some male friends to take the woman by force at a pre-arranged place. She would then pretend to scream for help, and her mother might pretend to chase after them to rescue her (*mus caum*), if she was in on the game. If the daughter really did not know the man well and was genuinely unwilling to marry him, the mother would shout abuse, raining blows on her abductors and asking them to release her. There would be much negotiation between the man's party and the girl's mother, and in the end the girl would go with the man with a great show of reluctance. The men in the girl's family would not be involved in this rescue, as they would have no roles to play until the wedding, when they would take full charge of all negotiations and other related tasks. Pre-arranged abduction is also regarded in some cases as a face-saving device to protect both the girl and her family should the marriage fail, as she would then be able to say that she was uncertain about the prospect all along and her family, too, can claim that they were not responsible for her failed marriage. For the same reason, a Hmong bride should not appear too pleased at her wedding.

By and large, Hmong get married through love and courtship after a certain period of time spent by the couple involved in becoming familiar

Modern Hmong wedding, Oklahoma, USA 2006. Courtesy of the authors.

with each other. They can then elope or "go silently" to his house (*mus ntsiag to*) without any noisy protests on the part of the girl.[16] Before this happens, the man will need his parents' approval because they have to help pay part or all of the dowry and wedding costs. Whether through "abduction" or elopement, the young man's parents send a message (*fi xov*) to the girl's parents' relatives informing them of her safety and asking for a convenient date to celebrate the wedding after the couple has arrived at the man's house and the chicken blessing ceremony has been completed.

The wedding costs consist of the bridewealth, fines for faults found or old clan scores, and miscellaneous expenses for pigs, food, and alcohol. They can all add up to a staggering amount of money, forcing many young men to depend on their parents for the payment. In China, the ceremony is much reduced and costs very little; the bridewealth is mainly paid in the form of furniture and clothes. The wedding ceremony elsewhere takes two days and a night of negotiations and feasting, firstly at the groom's house, then at the bride's house and again back to the groom's residence. As discussed earlier, each stage of the wedding is marked by particular songs sung by the go-betweens, and it is a very jolly affair. Many gallons of rice alcohol are consumed. Apart from the cost of food and ceremonial animals such as pigs

Modern Hmong wedding, Sydney, Australia, 2006. Courtesy of the authors.

and chickens, each of the helpers on both the groom's side and the side of the bride's family has to be paid. These payments and the cost of food items can amount to $2,000 or $3,000. In addition, the bridewealth,[17] which the Hmong call a "nurturing charge," ranges from $1,000 to $10,000. It is said that the more industrious, qualified, and beautiful a daughter is, the more her parents may ask for her bridewealth. The husband of a Hmong girl in California is rumored recently to have been asked for $30,000 for her because she has a master's degree. Many modern Hmong parents, however, do not levy this "nurturing charge" for their marrying daughter, as this is seen as "selling," which may later make her husband treat her as if she is owned by him. On the other hand, many Hmong still see the bridewealth as indemnity money to ensure that the husband will treat the wife well, as it is the personal and social values put on her person, which he is willing to pay in financial terms to marry her. The fines paid to make up for the past grievances suffered by members of the girl's clan in the hands of the groom's clansmen may range from $5 to $500, depending on how serious or how many wrongdoings occurred between the two groups in previous times.

A Hmong wedding can thus be very costly in terms of both time and money. For this reason, some couples may not be able to celebrate their marriages officially due to the lack of money. Some of them thus wait until they have saved enough money to have their marriage ceremony, although this does not stop them from living together as lawful husband and wife, and having a family. Some couples may also go to live with the wife's parents as a way to work off the payment of her bridewealth. These difficulties and the desire to embrace modernity have recently brought about new directions. In Laos, for example, urban young couples have adopted the Chinese style of modern weddings where guests bring envelopes with money as wedding gifts to the marriage ceremony. These donations can help to alleviate the overall costs of a wedding. In Thailand, couples travel to their weddings at the bride's village by car instead of going on foot as their parents did many years ago. Hmong couples in France, Australia, and the United States, especially those who have become Christian, now hold weddings with the bride dressed in a white wedding gown and long white gloves, in the tradition of all Western weddings, and with the men in Western suits, yet, they all still share some Hmong features—the use of the *mej koob* or marriage negotiators, dealing with the complex relations between clans, payment of the bride-price, and practicing the wedding rituals of 30 to 50 years ago.

Gender relations are rapidly changing for the Hmong, but some traditional attitudes still remain. Although Hmong women were never as submissive to their men as those in Chinese, Japanese, or Middle Eastern societies, daughters were still undervalued and sons prized as part of the kinship and ancestral lineage system. Today, Hmong women are speaking out for themselves, and forming their own associations even in Chiangmai, North Thailand.

NOTES

1. Geddes 1976, 128.

2. See Flinn, "World Beater: Long-Haired Record Smashed Twice," Thaifocus Travel News, August 1988. Available at http://www.thaifocus.com/news/stories/longhair.htm. Accessed 21 May 2010.

3. Young 2003, 116.

4. See its Web site at http://www.hmongwomenachieve.org. Accessed 21 May 2010.

5. See "Hmong Legislators Say Cultural Marriage Bill Is Unnecessary," *Minnesota Public Radio,* March 20, 2006, at http://minnesota.publicradio.org/display/web/2006/03/20/hmongmarriage/. Accessed 21 May 2010.

6. For a discussion on Hmong marriages based on an extensive survey in Thailand, see Kunstadter 2004, 375–420.

7. Lee 1994–1996, 44–60. Available at www.garyyialee.com. Accessed 21 May 2010.

8. De Beauclair 1970, 133.

9. Mickey 1947, 50.

10. Graham 1937, 27.

11. Chen and Wu 1942, 20.

12. Ruey 1960, 146.

13. Kunstadter 1983, 35, 39.

14. Bertrais 1978, as cited in Symonds 2004, 60.

15. Bertrais 1978, 35, 331.

16. This is also known as *tshoob coj*, or "leading" the girl to your house (Bertrais 1978).

17. This term is used here for want of a better word. "Bridewealth" is not a satisfactory term to describe this levy that the Hmong call "*nqi mis nqi hno*" (fee for milk and food or nurturing charge) for all the time and costs the parents spent on bringing up a daughter. The Lao and Thai have a similar charge they call "*xeen xot tong manh*."

9

Festivals and Leisure Activities

AS IN MOST societies, the Hmong have various forms of entertaining themselves and having fun. In a traditional village in Thailand, for instance, some men may play cards with a local Chinese shopkeeper and, although drinking is not common, alcohol may be consumed or, on rare occasions when a visitor from afar comes to stay, a few pipes of opium may be shared with the visitor. Singing is common among the young people and closely associated with courtship. Work in the fields is tiring and arduous, and generally the married women do not have much time for fun, although in the later evening, after the supper is done, a married woman may drop by a neighboring family to exchange some gossip perhaps with a female relative who has married into the same village. The men, too, more often than the women, tend to circulate to other houses in the evening, sitting by the fire and discussing affairs with other men. Generally, it is the younger and unmarried boys and girls who have the energy to go out in the late evening, and from the age of about 14 girls and boys of marriageable age will gather around the village square to chat and exchange riddles and songs. Sometimes lasting liaisons follow from these encounters, and a marriage will follow. The fact that women are allowed only one husband, while husbands may on rare occasions take a second, younger wife, or even a third wife, and the fact that premarital sex is permitted in Hmong society, means that married men enjoy much more liberty than their wives and they, too, may venture out in the villages to court a young girl, since it is always possible she will become his second wife, as we discussed in Chapter 8.

However, most leisure activities take place in the dry season toward the end of the calendar year, after the various harvests are brought in and farming work is not so intense. It is around this time that Hmong men and boys of all ages practice, sometimes for hours, a game of tops that consists of hitting down the spinning top of another. *Ntaus tuj lub*, as it is called, is a game of great skill and requires a lot of practice to master. The top is spun vigorously with a long piece of string and then released to knock another's top over. Indeed, a group of Hmong in Waterloo-Kitchener, Canada, have revived this pastime, which they practice in a grassy field outside town; they see it as having beneficial health and psychological effects. Today tops are mass-made for the Hmong outside Asia out of new materials that last better than the traditional wood, and the sport of "topspin" is becoming professionalized in the United States, with teams from different places playing each other. The Hmong also often play the Lao-Thai game *kataw* (or *takraw*), where a rattan or plastic/rubber ball is tossed between players in a ring who try to keep it in the air by kicking with their feet and without any use of hands. Other leisure activities may also be undertaken at this time; for example, a visit to town may be made, work sought outside the village (especially in China), skills such as archery with the crossbow and hunting learned and practiced, and cockfighting events arranged. This is the off-farming season, so one makes the most of it.

THE TRADITIONAL NEW YEAR

Playing tops is seen as a preparation for the greatest festival of the Hmong, the New Year, when spinning tops, wooden cart races, and other games of contest are put on show. In Laos there also used to be stick and sword dances, and this is one of the few occasions when a performance of the *qeej*, the Hmong reed pipe instrument, may be made just for fun, through solo and group performances. At the turn of the twentieth century, Christian missionaries introduced various sports such as football and athletics into Hmong villages, hoping to replace their traditional beliefs in spirits, and some of these survive and are played at the New Year. The New Year (*xyoo tsiab*) is often just known as *noj peb caug*, or "eating the thirtieth," because it takes place from the thirtieth day of the twelfth lunar month and a great feast is held by each family, after the pig for the New Year (*npua tsiab*) is slaughtered. It can also just be called *noj tsiab*, or "the feast of the new year." It is a time for socializing, for meeting people from other villages, for taking a rest from farm work, for boys to meet girls for courting, and above all a time for the family to be together and renew its ties to its ancestors. In Thailand, after the first day of the New Year (which lasts for a minimum of three days, but can stretch on up to 10, and on which no work is undertaken), it is common to see Toyota pickup trucks bearing whole crowds of gaily dressed young Hmong driving off over the mountains to meet the girls and boys of another village, often visiting more than one village. If a young man finds a likely partner in a village, he may stay in the village for some may. Although the festival should be celebrated from the last day of the lunar year, the Hmong do not usually consult formal calendars, and the exact date is fixed by a group of elder men in the village or in a cluster of villages or large settlement. This is often done in consultation with representatives of other villages and the dates staggered so that villages can attend each other's New Year celebrations.

Hmong ideas about the New Year have a lot in common with Chinese ones, and some very old customs in China have been preserved by the Hmong that have been forgotten by the Chinese. One is supposed to wear entirely new clothes for the New Year, so mothers and elder sisters are often very busy in the months leading up to the festival. making clothes for the whole family to wear on the day. The house is spring-cleaned, symbolically as well as actually, and all the rubbish and old things thrown out. Wine must be made, and wood collected and chopped for the fires. The Hmong make a delicious sweetmeat at this time, practically the only time of the year when sweet things were eaten in the past, called *ncuav nplej*, a kind of sourdough rice-flour cake, usually made without sugar, but eaten by being dipped into sugar cane juice (*suab thaj*). Everybody will wear their best costumes for the New Year, and a Hmong village is a very colorful sight at this time, with the young men dressed in their finery and adorned with silver, sunglasses, and expensive-looking watches, and the women wearing as elaborate dresses as they can find or make. It would be not only unseemly, but also positively inauspicious, if someone were to wear old clothes for the New Year, or to oversleep. Elders often stay up most of the night to see the New Year in. Before dawn on the first day of the New Year, young girls get up and compete to be the first to go the village spring or well to fetch water for the family in the belief that the one who is first will be the first to receive good harvest and fortune for the rest of the year. No work of any kind should be undertaken during the first three days of the New Year, so all agricultural and business activities cease at this time.

Soon after breakfast of the first day, the sight of long lines of couples of young Hmong men and women in a village, the men in one line, the women facing them in another, solemnly throwing a soft black cloth ball back and forth (*pov pob*) for hours on end has become a common one to the many tourists and visitors who today visit Hmong villages in Thailand or Laos. The Hmong in Western countries have kept up this custom at the New Year celebrations that now take place all over the world, often using tennis balls instead. But this is a deadly serious game in villages where opportunities for travel afar used to be so limited, since this is often a time when a boy may choose out the girl he most favors who may later become his bride. It can also be the girl who selects the man of her choice. The idea is, as we have explained, that if one of the partners in this game of catch drops the ball, he or she must either sing a traditional song (a *kwv txhiaj*) or forfeit a pledge of some sort such as a hair pin or handkerchief. This can serve as an excuse for a later meeting, since the boy can always arrange some time to give the pledge back to the girl on a less public occasion or more privately elsewhere at a later time, as noted in Chapter 8. As Westerners have their discos where young people choose a dancing partner, the Hmong have the courting game of catch at the New Year. This game has a very long history in China, being one of the very earliest customs reported there several thousands of years ago, when courting couples would meet at the mouth of two rivers (symbolizing the alliance of two families in marriage) and do just what the Hmong in Southeast Asia and overseas do today.[1] Although it has long died out among the Chinese, other ethnic minorities in southern China now play a similar game at the New Year with a feathered shuttlecock, as the Hmong in parts of northern Vietnam and southern China also do.

In the village setting of Southeast Asia, traditional singing often occurs during the New Year celebrations when young men and women from different clans and villages come together to play the ball game and sing the sort of love songs we described in Chapter 4 to court one another. The singing is not only a test of wit and cleverness with words, but it keeps the young people occupied and interested in the courting game. Each song may take up to 10 minutes, so in a competition between a young man and a young girl who reply to each other's song, it could take 30 minutes before they are finished. Those who are very good can go on for days, with one song after another as the competition may become fierce with one partner trying to outdo the other. Or they may become so enraptured in the singing that they really end up falling in love.

Beyond the obvious messages in the songs, however, there is a hidden side or meaning to Hmong traditional singing that is always public and attracts a big audience when the singers are good. As Lewis notes, parents may come and watch to assess the abilities of a potential son-in-law or a future daughter-in-law, for the singing reveals how quick-minded he or

New Year games, North Thailand. Courtesy of the authors.

she is, whether a pair of courting young people like each other by responding appropriately to each other's singing with one song after another, or
whether there is no romantic spark flying through the words of their singing.[2] A young woman may show her humorous side as she retorts to her
suitor in poetry, or she may show that she can only stumble along or
respond with a serious face and deep concentration. Thus, the personality
of the singer may also show through to the audience and the partner
engaged in the paired singing match.

In the past, particularly in Vietnam and China, the Hmong were also
famed for their bullfights, which attracted large crowds at the New Year and
on other calendrical festivals observed by the Hmong. Bullfights have largely
died out in Thailand, although they continue or have been revived in parts of
Laos and Vietnam. In China, some groups related to the Hmong, such as the
Hmu people of Southeast Guizhou, take part in the Dragon Boat races that
are commonly celebrated in southern China in the summer and are now an
international sport. In China, too, officials have recently revived many traditional local festivals for the purposes of attracting tourists, some of them quite
unknown to the people who are now expected to take part in them. One of
these is a Hua Shan or "Flower Mountain" (*nquam toj*) festival in the spring-
time that the Hmong now celebrate in Wenshan, formerly known as Kaihua,
or *Paj Tawg Lag* in Hmong. This is a festival that seems to have been based
on a traditional small-scale lineage ritual involving a sacrificial tree, but it has

now become an officially arranged event that is great fun not only for the Hmong but for the many other people who take part in it.

One popular feature of this *nquam toj* festival is the climbing of a slippery pole on top of which is tied a bag of goods as a reward for the first climber to reach it. Only those who are strong and agile can meet the challenge. The original small-scale lineage ritual, or the *lwm qaib*, however, is still performed by local descent groups or extended families on the afternoon of the last day of the old year. A small thorny tree, or *ntoo qaib* (chicken tree), is cut from the forest and placed in the ground some distance from the house, with a plaited grass rope attached to its top and foot, while the other end of the rope is held by the clan elder or another person. Under the tree all the dangerous weapons of the household are placed, such as rifles and sharp knives. The ritual can be called *ncig tus pos ntsaj* (to go around the thorn tree) or *ncig ncej ntxheb ncej ntxhoo* (to go round the decorated pillar). It is said this is a way of *lwm sub*, or exorcising the forces of evil influences. *Sub* is a kind of miasma that used to be associated with plague and pestilence. Everyone must walk under the cord while the lineage head or a lineage elder stands before it, blessing them by waving a rooster over their heads and murmuring a chant of blessings.[3] They walk three times backward to mark leaving behind the old year, and three times forward to welcome the new one. This *lwm qaib* (chicken blessing), and it is a ritual similar to that performed for a new bride when she enters her husband's home for the first time, to welcome her, as we saw in Chapter 8, except no grass rope and thorn tree are used in this instance. The point here is to demonstrate one's sense of family solidarity with related families living locally, and this is very much part of the fun and importance of the New Year festival when one's thoughts can turn to family matters and recreation.

Many other fun activities can take place at the New Year. In Laos, the New Year now includes stage shows and performances with microphones, theatre sketches, comedy acts, and band music with singers. There are often public singing contests between men and women, in Thailand, too, and the beauty contest has become an instituted part of the Laotian Hmong New Year since the time of Gen. Vang Pao in the early 1960s. In many places, there are bullfights and buffalo fights, horseracing, kicking or hitting fights between men, cockfighting, or crossbow contests between men. Games played by village children include *ua txws* (playing with rubbles), *xuab kev* (making a path in the village dust), *ua niam tais yawm txiv* (playing parents), *ua neeb poj qhe* (having "spoon" shaman trances), *txhiaj txhais* (a guessing game); and, of course, there is always storytelling (now often replaced by movie watching on TV), which is popular at this time. Some of these games take place at various times of the year, not necessarily only at the New Year, but they are performed with particular intensity and enjoyment at this time. Fighting bulls remain important symbols of wealth in Hmong society. Even in the United States, there is a Hmong Association of Owners of Fighting Bulls in Minnesota, with the bulls kept in the care of relatives in Laos where the fighting takes place and is videoed for these U.S.-based owners to watch. Everywhere, the end of the year is a time for catching up with distant relatives and, where appropriate, for love play.

THE RITUAL IMPORTANCE OF THE NEW YEAR

The importance of the New Year festival for the Hmong lies not only in the opportunities it offers for fun, social visits, and courtship games, but above all in that this is the most important time of the year for honoring the ancestral and domestic spirits of a family. In this section, we will discuss more of the rituals that take place at the New Year because they are so important at and integral to the New Year festivities. For a shaman, this is the time when he (or she) ritually dispatches his auxiliary spirits (the *neeb*) to the Otherworld for a few days' rest and then welcomes them back again, and there are major rituals associated with this that take place inside a Hmong house at this time.

For all households, with or without a shaman, this is a time of unity and togetherness. As described above, the New Year begins with the *lwm qaib* (New Year welcome and blessing) ceremony in which all local members of the same clan take part in a procession under a cord tied to a tree, as discussed above. In Western countries, however, participation in this ceremony is open to all clans as there may not be enough Hmong families of the same clan living in one city or there may be too many of them to hold many separate ceremonies for each clan. After the *lwm qaib*, the wandering souls of each individual family are called back to the home and ritually bound there in the ritual known as *hu plig* (calling the soul). This is usually done by the head of the household as we noted in Chapter 2. A large bowl is placed on a stool just inside the threshold of the house, on which is rice, with an egg in its shell for each member of the family, two live small chickens, and three sticks of incense. After throwing the divination horns, the souls of the household members are called in a soul-calling chant, and the chanter may beat a gong at the same time. These souls include not only those of people, but also of the household animals and crops, which are considered to form a unitary whole representing the household and its environs. Then the divination horns are thrown a number of times to ensure that the ceremony has succeeded in getting all the souls back into the house. The two live chickens are then held with the incense and are asked to exchange their own souls for any human souls in the family that may be held by evil spirits, so that such human souls are released and can return home. After these two chickens are sacrificed and cooked, and their tongues, legs, and claws inspected for good omens, they are placed together with the cooked eggs and rice in the bowl on a stool at the threshold for a second round of soul-calling chanting.

This is also the time of the year to pay respect to the *dab xwm kab*, the household fortune deity, symbolized by a piece of blank white paper stuck on the western interior wall of the house with three marks of a rooster's blood and feathers on its upper part and two tiny squares of folded golden and silver paper on its lower part. This is done through the renewal of the *xwm kab* altar with new gold and silver money pieces of paper so that good harvests and money will come to the family in the coming year. After changing the altar, a live cock is presented to the deity with a chant of offering, and after it is cooked, it is again offered to the deity with a further chant as a sacrifice. This ritual is coordinated with the ritual for calling the souls of the family members discussed above, so the chickens for both rituals can be cooked together. Beneath the *xwm kab*, a small table is set up that is adorned with a light, two pieces of spirit-paper, three small cups of alcohol, and a bowl of uncooked rice with eggs and three sticks of incense in it. The live cock is presented to the altar while the incense and spirit paper is burned and when the chant is finished, the divination horns are thrown several times, the bird is sacrificed and fresh blood daubed on the new paper altar. After the rooster is cooked it is again offered to the *xwm kab* deity, on a small stool or table set behind the first one, together with the cooked rice, egg, and some soup in another bowl.

The eve of the New Year is also one of the times of the year when Hmong families carry out an ancestral offering of food by the head of the family, called *laig dab*. In the *laig dab*, the ancestral spirits are honored by being ritually fed in the way explained in Chapter 2. Ancestors up to three generations will be invited to join in this New Year meal by having as many of them mentioned by name as possible, one generation after another, depending on how many names can be remembered. For this ritual, the head of the household will use alcohol, rice, and chicken meat from a different bird from the ones used in the soul-calling and *xwm kab* rituals, although they have been cooked together. The rice and meat for the *laig dab* are put on the family dining table in separate bowls with some spoons around their brims. He then recites an incantation in which he calls on the spirits of his dead relatives and immediate ancestors to come and share in the feast and to protect the family against illness and misfortune. He is seated alone while he does this as the rest of the family go about their normal business. When this ritual, which may take a few minutes to finish, is concluded, the whole family will sit down to eat together.

This is all done on the eve of the New Year, which usually falls on the thirtieth day of the twelfth lunar month (variously calculated), when the other household spirits such as the spirits of the hearths and the pillars, are also honored with offerings of spirit paper and incense, and all the utensils of the house and various parts of the house are protectively blessed. These rituals must be performed by the household to make the Hmong New Year meaningful. For this reason, the New Year is also the most important time when the unity of the household and the family, the bedrock of Hmong social organization, is affirmed and ritually sanctioned, apart from providing young people with fun activities.

New Year's Eve is a time for families to stay together, but the main fun and social activities begin once the New Year has started. During the first days of the New Year, younger male lineage members should *pe tsiab* or pay their New Year respects to the more senior (male) elders by going to visit them in a group in their homes to offer them drink, wish them long life, and kowtow three times with their heads to the floor while receiving blessings from their elders. This is still seen in some places, although it is becoming less common today.

The New Year is also the time when the *dab txhiaj meej*, the spirit of wealth and richness above the main door, should be renovated. In cases where a family has suffered repeated and continuous difficulties of an economic or medical kind, a shaman may diagnose that the reason for this is that the *txhiaj meej* spirit has deteriorated or "fallen," usually as a result of a sexual offense, and needs to be restored or "raised" (*tsa txhiaj meej*). For this ritual, in the early part of the year a bench will be set up as an altar just beneath the lintel of the front door, on which is placed a candle, a bowl of water, a bottle of wine, two cups of wine, and a cooked chicken. The head of the household, together with someone to assist him, will stand inside the house and hold a short but merry shouted conversation with two men just outside the door who pretend to have come to visit, and they will swap a piece of chicken for their wine. The two visitors are called the "messengers of heaven," and in the ritual they will symbolically raise and wash the sides of the door, and pin up new silver coins under the red and white cloth and tissue across the top of the door that forms the altar to the *txhiaj meej* and daub it with the blood of a sacrificed chicken. They throw paper money into the house, and all the old accoutrements of the altar are burned. Then a cock that has been struggling trussed inside the house is released and its behavior carefully observed as an omen of what the future will bring. This cock is seen as a mascot and is not killed. The messengers of heaven are invited into the house and take five steps toward the altar of the *dab xwm kab*, said to represent respectively an abundance of boy and girl children, chicken and pigs, horses and cattle, rice and corn, gold and silver, for the household in the coming year. Finally the door is ceremonially closed behind them to symbolize the shutting out of all diseases and misfortunes—all noxious influences—and the ritual is over. This ritual, however, is only rarely performed nowadays, according to Australian Hmong who say that families are reluctant to advertise the fact to others that they may have suffered misfortune, while new economic conditions overseas mean that a regular income is usually ensured.

For a shaman (*txiv neeb*), the New Year brings still other rituals; this is the time he must send off his helping spirits (*xa qhua neeb*) to the Otherworld to meet their Master, *Siv Yis,* and celebrate their own New Year with him in his mountain grotto, and then in a ritual a few days later, invite them back again. A household with a shaman in it is thus abuzz with rituals, feasting, and jolly excitement at this time of the year. Several chickens are sacrificed for the *neeb* or tutelary spirits of the shaman, and various people treated by the shaman during the course of the year may choose this time to make presents to him. The shaman must also clean and remake the shamanic altar and the threads that attach the shamanic altar to various parts of the house, the "bridge" of the *dab neeb*, along which they must travel, as on this occasion, whenever they leave the house, or when they return again. Three fine filaments of these threads run from the bowl of rice on the shaman's altar to a short bamboo pole suspended just above the altar, the middle one itself divided into three threads, and from there to a long bamboo pole running along the length of the house just underneath the ridgepole from where all except the leftmost one runs to a pole just above the front door; the last thread leads directly to the bedroom. The shaman has kept the lower jaws of all the pigs sacrificed at the rites he has officiated at during the course of the year hanging from the central pillar of his home, and at this time at the New Year, they are burnt and their own souls finally allowed to proceed on their normal path toward rebirth, having fulfilled the purposes for which they were sacrificed.

Such is the traditional Hmong New Year, in which ritual and secular elements intermingle together, and it is of such a complexity and richness as to render redundant the need for many other festivals in the course of the year. It must be said, however, that in their new homes in Western countries, the Hmong have celebrated this festival in very different and modern ways, and many now no longer perform the traditional New Year household rituals, particularly those who have become Christian.

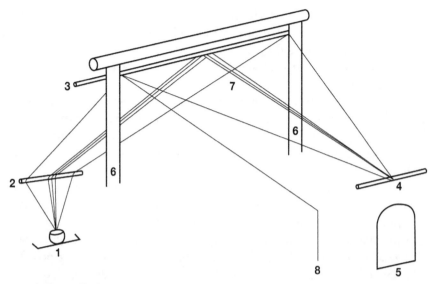

1. Altar and basket of rice.
2. Bamboo above the altar.
3. Bamboo under the support beam.
4. Bamboo above the door.
5. The door.
6. The two pillars supporting the ridge beam.
7. The thread.
8. End of the thread above the room.

Diagram of shamanic threads. Cartography Department, Australian National University, based on original drawing in Mottin 1982.

THE NEW NEW YEAR

Yang has described in detail some of the changes that have taken place.[4] The Hmong New Year in the United States is organized by different regional and national Hmong groupings and associations. Whether an admission fee is set is variously decided in different places. The timing of the event is affected by American public holidays, so that, for example, the Fresno Hmong New Year is held between Christmas and the American New Year. In California, where the climate is good, it takes place in large public park areas, while in the Twin Cities in Minnesota, with its heavy snow, it is held in a large community center. The idea of holding the New Year in such a formal way, and moreover in a public place, would still be quite foreign to most Hmong in Asia. Women are elegantly dressed in their traditional finery, now often in imaginative ethnic costumes bought from China or assembled elsewhere; most men wear suits but a small minority also dress in traditional Hmong attire. Commercial booths are set up to sell Hmong herbal medicines, and other stalls for car sales, clothes, Hmong video and DVD services, roller coasters and train rides, sales of ice cream and doughnuts, fried chicken and noodle soup, tacos and papaya salad, a glorious hybrid mixture of Asian cuisines. There are loan services and sales of health care and life insurance policies, student clubs, university recruitment booths, and even representatives of organizations such as the Mormon Church.

It is usually a major community event with full-blown electronic equipment used. There are modern group dance competitions, beauty contests for boys and girls, market stalls (even if only for window shopping), ball games (again), and so on. This kind of arrangement is now becoming more common among some urban Hmong in Southeast Asia, too. There may be political speeches by local politicians. An important change is that *pov pob* (the ball game) is now played by everyone, not just by the unmarried younger people, so it has lost most of its significance as an aspect of courting and become a sign of Hmong identity instead, although members of the same clan are still not allowed to play catch. The young peoples' behavior often demonstrates this departure from traditional courting norms; holding hands between the sexes, hugging, or kissing, which would still be regarded as somewhat shocking behavior in most Asian societies, is more and more becoming accepted. Colorful costumes alternate with mobile phones, shopping, taking photos, greeting friends and relatives. It becomes a day out for the family, as well as an important public expression of community identity and spirit.

To some extent these changes are occurring also in Southeast Asian countries, where girls dress up in all sort of fashions and Hmong New Year may be attended by visiting American Hmong and other non-Hmong fun-lovers. Large crowds gather in which the use of silver or tin earrings, mobile phones, and parasols against the sun are conspicuous, and public announcements and speeches are made from a podium. These events are true displayers of fashion. In 2000 a local regional minority association, IMPECT (the Inter-Mountain Peoples' Education and Culture in Thailand Association) organized a particularly public and large-scale Hmong New Year in the municipal stadium of Chiangmai.[5] Hmong in Canada arrange large Hmong picnics in the same sort of way, with stalls of barbequed food, displays, contests, sales of goods, and special areas marked off for young children, as in the Kitchener-Waterloo area.

Despite many changes in the New Year festival among Hmong living overseas and in Asia, particularly among the Christian Hmong, much of the joyous and remarkable flavor of the Hmong New Year is preserved in many ways through the performances of singing and dancing and the visits to other people and communities that still take place at this time, and it remains a most important family occasion.

OTHER LEISURE ACTIVITIES

Hmong fun and leisure activities are not limited to the months around the New Year festival, although this is certainly the most important time of the year dedicated to leisure activities of every kind, but do take place throughout the year and together with daily life wherever conditions permit. It is not only at weddings that feasting, drinking, and merry speeches and joking occur. Games of cards, betting of various kinds and other games, singing, and contests of different types have always been a common feature of Hmong existence.

Sports have played a big part in the life of the Hmong who live in urban areas in Laos. In traditional villages, as we have seen, tops and a kind of rudimentary badminton, using a bamboo base with chicken wing feathers stuck inside and two boards with a handle for striking it across a boundary line on the ground, are popular during New Year. However, more modern sports such as soccer and volleyball are also played at weekends in cities where teams can be formed and grounds are available. By the 1960s, soccer had become an entrenched part of Hmong urban life in Laos, was quickly taken up by those who escaped to the refugee camps in Thailand after 1975, and continued after their migration to the West. Whether in France, Canada, the United States, or Australia, soccer remains today a very trendy sport among young people in most Hmong communities. They may form teams to play after school or work, especially on weekends. Once a year, they may have competitions between teams from various states. In addition, sports of different kinds, including soccer, are often scheduled as part of the Hmong New Year celebrations. In December 2009, for example, two of the three days spent on the New Year celebration in Brisbane, Australia, were devoted to sports such as volleyball, *kataw* (see above), badminton, and soccer. On the last day, most members of the audience left the hall where stage entertainment was going on, and went out to watch the soccer game between local residents and interstate visitors. It rained intermittently, but both players and spectators paid little heed to the downpour. Such was their love for the sport.

Hmong living in Canada sometimes go to Detroit, Michigan, to compete in football tournaments where they are joined by teams from other American states. However, the biggest sports event takes place on the Fourth of July every year in St. Paul, Minnesota. Started around 2000, it has attracted such big crowds and so much commercial interest that it is now called the Fourth of July Hmong Festival. Devoted entirely to open-air sports, it runs the whole holiday weekend, with dozens of both male and female teams involved in baseball, American football, soccer, volleyball, and *kataw*. At this event, Hmong women, who are usually seen only at home and are often publicly invisible, openly display their full skills as sportswomen on an equal footing with Hmong men. Apart from its intense sports competition, the festival is one of the biggest Hmong community events in the United States, second only to the New Year, with Hmong sports people and spectators coming to participate from many states. It is reportedly attended by 40,000 to 60,000 people. The sports fields are surrounded by lines of market stalls selling Hmong DVDs, medicine, costumes, Hmong food, and many other goods. Stage entertainments are also available for those who are not keen on sporting activities.

A very important recreation activity for Hmong men is hunting. Traditionally hunting accorded some respite from the exigencies of everyday agriculture, besides contributing protein to the family staple diet. Hunting remains a favorite occupation of many men even in their new locations overseas today. In French Guyana, hunting and fishing are everyday occupations of the Hmong who live there, while in the woods of Wisconsin and Minnesota Hmong have become well-known for their hunting of deer, wild pig, squirrels, and game birds such as grouse, wild turkey, or quail. Sadly, tensions of an ethnic kind with white hunters have emerged that led to the slaying of six men by a Hmong man in 2004, and the murder of a Hmong hunter in 2007.[6] Now various public bodies such as the Department of Natural Resources have issued Hmong-language versions of hunting regulations, and Hmong hunting classes have been started to inform the Hmong better about hunting seasons, permits, and the laws of private property and trespass. However, the problems have not only been of Hmong ignorance, but also of bullying and ethnic chauvinism against them. Like top-playing as a leisure activity, hunting and other pastimes form an important release from tension for many Hmong in the stressed environments of urban life.

THE HMONG INTERNET AS RECREATION

Another huge area of fun and amusement, which has really opened up a whole new world of Hmong culture, has been found through the use of the Internet. We have mentioned the Internet in connection with oral literature and music, but here it is time to point out some of its extraordinary importance for entertainment, information, and communication of every kind. It may well be that, as Marshall McLuhan prophesied long ago, the oral traditions of the Hmong have proved particularly suitable to this new age of post-literate communications and an aural/oral and visual culture.[7] Soon after their arrival in the United States, the Hmong showed a particular propensity for telephone communications. By the 2000s, many people, including the elderly, in Australia, Canada, and the United States, were in the habit of making Internet phone calls to their relatives in other countries. As with some other diasporic communities, Hmong elites in the United States, Canada, and Australia have turned to the Internet as a major way of transcending the schisms of locality and overcoming the limitations of space, an attempt to create a unity formerly only dreamed of in utopian messianic movements and legends of a lost nation.

This new technology has enabled the production of new images of Hmong identity for a whole variety of audiences. It is not just elites who enjoy this access, but many ordinary people, too. Although Hmong Internet usage is most prevalent in the United States, Australia, and Canada, it is not used to the same extent in France, perhaps because of the dominance of the Internet by English, and the high costs of computers and Internet services there. Asia lags far behind these countries but even there Internet usage has taken off among the Hmong. It is most highly developed in Thailand, where a lot of Hmong Internet usage is in Thai. It is less common, but increasing day by day, in the socialist states of Laos, Vietnam, and China. Near the Central Post Office in Vientiane, capital of Laos, many Hmong, young and old, male and female, are using the Internet cafés operated by Hmong businessmen there, for a variety of different purposes, such as sending e-mails or browsing the Web. Similarly, outside the large Hmong settlement of Khek Noi in Thailand there is an Internet café run by local Hmong that is well used by young Thai teenagers besides Hmong.

Internet usage, as one might expect, is particularly common among teenagers, but not limited to them by any means. Many teenagers say that they use the Internet to find other Hmong friends and possible love matches. In Australia, where Hmong communities in Sydney, Melbourne, and Brisbane are separated by quite large distances, the Internet has also become an important means of staying in touch with family and friends, and making new ones. Across huge distances the structures of the Hmong kinship system are now maintained partly through Internet usage, with families scattered between France, Thailand, Laos, the United States, or Australia, staying in touch regularly by these means. Some families have a dedicated family Web page, with password access, while at least one clan (the Yang) has distributed a global questionnaire in trying to construct its genealogy through the Internet. In this way the Internet becomes almost a new extension of the kinship system, overcoming all barriers of space and time.

There is now an amazing variety of Hmong materials on the Internet in Hmong and English (besides pages in Thai, Vietnamese, and Chinese). In one snapshot in time of the Minnesota-based Hmong Electronic Resources project (and that is just one node), we found the following sites, among others, listed: Yamada Hmong WWW Guide, Ywj Pheej (Hmong Free Press), the well-known Hmong Homepage besides the early Hmong-Australia Homepage, Hmong Textiles, home pages for individual Hmong, a Lycos search page on the Hmong, and links to the University of Minnesota's Refugee Studies Center, Lao groups, U.S. State Department reports on Laos, and a report on the Minnesota Hmong.

One can buy CDs of traditional Hmong love music and learn all about the funeral rituals from a YouTube video, there are job announcements and conference calls, odds and ends on Hmong history, examples of creative Hmong work such as essays and embroideries, Hmong journals, newsletters, and newspapers (like *Hmong Today* and the *Hmong Times*), a bookshop specializing in Hmong publications, a host of Hmong discussion forums, and mailing lists.[8]

Some whole books are available online, like Lemoine's ethnography of Hmong material culture and social life in Laos, and Bertrais' Hmong-French Dictionary.[9] There have been several electronic Hmong studies journals, with articles ranging from adaptation, teenage truancy, and Hmong hip-hop, to shamanism, Hmong history in China, and many other subjects. There are online teenage magazines and culturally oriented journals like *18Xeem* in Wisconsin where the difficulties of growing up as Hmong (being neither exactly Laotian, nor Chinese) in the United States or Australia are frankly discussed. There are now millions of words in Hmong on the World Wide Web.

These materials fall into several different distinct types. Hmong-language pages are directed at an internal audience in the Hmong global community—the computer-literate Hmong. There are discussions of traditional Hmong society and customs, exchanges of business information, and debates about homeland politics, or crises of cultural practice such as a series of teenage gang rapes in St. Paul. More critical is the use of the Internet to commit what some see as cyber-adultery or to conduct "virtual" romances. Many a Hmong marriage and divorce has occurred in real life following these virtual encounters. The case of Pa Shia that involved the deaths of his family after an argument, it is said, about his wife's use of the Internet was much discussed in chatrooms and discussion forums. This highlighted tensions about Internet usage between the young and old, men and women. The 2004 killing of white hunters by a Hmong in Wisconsin, mentioned above, and his subsequent trial was also much discussed from the point of view of relations between the Hmong and others. The Internet is a space for serious cultural discussions as well as fun, with many Hmong spending large amounts of their spare time on it, especially in the chatrooms and discussion groups.

English-language materials on the Hmong, the majority of which are also authored by Hmong, do not deal so much with these internal issues. A large amount of this is more educational or informational in purpose, directing researchers, particularly those working with the Hmong in capacities such as language teachers or health workers, to publications and sources on the history, culture, and background of the Hmong (for instance, see the Hmong-Australia homepage at http://www.hmongnet.org.hmong-au/ozintro.htm, accessed 22 May 2010). Some of the English-language material on the Hmong on the Internet is more like a kind of public announcement for a particular purpose, such as getting funding for community projects or for political campaigns like the successful campaign to have ex-Hmong fighters recognized as Vietnam War veterans.

American Hmong voices on the Internet, together with those of others associated with them writing about them,[10] summarizing their history and organizing their materials, speak not only of a dynamic and lively community, but also of a people with a highly articulate, sophisticated sense of their own identity, together with a growing knowledge of how to convey it. Through the Internet and Web, many voices with a concern for and interest in Hmong culture and identity have found their fullest expression, although they do not always sing to the same tune. Even where they do not, however, the theme of an imagined greater Hmong harmony and unity projected onto an ideal future very often runs through these varied representations. Perhaps more importantly, what has been occurring on the Internet points to the fact that it has become a focal point for Hmong leisure activities and spare-time intellectual exchanges on a global scale.

NOTES

1. Granet 1930.
2. Lewis 1993, 76.
3. See Mottin 1979, 128–31.
4. Kou Yang 2007.
5. Tomforde 2007.
6. See Siegle, "Wisconsin Man Charged with Murder in Hmong Hunter's Death," *USA Today*, January 16, 2007. Online at http://www.usatoday.com/news/nation/2007-01-16-hunter-homicide_x.htm. Accessed 23 May 2010.

7. McLuhan 1962.

8. The materials in this section have been taken from a sub-project on Internet usage as part of a research project on the Hmong diaspora undertaken by the authors in 2001–2002 funded by the Chiang Ching-Kuo Foundation, Taiwan, and has been reported on to the Foundation and elsewhere (e.g. Tapp 2006; 2007). We would like to express our thanks to Jo Stacey and Yeu Lee in Canberra, who helped with this project and drew diagrams of the main nodes of the Hmong-related Internet for us.

9. Lemoine 1972a; Bertrais 1964, both available from www.reninc.org. Accessed 22 May 2010.

10. See Pfeifer 2007.

10

Social Organization, Customs, and Lifestyles

THIS CHAPTER WILL look at Hmong social customs, traditions, and lifestyles, and the general nature of Hmong social organization. It will delve into some of the issues discussed in this book from a broader perspective as well as some issues that have not been previously dealt with. The aim is to highlight Hmong social behavior together with the main features of Hmong society that are important for maintaining their social organization as well as being major challenges to them in the face of modernity, a radically new lifestyle in the West, and globalization.

For many centuries, the Hmong have been subject to the domination of other more powerful people such as the Chinese. When they migrated to Southeast Asia, they lived as minorities under the rule of more numerous groups or people who controlled the territories they found themselves in such as the Vietnamese, Lao, and Thai. They are thus a subaltern people, people always living in subordination to others. The Vietnamese and Lao, in turn, were dominated for many years, from the late nineteenth century until the end of the Vietnam War in 1973, by more powerful French colonialists or their anti-communist American and other allies. In all these situations, the Hmong have been greatly influenced by the people they have been surrounded by. Many Hmong beliefs and customs have been assimilated or borrowed from these cultures or have been changed through contacts with them.

SOCIAL ORGANIZATION

Social customs and rules of social conduct are dictated by society, and are based on certain norms and values that are often translated into moral and religious codes considered sacred to the group concerned. These ethical sanctions help sustain, and are in turned sustained by, the various spheres of social organization of the group such as the family and clan system, religion, the economy, and the legal system. They are enforced by various agencies like the police, the church, the military, and those in positions of power within the political system. Although Graham states that the Hmong in Sichuan, China, where he spent a number of years studying, have "no tribal organization," what he says is far from the truth.[1] The Hmong, indeed, have a very clear-cut social organization at various levels starting from the family to the lineage and the clan, each with its own demarcating sets of rules and behavior expectations.

If we take society as a group of people that is distinguished from other groups by mutual interests with their own sets of social relationships, shared institutions, and a common culture, then Hmong society would be one with a family and group organization based on a patriarchal system, where men dominate in power relationships and are given more prominence in family and community affairs, while daughters are seen as "other people's women" because they marry out into other families and clans. Some daughters, of course, may stay unmarried, and they can always remain in the family.

The Family

After their wedding, a Hmong young couple almost always goes to live in the house of the groom's parents. This is not only because the latter have paid for his bridewealth, but also because the newly married couple wants to profit from the advice of his family elders regarding marital problems, to show their gratitude for the help they have received, and to assist with any household tasks.[2] The strength of this rule of post-marital residence, however, varies from one regional group to another. A married man, for instance, may not get along with his parents, or may only be able to find work elsewhere and is thus forced to move his family away from the original kin group. It is probable that the present Hmong patrilineal kinship system with patrilocal residence has developed from the influence of the Han Chinese, but variations exist due to poor assimilation of Chinese culture.

Regardless of these variations, most newly married sons tend to remain in the house of their fathers, especially among the Hmong in Southeast

Asia. The new couple and other married brothers thus form an extended household with their parents. This extended social unit may survive for many years until one or more of the married couples can set up house for themselves, often when they have two or three children. The parental household will be overcrowded by that time for all the married brothers to remain under one roof. The couple who move out will then build a house for themselves, often not far from the man's father and his household if all is well between them. The new household will then consist only of a nuclear family. Lee found that half of the 30 households he studied in Khun Wang, Thailand, were nuclear families while the other half were extended households.[3] This household composition appears to be similar elsewhere in other Hmong settlements in Thailand. Mark also notes that the nuclear family was the predominant household form with the Magpie Hmong (Hmoob Yob Tshuab, Yaque Miao, or Hmoob Ntsw) in China; stem families were next in frequency; and 5 percent of the households had extended joint families.[4]

In terms of the number of persons in a household, this usually ranges from six to eight. As extended families are common in Hmong society, household size is bigger than family size, a factor attributed by Geddes and Kunstadter to the need for manpower in the Hmong cash-crop economy by combining the human resources of two or more families into one single unit to increase farming production and cash income.[5] This prevalent larger household size is also an indicator of the Hmong desire and ability to maintain cohesive social groupings at the household level. By Western standards, Hmong household size is rather large, because of the Hmong extended family system. It may also be due to the Hmong's desire for sons so that parents will try to have as many children as they can in the hope that some of them will be sons who will grow up to fulfill their roles as carriers of the family descent line and as providers for the spiritual needs of their parents after the latter's death.

Today, much of these family norms and practices have undergone transformations, due to the impact of education and exposure to Western social values as well as the realities of economic survival in the diaspora. Apart from marrying late because of the need to complete their studies and to find stable employment first, many young Hmong also prefer living as nuclear families rather than as traditional extended households. This is mainly because houses in Western countries and in overcrowded Asian cities are small and cannot accommodate large extended families. The need to have cars as modern transport further reinforces the preference for smaller families, as the average American house only has a double garage, forcing many Hmong families to park their many cars on the front lawn.

There is a saying among visitors to the Hmong in the United States that a house with many cars parked around it is sure to be a Hmong house. Education, the availability of contraceptives, and the fact that labor is now not needed for farming are all contributory factors to the decreasing size of Hmong families. A smaller family is more practical and economically more viable today now that many Hmong no longer work as subsistence farmers but are wage earners who often find it difficult to cope financially with a large number of children, especially in regard to health care and educational costs. The preference for nuclear families will thus continue into the immediate future as more and more Hmong become wage earners, even for those in the old homeland of Laos, as is already the case for those living in China and the diaspora.

Lineage and Clan

The next level in Hmong social organization is the lineage. A lineage consists of all those members of a group who share the same family name and can trace descent to a known ancestor. They follow the same sets of religious practices or rituals for the door ceremony (*dab roog*) and the bull ritual (*nyuj dab*) such as having 5 bowls of sacrificial meat while another lineage may have 7 or 12 bowls, called *txim* in Hmong. There may be other features that distinguish one lineage from another such as prohibitions regarding the relationships between fathers and daughters-in-law. These taboos are discussed by Chindarsi for the Blue Mong, but they also apply to the White Hmong.[6] As noted in the chapters on religion and on the house, certain clans (such as the Lee and Yang) have some lineages whose daughters-in-law cannot climb up to the loft to store or retrieve goods. To do this, they would have to pass the central beam that is held by the central post, the domain of important household spirits and rituals. Trespassing on this area would amount to showing disrespect to family ancestors, and this would bring harm to members of the household since the house formally belongs to the parents of their husbands. This example illustrates a lineage taboo regarding the relationships and obligations of parents and their daughters-in-law. There are other prohibitions and variations applicable to other sets of relationships or other Hmong clans. Some lineages, for instance, leave the bodies of their dead on a platform on the house floor during a funeral, while others of the same clan put the bodies on a wooden stretcher on the main wall facing the southern door.

Above the lineage is membership of two broader groups: the clan and sub-clan. Clan identification is made on the basis of a common surname. Hmong clan names are similar to the surnames of the Chinese, and may have been based on them. When two persons have a similar surname, they are said to belong to the same clan, but are often not related by blood. People who share similar rituals but have no known genealogical connection are said to belong to the same sub-clan, a grouping intermediate between the clan and the lineage. The Hmong call members of a lineage a "cluster of brothers" (*ib cuab kwv tij*), and those of a sub-clan "one ceremonial household" (*ib tus dab qhuas*). One distinguishing feature of a lineage is that its members can die in one another's house and will be given funerals there, but not people who only share clan or sub-clan membership. This applies to birth, too; a child should be born in a house of its father's clan members if not in the house of its own parents.

Although Chinese of the same surnames can marry each other, this is forbidden among the Hmong due to the incest taboo. The clan system thus unites as well as divides the Hmong into separate social categories. It helps a person to identify the groups that he or she can count on for closer ties and support, despite the fact that the bond of mutual obligations will not be as strong as that between members of a lineage. Other criteria used for the identification of sub-clan membership include the type of grave construction. Hmong graves can be a mound of earth with some tree branches on top to protect the corpse from wild animals, a mound of earth surrounded by a plaited bamboo fence, or a mound of earth protected by boulders. Each type of grave is strictly observed by each sub-clan. These various types of graves, however, no longer distinguish members of different sub-clans among the Hmong in the West, where all the dead are buried in a common cemetery together with the corpses of other people.

Above the sub-clan, the clan or *xeem* (xeng) classifies the Hmong into kin or non-kin. Although it unites them into organized kinship groups, it also divides them along mutually exclusive patrilineal lines. Male persons of the same clan or sub-clan without any known blood links refer to each other as *kwv tij* or brotherly relatives in the broader sense of the term. Based on the various surnames found in Thailand and Laos, Binney groups them into 12 clans: Chang, Hang, Heu, Lee, Lo, Mua, Pang, Thao, Vang, Vue, Xiong, and Yang.[7] Other clan names also exist, but it is difficult to know how many altogether because of the Hmong's wide dispersion across many countries. The Blue Mong or *Moob Ntsuab*, for instance, share some clan names with the White Hmong or *Hmoob Dawb*, but also have others of their own.[8] In America, it is believed that there are 18 clans of Hmong, so leaders of the Hmong there have set up an 18-Clan Council to assist members with advice, to resolve inter-clan disputes, and to carry out activities that will benefit the Hmong as a whole. There are between 40 and 60 surnames for the Hmong in China, again with names similar to Chinese surnames.

The Community

Beyond the clan are the village and the general Hmong community. The first is based on membership in a geographical settlement involving the concept of physical space and all that it entails. The second may encompass the physical boundaries of a settlement or may refer to all Hmong living within a region or even a country, or the global Hmong population. The community is a broader and more fluid concept that identifies Hmong on the basis of being born into Hmong society, speaking the Hmong language and sharing the Hmong culture. It includes the identification of all Hmong as a tribe or a minority within the nation-state in which they are citizens and live. In China, this is commonly known as a "nationality" (*minzu*). At the highest level, the concept of community includes the notion of the Hmong nation as a global transnational entity.

As a minority living among many other diverse groups and members of the dominant society wherever they are, many Hmong often have a conflicting sense of their own nationhood. On the one hand, they live in different countries under different governments and show loyalty to the country of which they are rightful citizens. On the other hand, many have become aware that they are part of a bigger Hmong global community, a transnational Hmong nation without physical boundaries. They may identify more consciously with the nation-state in which they live physically, but also feel they belong emotionally to this broader imagined ethnicity. Because the Hmong have never had a country of their own, it is difficult to feel too strongly about a Hmong nation; yet it may be equally difficult to feel wanted by the nations in which they live, as the host nations may require them to shed vestiges of their ethnic identity, such as names and dress, in order to be socially accepted, to benefit from social services, or to obtain government employment. Thailand is a case in point. On the other hand, they may also suffer from discrimination or direct political persecution as is the situation in Laos, making some of them long for a country of their own.

BELIEFS AND AUTHORITY

Organization into different levels of social groupings and hierarchy by itself is like dividing a house into different rooms to give them order and functions. However, their functions have to derive legitimacy from some mandates, some belief system that gives them sanction and approval. The most fundamental source of moral authority is the religious system. The Hmong religious system gives rise to their faith in relation to human existence and to the moral doctrines or codes of ethics that guide their everyday conduct. They have had neither Bible nor any written rules, but they hand down their beliefs orally from generation to generation. This trust in their religious teachings is one based on practices and self-learning, not the preaching of any priest or religious leader because they do not have an organized religion. To have morality is to conform to the prescribed standards of approved conduct, according to what is deemed right and wrong.

Among other things, Hmong morality includes such social values as honesty, hard work, family duties with family and in-group interests placed above individual interests, the importance of "face" (*ntsej muag*) and the need to safeguard family honor, maintaining individual and group reputation (*koob meej*), respect for elders and their wisdom, and offering generosity and hospitality to fellow human beings. Along with these basic values are certain norms such as: (1) Hmong have to love other Hmong and look after their own people; (2) the clan system is a means to regulate marriage and social relationships with clan and non-clan members; (3) the authority structure of the patriarchal family has clear gender roles and privileges; and (4) the obligations of male descendants dictate that they care for living parents and revere dead ancestors. These are only some examples. There are, of course, other values and norms that the Hmong follow, depending on the circumstances. There have been important changes in the sense of morality, and we have noted the importance of Confucian ideas of etiquette and social relations for the Hmong. Hmong young people are brought up not to lie or steal, and are particularly averse to speaking ill of others. This is why problems and issues that are thought of as internal to the community are rarely discussed with those perceived as outsiders.

Class and Power Structure

If we take power as the ability to perform an action due to one's personal attributes or achievements, then there are a number of individuals who fulfill roles of power within Hmong society. Such persons would include the shaman, the herbalist, the expert performer of a particular ritual or ceremony, and the informal leader in particular tasks. We have seen that shamans acquire their positions of power through being called on by healing spirits that inspire them through sickness to learn the art of the shaman and become skilled in their field of expertise. Other ritual experts, however, learn to perform rituals out of personal interest and gradually become adept in their performance as well as gaining a wealth of knowledge in rituals through experience. They have the personal attributes required for their roles, and are given the power in their particular field through personal achievements. In other words, they have become authorities in their field of specialization. In a Hmong settlement, there are only a few shamans or one renowned herbalist. Ritual performers exist in nearly all clans, as religious ceremonies are different from one clan to another, so a ritual expert in one clan does not always know those in another clan and is not always called on to perform for members of another clan.

In terms of authority or the ability to occupy a formal role or an approved office, many Hmong hold such positions by being born into them or through acquisition and official appointment. Those with authority may include the male head of the family, the household head, elders in a family and community, the village chief, and people who occupy government positions at various levels. Within a Hmong family, for example, the mother has authority over her children by virtue of her role as the one who gives birth to them and raises them.[9] This authority is especially important in relation to her daughters. In the village, all Hmong mothers breast-feed their babies, and carry them around on their backs in an apron-style embroidered baby carrier when they are busy with household chores or farming activities. Thus, mothers spend more time than fathers on childcare, although the fathers share in looking after small children when their wives are too busy or when there are no older children to help.

With older children, a mother is responsible for the training of her daughters in household work and all matters of female comportment. A father's role is primarily to train his sons in the knowledge and performance of male responsibilities in such areas as agriculture, socializing, and ritual performance. If a father dies before his children are married, their physical upbringing and care are assumed by paternal grandparents, a paternal uncle and his wife, an older son, or an unmarried daughter.[10] Preference in such cases is for the surviving wife and male siblings of the dead father, but a lot also depends on who can assume such undertaking.

Authority and respect are also vested on the basis of age and gender. The older one becomes, the more authority one is given, along with more responsibilities. As in most Asian societies, age means wisdom for the Hmong. This is true not only for the living, but also for the dead. One has to respect and listen to the counsel of one's parents or community elders. For the dead ancestors, ritual offerings have to be observed and their names remembered. Men tend to have more power than women, and more men are involved in community affairs and in settling family or village disputes, due to the patriarchal nature of Hmong society.

Beyond the authority gained through age and gender, leaders at the lineage and clan level are usually appointed by members of their own groups, again mostly men. Lineage heads are usually the oldest living male descendants of a lineage. These lineage leaders carry the title of *tus coj plaub* (trouble bearer or all-purpose leader), and *tus coj dab* (ceremonial bearer or ritual leader) for their members. The trouble bearer assumes responsibilities over all social and legal matters pertaining to members, while the ritual leader sees to or performs all tasks related to religious needs and has to be skilled in ritual performance. These lineage and ritual leaders may be, but are not always, also village heads who are formally appointed or elected for the whole village or a group of villages that contain many lineages. The lineage and ritual leaders are often chosen informally by their own cluster of close relatives. There is only one village head man or woman, but there are many lineage and informal leaders within a settlement.

There are other figures of authority in Hmong society. These are people who hold official positions such as local police officer, or teacher. In some countries such as Laos and China, the Hmong are appointed to higher positions beyond the village level. In Laos, the Hmong were able to gain office as *Kiatong* or canton chiefs after their first uprisings against French colonial taxes in 1896 when they organized an ambush against tax collectors at Ban Khang Phanieng in Muong Kham, Xieng Khouang province.[11] The most famous kiatong was Lo Bliayao who helped the French to pacify the Pachai rebellion from 1918 to 1921 that involved many Hmong in northeastern Laos, who had been led to believe that a Hmong king would emerge to establish their own Hmong country. The *Kiatong* office was later changed to *Tasseng*. The first Hmong Tasseng position in Laos was given to Kiatong Mua Yong Kai (Muas Zoov Kaim) in Nong Het, and a second Tasseng was created near Xieng Khouang town for Ya Yang Her (Zam Yaj Hawj). This new arrangement was intended to allow all Hmong leaders to collect taxes from their own people and to have their own autonomy in local village administration, bypassing Tai or Lao officials at the Tasseng and Muong or district levels.[12]

Touby Lyfoung, one of the first Hmong to be educated in the French education system and a strong ally of the French colonial administration in Laos, was made Chao Muong or district administrator in 1950 to oversee the Hmong in Xieng Khouang province. He later became a deputy in the Lao National Assembly, minister of Social Welfare and Minister for Telecommunications in the Royal Lao Government. Touby's cousin, Faydang Lobliayao, who sided with the opposition in the Lao civil war, the communist Pathet Lao (PL), was made vice-chairman of the National Assembly. He was also nominated one of the "Heroes of the Revolution," after the Pathet Lao took control of Laos in 1975. On the military front, a young Hmong named Vang Pao joined the Royal Lao Army in 1947 as a military police officer, and became a general and the commander of the

Second Military Region in 1962 in northeastern Laos. When the Lao civil war was in full swing in 1961, Vang Pao received support from the U.S. Central Intelligence Agency (CIA) to set up the so-called "secret army" to combat the advances of PL troops. This support lasted until the Paris Cease-Fire Agreement in 1973, leading to the dislocation and deaths of thousands of Hmong in the highlands of northern Laos, and their subsequent settlement in many Western countries.

As of 2010, the Hmong in Laos have gained many notable positions of authority, from provincial governor to Chairman of the Lao National Reconstruction Front (*Neo Hom Xang Xat*), Vice-Chairman of the National Assembly (House of Representatives), and ministers in the Lao Government. In the five years before 2010, there were three ministers of Hmong background in Laos: Chaleun Heu, Minister for Justice; Lycheng, Minister Assisting the Prime Minister in Rural Development; and Lytou Bouapao, Deputy Minister of Education. There are also Hmong in various management levels of the Lao public service. In China, the situation is very similar, at least at the prefecture and provincial levels. Some degree of formal leadership has been attained in Vietnam, but the Hmong in Thailand and in most Western countries have been lagging behind with formal leadership positions gained only at the group or village level.

It can thus be seen that although the Hmong are a subaltern people who live under other people's rules, they have structured their power base on their own traditional system based on the household, lineage, and the clan. They have also attained positions of power in the administrative system of the majority societies in which they live, from village chief up to provincial governor and government ministers. Beyond the village, however, the Hmong have to follow the official power or administrative system of the country in which they live and have to compete with other groups to be included in the broader power structure.

Do the Hmong have social classes, based on these many levels of social and political organizations? Before their exodus to Western countries in 1975, the Hmong of Laos were mostly subsistence farmers in the hills, although some went to schools in the cities, were in the army and public service, or attained high positions. Those living in Vietnam and Thailand were nearly all confined to a life of village farming and did not receive much education until the 1980s. Their social organization was not based on wealth and educational privileges, but on the principles of age and sex within their lineage and clan system that only differentiated them on the basis of birth into different clans and not on any economic criteria. On the whole, their wealth difference was too minimal and those in ruling positions were too few to constitute social classes of their own. The

Hmong have been until now more or less an egalitarian society, without the formation of marked class differences and where decision making is made on a democratic basis. However, social classes may emerge in the future with more urban living and diversification into other means of livelihood, power acquisition, and wealth accumulation.

LIFESTYLES

Traditionally, the Hmong have based their way of life on village subsistence agriculture, supplemented by some cash cropping, herding, hunting, and gathering. As rural farmers, their major energy is aimed at growing enough rice and other crops for the consumption of the family. From dawn to dusk, they spend most of their waking hours in the fields, followed by gathering firewood and animal feed from the jungle on their way back home. The evening is used for relaxing after dinner with social visits, gossip, story-telling, and courting for young people. The next day starts again with much the same farm activities. A variety of crops are grown, including rice, corn, and vegetables. There may be time when this farm work slows down enough for them to visit relatives in distant villages, or go to the city to purchase essential products like salt, materials, and medicine. Most social visits take place during the New Year festival in November or December after the harvest has been done.

Subsistence farming as a way of life has profoundly affected the Hmong and their life style. Many of their traditions and religious beliefs have been formed and shaped by this economic system.[13] An example of this impact is the Hmong's conceptualization of time. As a people without writing until recently, they did not have the means to keep records of time. Few members of the older generation knew how to read and write, so births and deaths were rarely recorded on paper. As they lived in remote areas, there was no official registration of these major life events anyway. Few Hmong thus knew their true ages, as births were usually reckoned by reference to some natural phenomenon such as the year of a local landslide or a political event like the year the Japanese occupied the country.

The Hmong only had access to the use of a clock or watch 30 to 40 years ago. Until then, they did not conceive time in term of seconds, minutes, and hours. In fact, they had no words for these time divisions in their own language. Despite this, the Hmong have had their own system of looking at time.[14] For example, a day is divided into 5 periods: (1) morning or *sawv ntxov*, approximately from 5:00 A.M. to 8:00 A.M.; (2) after breakfast or *caij noj tshais tas*, from 8:00 A.M. to 12:00 P.M.; (3) midday or *tav su*, from 12:00 P.M. to 1:00 P.M.; (4) afternoon or *hnub qaij*, from

1:00 P.M. to 5:00 P.M.; and (5) nighttime or *tsaus ntuj*, from 5:00 P.M. to 5:00 A.M. The day starts at 5 A.M. because the Hmong have to get up early to go and work on the farm. A night is divided into 5 periods: (1) nightfall or *tsaus ntuj*, from 5:00 P.M. to 8:00 P.M.; (2) after dinner or *noj hmo*, from 8:00 P.M. to 10:00 P.M.; (3) midnight or *ib tag hmo*, from 10:00 P.M. to 1:00 A.M.; (4) after midnight or *hli qaij*, from 1:00 A.M. to 4:00 A.M.; and (5) dawn or *kaj ntug*, from 4:00 A.M. to 6:00 A.M. It is worthy of note that dinner time was after 8:00 P.M., because most families did not return from the farm until 7 P.M., and it took at least one hour for the women of the house to get dinner ready, again a family event imposed by the rigor of farming. The early hours were also reckoned by the crowing of the cock; thus, first cock's crow, second cock's crow, and so on.

The Hmong do not have any formal week and they have no term in their vocabulary for such a week and no names of each day of the week. A month has 29 or 30 days, reckoned by the waxing and waning phases of the moon. A year has 12 months, beginning around November when most Hmong celebrate the New Year after harvest has been completed for all crops. There is no separate name for each month of the year. The months are given numerical names such as First Month, Second Month, and so on, just as the Chinese months are numbered still today. The Hmong year is once more dictated by the agricultural cycle they are subject to in the highlands of China and Southeast Asia. There are four seasons: (1) dry season or *caij ntuj qhua* from February to April; (2) wet season or *caij ntuj nag* from May to July; (3) summer or *caij ntuj sov* from August to October; and (4) winter or *caij ntuj no* from November to January. If a lunar calendar is strictly calculated, however, after some time the seasons will get out of joint, because a year is not exactly divisible into 12 (and actually there are not exactly 30 days in a lunar month). So months either have 30 or 29 days alternately; approximately every three years there will be a meeting of local elders to decide to add an extra month to bring it into line with the solar calendar.

One of the consequences of not having mechanical time or a rigid calendar is that the Hmong sometimes have a carefree attitude to long-term time beyond today and tomorrow. This issue with time reckoning may mean that some people are late for appointments and meetings. Others may deliberately turn up late, because they do not want to be seen to be too eager by coming on time. This is often referred to as "Hmong time" (like "Lao time," or "Thai time"), the need to be late for a dinner or a social event, to have good manners by showing reluctance despite being keen. The Hmong work very hard and make good use of their time, but they are not controlled by the clock if they work for themselves as farmers or are running their own businesses.

Apart from differences in time conceptualization, there are issues in regard to the traditional lifestyles of the Hmong in the context of the diaspora. In addition to the problem of some Hmong traditions being at odds with the law in Western countries, the Hmong also have their own difficulties in relation to the maintenance of these traditions. When suffering from ill health, for example, the Hmong resort to three main methods of curing sickness apart from the soul-calling: (1) the use of medicinal herbs (*tshuaj*), roots, or plants either by drinking a boiled concoction or by applying mashed leaves of a plant directly onto a wound, usually on the advice of an herbal medicine man or woman; (2) the use of a shaman (*txiv neeb*) to bring back the lost or separated soul to the body of the sick person through shamanic trances in two sessions: one to diagnose (*saib*) the cause of the sickness and a second session to cure (*kho*) it through the sacrifice of animals, usually a piglet but it may in very special circumstances be a dog or a goat; and (3) the use of "magic formulas" or *khawv koob* on a wound or a burnt area. Massage and a form of moxibustion cupping are also known and practiced.

In the Western context, the Hmong usually resort to modern medical care as a first option by consulting their local doctors or going to the nearest hospital. However, language barriers, health insurance costs, negative experiences with the official health care system, or a firm belief in the old Hmong healing practices may lead some Hmong to continue using the Hmong methods of curing illnesses, especially among the elderly. Many thus continue to use the shaman, although his need for live sacrificial animals has been a major problem as detailed above. It is difficult to find such animals for use, and killing them in one's house is against the law. Shamanic performances are also rather noisy, with the gong used and the shaman chanting loudly. It may not be conducive for good relations with neighbors, and complaints from them can attract the attention of local law-enforcement agents. Thus, it is a difficult issue to resolve.

The problem is further complicated when there is a significant lack of interest among the young Western-educated Hmong in taking on the calling of being ritual performers. Few have been touched by the shamanic spirits in their search for new people to become shamans. With the Hmong still dependent so much on shamans to cure their sickness in U.S. urban enclaves, the dwindling number of spiritual healers within their ranks is a worrying trend. Already, the few shamans in existence in the United States have become rather untraditional in their approach. Some seem to perform their shamanic séances for financial gain with a set fee rather than as a community service for which they accept whatever the client offers them, be it meat from the sacrificial animals used for their performance or a small fee affordable to the client. These new fee-charging shamans can be seen as changing their traditional role, as they rush from one patient to another in the hope of making money, instead of taking time to ensure that all rituals are properly carried out and all the necessary spiritual support given to the sick person. Thus, Hmong lifestyles in the new countries are also changing from within their own society, due to new attitudes and needs.

There are other examples of assimilation to a new Western life with unintended consequences. One physical adjustment that has brought many health problems is the new rich diet the new settlers face. Many Hmong in the United States have fallen into the "fat trap," as it were. Having lived a frugal life in the hills of Southeast Asia with rice and vegetables as the dominant diet, they now have easy access to fatty meat and sweet food ingredients and seem to have developed a special appetite for them. Urban living and full-time employment also prevent many from physical exercises. The result is that many have become obese and suffer from diabetes, high blood pressure and other health problems resulting in stroke or death, as discussed in Chapter 7.[15]

Another major challenge to the traditional values in the face of the new lifestyles is ageing. In traditional Hmong society, the elderly are well respected and cared for by their own families. Reaching old age is a time to reap the rewards of younger years, from productive farming life to one of providing gentle advice and support for the family. It is a time to impart wisdom and to gain community respect. In Western countries, however, sons and daughters are trapped into making a living by the clock and have little time for elderly parents who are stuck at home like prisoners, neither daring to venture outside nor able to watch television or read due to their lack of English. Their words of wisdom are irrelevant to the new needs in the new societies. Some children, because of work commitments, cannot care for their frail aged and have to settle them in assisted living or nursing homes where they suffer from isolation and heartbreak when unable to communicate with English-speaking staff and other residents. It is sad to think that many succeeded in escaping from Laos after the communist takeover in 1975 only to end their lives in this way.

SOCIAL CUSTOMS AND BASIC VALUES

According to Hobsbawm, social customs are established practices governed by collectively accepted rules, which seek to inculcate certain values and norms of behavior related to precedents set in the past.[16] As conventional ways of doing things, they are usually passed down from one generation to another. The Hmong have very strong beliefs about proper behavior practices toward each other within their own society and toward other people outside their community. We will start with the values customarily expected of a Hmong toward other fellow Hmong, although the discussion is not aimed to be comprehensive but only to give some basic examples.

Within the Family and the Household

In a family, the husband acts as head and is expected to make major decisions affecting the welfare of its members. He is to fulfill his role with a measure of gentleness mixed with authoritative enforcement but not become authoritarian. He is to lead in economic activities and be the main breadwinner. A wife is to follow her husband's advice and be his partner in decision making and in implementing such decisions. Both husband and wife are to treat each other with respect, although in practice many Hmong husbands appear to play the dominant role in most family matters, except in relation to household chores like cleaning and cooking that Hmong men, like men in other societies, tend to leave to the women. Some Hmong men even see helping their wives with dish-washing and cleaning as demeaning to their status. However, the new lifestyle in Western countries where both husband and wife work for a living requires that such traditional attitudes regarding gender roles have to be discarded.

Children are expected to listen to their parents, to follow their advice and respect their wishes. They are to help parents care for younger siblings and learn to carry out their role expectations as daughters and sons. Parents have the duty to guide and teach their children about proper behavior, and to provide for both their physical and moral upbringing. Brothers are to protect their sisters, and the latter are expected to follow the advice of their brothers. Family problems are to be resolved within the family, and if this is not possible, then through the lineage or clan head of the family. Children, especially sons and their wives, are expected to care for their elderly parents, and to offer them food and paper money after death as a mark of respect so that the souls of the departed parents and other ancestors will protect them from sickness and harm. To this end, sons should learn all the family's religious rituals and be able to perform them properly.

As Lineage and Clan Members

Lineage heads are expected to represent the interests of their members, and ensure their welfare. They are to lead members in any undertakings required of the group. The members of a lineage, in turn, are to respect their lineage leaders and hold mutual consultations on major issues affecting the lineage.

If a man is of a particular clan, he will be welcome to the house of another Hmong with the same clan name, even if they have never met or known one another before. Their relationships will be closer still if they are also of the same sub-clan that share similar household rituals. Members of the same clan have to observe their clan taboos such as not eating the heart of animals for the Yang clan, or daughters-in-law not entering the bedroom of fathers-in-law for the Vang clan, as we have noted. More importantly, they are not allowed to marry members of the same clan, people bearing the same clan names even if they are not related by blood and have never seen each other previously. Members of the same clan are believed to descend from the same original ancestor, and are regarded as brothers and sisters who should welcome each other into their house like family members.

In the Community and Village

The Hmong today normally share villages with Hmong of other clans, and in some instances, with non-Hmong people such as Chinese, Iu Mien, or Khmu. Apart from showing a general tolerance and acceptance of fellow villagers, there are occasional community events that village people are obliged to join. There may be village meetings called by the village chiefs, to discuss matters of common interest or local problems and decisions. There may also be village celebrations. Each household is expected to send at least one male representative to help and to take part in the event, as was the case in previous times when the Hmong went to war. The most important requirement is labor requisition for a major community project such as village clean-up, repairs to the water pipe system used to bring water to the village for all to use, fencing or fencing repairs to protect the village from domestic animals and other threats. Each household is expected to send an able-bodied member to join this pooled labor for however long it takes.

During seasons of intense farm activities, households may undertake labor exchanges with other households in the village. One family may agree to work in the field of another family for so many days until an activity such as weeding is completed. The other family will then send an equal number of persons to work with the first family on their farm. This arrangement is by mutual agreement, and often occurs between closely related households.[17]

Co-ethnics or Other Hmong

There is a saying that the "Hmong boil Hmong herbal medicine, the Chinese boil Chinese herbal medicine" (*Hmoob tshuaj Hmoob rhaub, Suav tshuaj Suav rhaub*). It is often used to support the fact that a Hmong problem is best dealt with by Hmong people within their own community. It should not be spilled over to other non-Hmong ears or hands, for this may only spell more problems. The reason for this is that the Hmong believe they know best about other Hmong and their needs; they know the culture and have the wisdom to know how to best solve Hmong problems. Apart from the natural reluctance to talk ill of others, there may also be the need to hide unsavory Hmong issues from non-Hmong and the authorities in case they bring shame to the community or incur bigger punishment from officials. If dealt with by the Hmong themselves, all they need may be a ceremony to negotiate between the parties concerned, and the amends may be made to the wronged party through a feast or a payment. The wronged person will be asked by village elders "to forgive and forget" through a *sib thov* (asking for forgiveness) ceremony.

Another very common saying is that the Hmong have to love Hmong or look after their own (*Hmoob yuav tsum hlub Hmoob*). This means that no matter where, a Hmong should not abandon another Hmong and should give help, provide hospitality, and be kind or caring toward other Hmong people. There are other precepts that offer guidance on how Hmong should behave toward each other, but these two examples are sufficient to show us what is expected in this context.

Strangers

The Hmong see non-Hmong as *Mab Suav* or Chinese strangers, a carryover from the old days when they lived in China. The term *mab* really means people from the wilds, the unknown. Regardless of their status as strangers, the Hmong are expected to welcome them into their abode and to share food and drink with them. In most situations, however, giving hospitality to strangers is the responsibility of the village chief, so that villagers may send strangers to his house rather than taking them in directly.

Whether in strangers or Hmong, the following characteristics in a person are not looked on with approval: boastfulness and arrogance, disrespectfulness to other people, drunkenness, extravagant and wasteful behavior, ignorance of other cultures, insensitivity to others, or being lazy and free-loading, loud and obnoxious, promiscuous, racist, rude, childish, mean, snobbish, and all-knowing. The Hmong are taught to be humble by their own culture and by mainstream authorities who often show them who are the masters and who are servants. For this reason, the Hmong often act their part of being downtrodden and oppressed, but they still intensely dislike people who think they know best or who believe they are the best and that everyone else should follow their ways. They are very democratic and freedom-loving.

Smiles and Laughter

The Hmong appreciate laughter and smiles, especially in children, because it indicates happiness. Hmong will always greet visitors with a smile, but they do not like to joke with people unless they know each other well. When by themselves, they enjoy a few jokes together, and men may tell the occasional blue jokes. By and large, however, the Hmong do not like a person who jokes too much, or someone who laughs too often and loudly, especially a woman. For a girl, such comportment shows a flirtatious attitude, something the Hmong refer to as *plees tshis* (behaving like a goat) and highly disapprove of. Nor do they like young women to be too playful with their male mates in front of others, so no public cuddling or kissing is the rule.

Body Language

This is an area that is relatively undeveloped among the Hmong who prefer to convey their messages directly in words rather than in bodily signs. This does not mean that people do not use body language, but it is not seen and used as deliberately as it sometimes is in the West. People may smile, contort their faces, or grimace in pain. Such messages are easily understood, but people do not generally try to convey subtle or complicated meanings through body language as it is felt that they may be misunderstood or go completely unnoticed. It is considered rude to interpret people's body language and remark on what it may mean when this is an alien concept in Hmong culture. Hmong do, however, use their hands and fingers to convey messages, and shake hands when greeting visitors—a practice adopted from French colonial days in Laos and Vietnam.

Humor

A good sense of humor often helps to make things better, and the Hmong accept this reality. People will try to tell jokes to lighten the atmosphere of a tense situation. A storyteller may add jokes to spice up his or her narrative. In general, however, the Hmong do not like someone who has too much sense of humor. Such a person is seen as not being serious enough about himself and about life, thus not deserving the respect of other people. Often, Hmong are seen as people who are too serious, without a good sense of humor. For this reason, there are not many Hmong who can make a living as comedians, although there are some comical actors in films.

Anger and Aggression

The Hmong have a reputation as some of the best soldiers in the world and were recruited by the French into their colonial army, and later by the CIA into its "secret army" in Laos. This does not mean that they are an aggressive people who would not hesitate to kill or force their way through enemy territories. In general, the Hmong condemn aggression in a person and usually do not approve of pushy assertive types. When angry, the Hmong will scream and shout to let go of the anger. They do not hold it back and suppress it, as they believe it will not go away in this way. For this reason, it is normal to see a husband or wife shouting at each other or at their children when they become angry or frustrated.

Being a Guest

The Hmong traditionally do not ask guests to remove their shoes at the door as the Lao or Thai do, even after they have settled in Western countries and have nice carpeted floors. Some families, however, may now make it a rule. In general, it is best to keep an eye on whether there are a lot of shoes at the front door. If there are, then it is best to remove your shoes. In the villages, where houses have dirt floors, this is not a customary practice. Nor is it the practice in Hmong culture to worry about the sacredness of the head, or the filthiness of feet, as is so important to the Lao or Thai, although some Hmong now have adopted these practices as part of being Southeast Asian settlers in new lands. The Hmong do not expect visitors to give gifts, even if they visit by invitation. This does not mean that gifts cannot be given, but unlike the Japanese, there are no special ways in which to wrap the gift or to hand it over to the host. Gifts may also be exchanged between people who expect favors from each other, whether it is for business or personal reasons. However, visitors will have to be careful not to make the host "lose face" (*poob ntsej muag*). Like other Asian cultures, the Hmong take particular care not to offend other people, and try not to make them "break heart" (*tu siab*). Once a Hmong *tu siab*, it will be forever. It is not something that can be easily "forgiven and forgotten." After an embarrassing exchange or a physical fight, the Hmong do not simply reach out to their opponents and shake hands in the American fashion, to make things get back to normal. This is a big problem with Hmong attitudes and social customs.

GLOBALIZATION AND A NEW GLOBAL IDENTITY

To "globalize" means to extend to other or all parts of the globe; and to make something grow worldwide. Hmong globalization means the spread of the Hmong population and culture into different parts of the world. It can be in several forms, such as:

- settlement of Hmong population as migrants and refugees in different countries, especially after the end of the Indochina war in 1975
- trade and business connections between Hmong living in the United States and other countries
- remittances and economic assistance from relatives in Western countries to those left behind in the old homeland
- visits and travels made by Hmong to other Hmong areas for cultural exchanges, tourism, business, or missionary work
- dissemination and exchange of information through meetings and the media such as videos, radio broadcasting, books, newspapers, and magazines
- raising Hmong profile and global awareness of issues affecting the Hmong in various countries with the U.S. Congress, the European Union Parliament, and the UN by Hmong groups like the Chao Fa's political movement
- transnational translation and mutual borrowing by Hmong of various cultural forms such as costumes, rituals, food and music
- global commercialization of Hmong artifacts such as Hmong herbal medicine and women's costumes
- cyber-community formation through the World Wide Web by Hmong Internet users.

This globalization has now resulted in a new Hmong global consciousness, a new cultural enrichment through diversity. It has brought the Hmong a transnational identity that sharpens mutual awareness between Hmong communities around the world—often, as in the case of Hmong videos, without leaving the comfort of their living rooms and television sets. This new identity and transnational consciousness has made many thousands of Hmong in the diaspora undertake travels each year not only to nearby cities and states but also to other countries, across national and international borders to engage in recreational, social, and economic activities. They are involved in transnational traveling as business people, as visitors to relatives in other far-flung places, as missionaries and propagandists, as searchers after traditional medical remedies for illnesses, and as tourists. Much of this transnational traveling is done to fulfill some deep-seated nostalgia for a village traditional lifestyle that is no longer available in their new settings in Western countries, but above all, to get a taste of "real" Hmong culture by being in a place where they can freely buy and wear traditional costumes or attend the New Year festival or major religious events.

Together with the widespread use of the Internet, this has further helped reinforce the new transnational Hmong identity, making it possible for the Hmong worldwide to affirm the relevance of their changing culture and to keep it alive so that its followers can feel pride in themselves and be seen to contribute to their own and to mainstream society.

Notes

1. Graham 1926, 304.
2. Chindarsi 1976, 77.
3. Lee 1981, 54.
4. Mark 1967, 57. The Chinese call them Yaque Miao, or Magpe Miao, which in Hmong would be Hmoob Yob Tshuab. But they call themselves Hmoob Ntswv.
5. Geddes 1976, 128; Kunstadter 1983, 38.
6. Chindarsi 1976, 79.
7. Binney 1968, 380.
8. Yang, Kao-ly 2004, 108.
9. See also Symonds 2004, ch. 5.
10. Ruey 1960, 154.
11. Yang Dao 1975, 46.
12. Savina 1924, 238.
13. Lee 2005b.
14. Xiong 2004, 149–50.
15. Kim, L., Harrison, G., and Kagawa-Singer, M., 2007. See also Kunstadter, 1992.
16. Hobsbawm 1983, 1–2.
17. Cooper 1980.

Glossary

Englishes

Affinal relations relationships formed through marriage; thus, in-law relationships

Appliqué sewing one piece of material on top of another one

Bridewealth a marriage payment made to the family of the bride

Calabash pumpkin or gourd

Clan a social unit comprising all descendants believed to be related through a common ancestor whose name is, however, unknown

Corvée Labor enforced or unpaid labor owed to a feudal lord or government, compulsory labor as part of the dues owed to an overlord

Cross-cousin (opposite of parallel cousin) a cousin whose parent is of the opposite sex to your own parent, for example, your father's sisters' children or your mother's brothers' children

Culottes knee-length trousers or split skirts

Diaspora the spreading out and expansion of a people from an original central point of origin, such as the Jews from Israel

Euphony pleasing or sweet sound; adding words or particles just for their nice sounds

Exogamy marriage out of one's group

Extended family a family of three or more generations that may include the children of several siblings, such as a joint family (see below) or a stem family (the parents with one married child and spouse)

Geomancy   literally, a system for divining future fortunes through the shapes of the landscape

Insurgent   rebel, rebellious

Joint family   family composed of one or more siblings and their children

Kinship system   a way of reckoning relatedness through ties of blood or marriage

Levirate   worldwide custom of a younger brother marrying the widow of an older brother

Lineage   a social unit comprising all descendants believed to be related through a common ancestor whose name is known

Matrilineal   descending through the female line

Matrilocal   where a newly married couple live in the wife's family's place (in the mother's place, meaning the mother of their children)

Messianic religion   a religion focused on the belief in a savior or Messiah who will bring salvation

Mortise   part of a wooden joint, the cavity in a piece of wood into which the projection from another piece of wood (the tenon) is inserted

Mortuary ritual   ritual associated with death, including the funeral and/or any commemorative rituals later

Moxibustion   burning of an herb, traditionally mugort, on the affected part to increase circulation

Neolocal residence   where a newly married couple live in a place that is not where their parents live

Nuclear family   family composed of parents and children

Pathet Lao   "Lao Country," name for the Lao Communist Party and current government of Laos

Patriarchal   rule of authority by men

Patrilineal   descending in the male line

Patrilocal   where a newly married couple live in the husband's family's place (in the father's place, meaning the father of their children)

Pentatonic   a scale based on five notes, rather than eight as in the octave (as normally understood)

Politburo   short for the Political Bureau, members of the Central Committee of the Communist Party in socialist states

Polyandry   marriage with several husbands

Polygamy   marriage with several wives or husbands

Polygyny   marriage with several wives

Rattan   vine-like forest palm used for making furniture and baskets

Re-education sessions/camps brainwashing and propaganda centers where communists tortured and indoctrinated those they believed to be enemies of the regime

Reincarnation rebirth, the belief that a soul returns to this world after death in another body

Reverse appliqué cutting away a piece of fabric to reveal a design on the material beneath it

Ridgepole horizontal roof beam or timber to which rafters are attached

Segmentary organization a technical term applied by anthropologists to describe a type of political and kinship organization in which each lower-level unit is pitted against each other, but unites against a common enemy against a higher level; example: local football teams play against each other, but may unite together against the teams from another city or area

Shamanism a form of religious practice in which a ritual specialist (the shaman) enters into a state of possessive trance in which he or she is believed to visit or communicate with the supernatural world to search out the causes of human affliction and heal or cure them

Shifting cultivation also known as swidden cultivation, or negatively as slash-and-burn; a method of agriculture in which the land is cleared of growth by burning, then planted and farmed for a number of years after which the land is left fallow and allowed to revert to its natural growth; the cultivation moves to another piece of land

Shingles thin overlapping planks

Subsistence farming farming that is only sufficient to ensure survival, with no surplus production for sale or exchange

Taboo ritual prohibition

Tamping packing something down tightly by a series of repeated blows

Tenon part of a wooden joint, the piece of wood that is inserted into a cavity (the mortise) in another piece of wood

Tributary allegiance refers to tributary system common to pre-colonial Asia; the rulers of small states would pay annual tribute to the rulers of larger states or empires, sometimes to two or three at once, in return for their nominal protection; kengtung, for instance, paid tribute to both Burma and China, and sometimes to Siam

Vernacular common, folk, popular

Vernacular architecture architecture of a folk or local design

Viet Minh North Vietnam communist movement

Winnowing basket a basket in which the rice is tossed repeatedly to separate the chaff from the grain

LATIN

Deus otiosis   a god who has become absent but may be called on or appears at times of human need

CHINESE

Feng shui   (literally winds and waters) a system for aligning houses, villages, and graves with the contours of the landscape, according to a system of beliefs relating time with space and the social with the natural, for example, the north direction is equivalent to winter and is represented by the symbol of the Black Tortoise

Kanyu   the literary term for feng shui

Kuomintang   the Chinese Nationalist Party

Minzu   the official term for an ethnic 'nationality' in China

HMONG

Cab   the tool used for batik

Caiv   taboo, prohibition

Dab   spirits

Dab nyeg   domestic, or household spirits

Dab qhuas   a term which can be used to refer to the household spirits; those identifying as of one *dab qhuas* (*ib tus dab qhuas*) share the same ancestral spirits and are therefore considered to be closely related, of one sub-lineage

Dab qus   wild spirits

Daim   an amulet in the form of a square engraved silver platelet suspended from the neck

Faib dab tshuaj   to separate the spirits of medicine

Hu plig   to call (re-call) the soul

Kab ke   customs, ways

Kev cai   customs, ways

Khi tes   tying the wrists, in a ritual to conserve the soul with the body

Kuam neeb   divination horns

Kwv txhiaj   a category of songs (*kwv txhiaj plees* are lovesongs)

Lub qhov cub   the main hearth

Lub ntos   weaving loom

Lwm qaib   to exorcise (malign influences) through the use of a fowl

Lwm sub   to exorcise malign influences

Me nyuam hav zoo   a "wild" child (a child with no living father)

Me nyuam tsaub   a child born out of wedlock

Muag   face

Nees   horse

Neeb   tutelary spirits of the shaman

Noj mov   eat rice

Noj peb caug   "eat 30th" (the New Year)

Noj tsuas   eat food

Ntaus kuam   to throw the divination horns

Ntaus tuj lub   play tops

Ntoo xeeb   holy tree

Ntuj   heaven

Nyiav   lament

Paj ntaub   embroidery

Pe   to pay respects by prostrating on the floor (different from *ua tsaug* or thanking standing up with cupped hands)

Plig   soul

Pov pob   play catch

Qeej   the reed pipes

Qeej tu siav   the piped tune for the expiry of life

Qhov rooj   the door

Qhuab ke   opening the way—the song sung at death to open or point or guide the Way to the Beyond for the dead person

Rab hneev   crossbow

Saib loojmem   to search out or "sight" the "veins of the dragon" (see Geomancy)

Tis npe   giving a name

Tshuab qeej   blow the pipes

Tso plig   ritual to "release the soul" held some months or years after death

Txiv neeb   shaman (whether male or female)

Ua   to do, make

Ua dab   to perform rituals for/to the spirits (excluding shamanism)

Ua neeb   shamanism, to do a shamanic trance

Ua neeb kho   shamanism to heal

Ua neeb saib   shamanism to "see" or diagnose

Ua nyuj dab   ritual that may be performed, using a sacrificial bull, some years after death for the soul of a deceased parent

Xi plig   ritual to invite the soul of the recently buried dead home for a final meal before dispatch for rebirth

Xyooj tshiab   New Year

Yaj ceeb   this world, the world of the living

Yeej ceeb   the spiritual world

Further Readings

Castle, Timothy. *At War in the Shadow of Vietnam*. New York: Columbia University Press, 1993.

Cha, Dia, Steve Carmen, and Mai Zong Vue. *Field Guide to Hmong Culture*. Madison, WI: Madison Children's Museum, 2004.

Chan, Sucheng, ed. *Hmong Means Free: Life in Laos and America*. Philadelphia: Temple University Press, 1994.

Cohen, Erik. *The Commercialized Crafts of Thailand: Hill Tribes and Lowland Villages*. Richmond, VA: Curzon Press, 2000.

Colboy, Kenneth. *Shadow War: The CIA's Secret War in Laos*. Boulder, CO: Paladin Press, 1995.

Cooper, Robert, ed. *The Hmong*. Singapore: Times Editions, 1998.

Culhane-Pera, Kathleen A., Dorothy E. Vawter, Phua Xiong, and Barbara Babbitt. *Healing by Heart: Clinical and Ethical Case Stories of Hmong Families and Western Providers*. Nashville, TN: Vanderbilt University Press, 2003.

Detzner, Daniel F. *Elder Voices: Southeast Asian Families in the United States*. Walnut Creek, CA: AltaMira Press, 2004.

Downing, Bruce T., and Douglas Olney, eds. *The Hmong in the West*. Minneapolis: Center for Urban and Regional Affairs, University of Minnesota, 1982.

DC Everest Area Schools. *The Hmong and Their Stories*. Weston, WI: DC Everest Schools Publications, 2001.

———. *The Hmong in the Modern World*. Weston, WI: DC Everest Schools Publications, 2005.

———. *Looking Back, Stepping Forward: The Hmong People*. Weston, WI: DC Everest Schools Publications, 2008.

Fadiman, Anne. *The Spirit Catches You and You Fall Down*. New York: Farrar, Straus and Giroux, 1997.

Geddes, William. *Migrants of the Mountains*. Oxford, UK: Clarendon Press, 1976.

Hamilton-Merritt, Jane. *Tragic Mountains: The Hmong, the Americans, and the Secret War for Laos, 1942–1992*. Bloomington: Indiana University Press, 1999.

Hassoun, Pierre. *Les Hmong du Laos en France*. Paris: Presse Universitaire de France, 1997.

Hendricks, Glenn, Bruce Downing, and Amos Deinard, eds. *The Hmong in Transition*. New York: Center for Migration Studies, 1986.

John Michael Kohler Arts Center. *Hmong Art: Tradition and Change*. Sheboygan, WI: JMKA Center, 1986.

Graham, D.C. *Songs and Stories of the Ch'uan Miao*. Washington, DC: Smithsonian Institution, 1954.

Johnson, Charles. *Myths, Legends and Folk Tales from the Hmong of Laos*. St. Paul, MN: Linguistics Department, Macalester College, 1998.

Keown-Bomar, Julie. *Kinship Networks among Hmong-American Refugees*. New York: LFB Scholarly Publishing, 2004, Ch. 5.

Livo, Norma, and Dia Cha. *Folk Stories of the Hmong: Peoples of Laos, Thailand and Vietnam*. Boulder, CO: Libraries Unlimited, 1991.

Long, Lynellyn. *Ban Vinai: The Refugee Camp*. New York: Columbia University Press, 1992.

McLuhan, Marshall. *The Gutenberg Galaxy: The Making of Typographic Man*. Toronto: University of Toronto Press, 1962.

Mote, Sue Murphy. *Hmong and American: Stories of Transition to a Strange Land*. Jefferson, NC: McFarland, 2004.

Mottin, Jean. *History of the Hmong*. Bangkok: Odeon Stores, 1980.

Moua, M. N., ed. *Bamboo among the Oaks: Contemporary Writing by Hmong Americans*. St. Paul, MN: Minnesota Historical Society, 2002.

Mua, Naw-Karl. *Hmong Marriage in America: The Paradigm Shift for a Healthy Generation*. Bangkok: Prachoomthong Printing, 2002.

Pfeifer, Mark. *Hmong-Related Research and Literature: Past, Present and Future Directions*. St. Paul, MN: Hmong Culture Center, 2003. See also other bibliographies by Pfeiffer available at http://hmongcultural.stores.yahoo.net/hmonres1800p.html.

———. *Hmong Related Works, 1996–2006: An Annotated Bibliography*. Lanham, MD: Scarecrow Press, 2007.

Quincy, Keith. *Harvesting Pa Chay's Wheat*. Cheney, WA: East Washington State University Press, 2000.

Ranard, Donald A. *The Hmong: An Introduction to Their History and Culture*. Washington, DC: Center for Applied Linguistics, 2005.

Savina, F. M. *Histoire des Miao*. Hong Kong: Société des Missions Étrangères, 1924.

Symonds, Patricia V. *Calling in the Soul: Gender and the Cycle of Life in a Hmong Village*. Seattle: University of Washington Press, 2004.

Tapp, Nicholas. *Sovereignty and Rebellion: The White Hmong of Northern Thailand*. Singapore: Oxford University Press, 1989.

———. *The Hmong of China: Context, Agency and the Imaginary*. Leiden: Brill, 2001.

———. "Problems of Cultural Translation among the Canadian Hmong," *Australasian Canadian Studies* 22, no. 2; 23, no. 1 2005.

———. "Hmong Diaspora." In *Encyclopedia of Diasporas: Immigrant and Refugee Cultures around the World*. Vol. 1, *Overviews and Topics*, edited by Melvin Ember, Carol R. Ember, and Ian Skoggard. New York: Kluwer Academic/Plenum, in association with the Human Relations Area Files (Yale University), 2004.

Tapp, Nicholas, J. Michaud, C. Culas, and G. Lee, eds. *Hmong/Miao in Asia*. Chiangmai: Silkworms Books, 2004.

Tapp, Nicholas, and Gary Lee, eds. *The Hmong People of Australia: Culture and Diaspora*. Canberra: Pandanus Books, 2004.

Tomforde, Maren. *The Hmong Mountains: Cultural Spatiality of the Hmong in Northern Thailand*. Hamburg: Lit Verlag, 2006.

Tsheej, Vwj Zoov. *Haiv Hmoob Lij Xwm*. Quezon City: Patrimoine Hmong, 2004.

Warner, Roger. *Shooting at the Moon: The Story of America's Clandestine War in Laos*. Hanover, NH: Steerforth Press, 1998.

Vang, Lue, and Judy Lewis. *Grandmother's Way, Grandfather's Path*. Rancho Cordova, CA: Authors, 1990.

Yang, Dao. *Hmong at the Turning Point*. Minneapolis: WorldBridge Associates, 1993.

Yang, Kao Kalia. *The Latehomecomers: A Hmong Family Memoir*. Minneapolis: Coffee House Press, 2008.

LPs, Videos, and DVDs

US Central Intelligence Agency, *Journey from Pha Dong: a Decision in the Hill*, 1967. Produced by the CIA, this video documented the alliance between the Hmong led by Gen. Vang Pao and the United States as they jointly fought to contain the spread of communism in Southeast Asia. Available from Hmong Arts, Books and Crafts shop, St. Paul, Minnesota, and online at http://www.hmongabc.com.

Geddes, W. R. *Miao Year*. 62 mins. CRM McGraw Hill Films, 1968; 1971. An ethnographic film made by a pioneer in Hmong studies about Hmong traditional village life in Thiland in the 1960s. Available from McGraw Hill, and some tertiary libraries.

Granada Television. *The Meo* (*Disappearing World* series), 1972. 52 mins. color. DVD or VHS/PAL. Directors Brian Moser, Jacques Lemoine. Available for sale from the Royal Anthropological Institute, London (http://www.therai.org.uk/film/), and many school and university libraries.

Musique des Hmong du Laos: Cour d'Amour et Culte des Ancêtres (Anthologie de la musique des peuples). Long-playing record issued by SFPP (Société Française de productions Phonographiques—Paris); FP8: 8-2911. Also on

CD (CDQ-74CN) with the same title, by Sony France S.A. (made in Taiwan), 1981.

Rob, G. *Secret War: an Exit Strategy in Action*, 2007. This DVD is based on interviews with Hmong and CIA leaders involved in the secret war in Laos and shows how they tried to find a way out. Available from Hmongabc.com

Schofield, Steve. *A Brief History of the Hmong and the Secret War in Laos*, 2004. Available from the Hmong Archives, 298 1/2 University Avenue West, St. Paul, MN, and online at http://www.hmongarchives.org/.

Xiong, Yuepheng. *Taug Txoj Lw Ntshav (Follow the Blood Trail)*. vols. 1, 2, and 3.

———. *Hmong Gen. Vang Pao and the Secret War in Laos*, vols.1 and 2, These videos document Hmong history in China and Laos, and are available from Hmong ABC shop at 298 University Avenue West, St. Paul, MN 55103; and online at http://www.hmongabc.com

Bibliography

Anderson, J. *Mandalay to Momien: A Narrative of Two Expeditions to Western China of 1868 and 1875*. London: Macmillan, 1876.

Armstrong, J. A. "Mobilized and Proletarian Diasporas," *The American Political Science Review* 70, no. 2 (1976): 393–408.

Barney, George Linwood. "Christianity and Innovation in Meo Culture: A Case Study in Missionization." Unpub. MA thesis, University of Minnesota, 1957.

Bender, Mark. Review of *Miaozu guge yu Miaozu lishi wenhua yanjiu (A Study of the Ancient Songs of the Miao Nationality and Miao Naionality History and Culture)*, by Wu Yiwen and Tan Dongping. *Asian Folklore Studies* 60, no. 2 (2001): 368–69.

———. *Plum and Bamboo: China's Suzhou Chantefable Tradition*. Urbana: University of Illinois Press, 2003.

———. *Butterfly Mother: Miao (Hmong) Creation Epics from Guizhou, China*. Indianapolis: Hackett Publishing, 2006.

Bernatzik, H. R. *Akha and Miao: Problems of Applied Ethnography in Farther India*. New Haven, CT: Human Relations Area Files, Yale University, 1970.

Bertrais, Yves. *Dictionnaire Hmong-Francaise*. Vientiane: Mission Catholique, 1964.

———. *Traditional Marriage among the White Hmong of Thailand and Laos*. Chiangmai: Hmong Studies Center, 1978.

———. *Dab Neeg Hmoob* (3 volumes). Javouhey: Patrimoine Culturel Hmong, 1985.

————. *Kab Ke Pam Tuag: Cov Zaj (Funeral Rites: Chants and Recitations)*. Javouhey: Patrimoine Hmong Culturel, 1986.

————. *Dab Neeg Kwv Txhiaj Keeb Kwm Nyob Moos Laj*. Javouhey: Patrimoine Culturel Hmong, 1992.

————. *How the Hmong RPA Was Created and Has Spread from 1953 to 1991*. Javouhey: Patrimoine Culturel Hmong, 2002.

Bessac, S. L. *Embroidered Hmong Story Cloths*. Missoula: University of Montana, 1988.

Binney, G. A. *Social Structure and Shifting Agriculture of the White Meo*, Final Technical Report, Washington, DC: Wildlife Management Institute, 1968.

Blackburn, Stuart. "Oral Stories and Culture Areas: from Northeast India to Southwest China," *South Asia: Journal of South Asian Studies* N.S. 30, no.3 (2007): 419–37.

Bliatout, Bruce. *Hmong Sudden Unexpected Nocturnal Death Syndrome: A Cultural Study*. Portland, Oregon: Sparkle Inc., 1982.

Catlin, A., and D. Swift. *Textiles as Texts: Arts of Hmong Women from Laos*. Los Angeles: The Women's Building, 1987.

Cha, Dia. *Hmong American Concepts of Health, Healing and Conventional Medicine*. New York and London: Routledge, 2003.

————, S. Carmen, and M. Z. Vue. *Field Guide to Hmong Culture*. Madison, WI: Madison Children's Museum, 2004.

Chan, A., and N. Livo. *Hmong Textile Designs*. Owings Mills, MD: Stemmer House, 1990.

Chen, K. C., and T. L. Wu. *Studies of the Society of Miao and Yi Tribes of Kwei-chow*. Kwei Yang: Kwei Yang Wen Shu T'ung Chii. [In Chinese], 1942.

Chindarsi, Nusit. *The Religion of the Hmong Njua*. Bangkok: The Siam Society, 1976.

Clarke, Samuel W. *Among the Tribes in South-West China*. London: China Inland Mission, 1911.

Clifford, James. *Routes: Travel and Translation in the Late Twentieth Century*. Cambridge, MA: Harvard University Press, 1997.

Cohen, Erik. *The Commercialized Crafts of Thailand: Hill Tribes and Lowland Villages*. Richmond, VA: Curzon Press, 2000.

Cohen, Robin. "Diasporas and the Nation-State: From Victims to Challengers," *International Affairs* 72, no. 3 (1996): 507–20.

————. *Global Diasporas: An Introduction*. London: University College of London Press, 1997.

Conquergood, D. "Health Theatre in a Hmong Refugee Camp: Performance, Communication and Culture." In *Internationalizing Cultural Studies: An Anthology*, edited by Ackbar Abbas and John Nguyet Erni. Malden, MA: Blackwell, 2005.

Cooper, Robert. "Unity and Division in Hmong Social Categories in Thailand." In *Studies in ASEAN Sociology*, edited by P. S. J. Chen and H. D. Evers. Singapore: Chopmen, 1978.

————. *Patterns of Work Organization in a Situation of Agricultural Transition*. (Occasional Paper no. 62). Singapore: Institute of Southeast Asian Studies, 1980.

————. *Resource Scarcity and the Hmong Response: Patterns of Settlement and Economy in Transition*. Singapore: National University of Singapore, 1984.

————. *The Hmong: A Guide to Current Lifestyles*. Singapore: Times Editions, 1998.

Culas, Christian, and Jean Michaud. "A Contribution to the Study of Hmong (Miao) Migrations and History." In *Hmong/Miao in Asia*, edited by Nicholas Tapp, Jean Michaud, Christian Culas, and Gary Yia Lee. Chiangmai: Silkworm Books, 2004.

Culhane-Pera, Kathleen, Dorothy Vawter, Phua Xiong, Barbara Babbitt, and Mary Solberg, eds. *Healing by Heart: Clinical and Ethical Case Studies of Hmong Families and Western Providers*. Nashville: Vanderbilt University Press, 2003.

————, Dia Cha, and Peter Kunstadter. "Hmong in Laos and the United States." In *Encyclopaedia of Medical Anthropology: Health and Illness in the World's Cultures*, edited by Carol and Melvyn Ember. Berlin: Springer, 2004.

Culler, Jonathan. *Literary Theory: A Very Short Introduction*. Oxford: Oxford University Press, 1997.

De Beauclair, Inez. "A Miao Tribe of Southeast Kweichow and Its Cultural Configuration." In *Tribal Cultures of Southwest China*. Taipei: The Orient Cultural Service, 1970.

Diamond, Norma. "Defining the Miao: Ming, Qing, and Contemporary Views." In *Cultural Encounters on China's Ethnic Frontiers*, edited by Stevan Harrell. Seattle: University of Washington Press, 1995.

Donnelly, Nancy. *Changing Lives of Refugee Hmong Women*. Seattle: University of Washington Press, 1994.

Dowman, Scott. "Intra-Ethnic Conflict among the Hmong in Australia and Thailand." Unpub. PhD diss., Griffith University, 2004.

Eliade, Mircea. *Shamanism: Archaic Techniques of Ecstasy*. London: Routledge and Kegan Paul, 1964.

Errington, S. *The Death of Authentic Primitive Art and Other Tales of Progress*. Berkeley: University of California Press, 1998.

Evans, Grant. *The Yellow Rainmakers: Are Chemical Weapons Being Used in Southeast Asia?* London: Verso Editions, 1983.

Falk, C. "Hmong Instructions to the Dead: What the Mouth Organ Qeej Says," *Asian Folklore Studies* 63 (2004): 1–29.

Feith, David. *Stalemate: Refugees in Asia*. Parkville, Victoria: Asian Bureau Australia, 1988.

Feng, D. R., and L. G. Kilborn. "Dyestuffs Used by the Ch'uan Miao," *Journal of the West China Border Research Society* 10 (1937): 144–51.

Feuchtwang, Stephan. *An Anthropological Analysis of Chinese Geomancy*. Vientiane: Editions Vithagna, 1974.

Fichner-Rathus, L. *Understanding Art*. Englewood Cliffs, NJ: Prentice Hall, 1995.

Finkle, Kathy. *Hmong Recipe Cook Book*. St. Paul, MN: United Presbyterian Church, 2003.

Flinn, Adam. "World Beater: Long-Haired Record Smashed Twice," *Thaifocus Travel News*, August 1988. Available at http://www.thaifocus.com/news/stories/longhair.htm.

Forsyth, Tim, and Andrew Walker. *Forest Guardians, Forest Destroyers: The Politics of Environmental Knowledge in Northern Thailand*. Seattle: University of Washington Press, 2008.

Freedman, Maurice. "Geomancy." In *The Study of Chinese Society: Essays by Maurice Freedman*, edited by George Skinner. Palo Alto, CA: Stanford University Press, 1979.

Gallego, Carlos. "The Significance of Culture in Hmong Art," *Asian American Press* (March 23 [Part 1] and April 7 [Part 2], 2008).

Garrett, W. E. "The Hmong of Laos: No Place to Run," *National Geographic* 154, no.1 (January 1974): 78–111.

Geddes, William R. *Migrants of the Mountains: The Cultural Ecology of the Blue Miao (Hmong Njua) of Thailand*. Oxford, UK: The Clarendon Press. 1976.

Giacchino-Baker, R., ed. *Stories from Laos: Folktales and Cultures of the Lao, Hmong, Khammu and Iu-Mien*. El Monte, CA: Pacific Asia Press, 1995.

Graham, David C. "The Chuan Miao of West China," *Journal of Religion* 6, no. 3 (1926): 302–307.

———. "The Customs of the Ch'uan Miao," *Journal of the West China Border Research Society* 9 (1937): 13–71.

———. *Songs and Stories of the Ch'uan Miao*. Washington, DC: The Smithsonian Institution, 1954.

Granet, Marcel. *Chinese Civilization*. London: Kegan Paul, 1930.

Hamilton-Merritt, Jane. "Poison Gas War in Laos," *Reader's Digest* (October 1980).

———. *Tragic Mountains: The Hmong, the Americans, and the Secret Wars for Laos, 1942–1992*. Bloomington and Indianapolis: Indiana University Press, 1993.

Hartley, L. P. *The Go-Between*. Harmonsworth, UK: Penguin Books, 1988.

Heimbach, Ernest. *White Hmong-English Dictionary* (rev. ed.). Southeast Asia Program Data Papers, No. 75. Ithaca, NY: Cornell Southeast Asia Program, 1979.

"Hmong Legislators Say Cultural Marriage Bill Is Unnecessary," *Minnesota Public Radio*, March 20, 2006, at http://minnesota.publicradio.org/display/web/2006/03/20/hmongmarriage/.

Hobsbawm, E. "Introduction: Inventing Traditions." In *The Invention of Tradition*, edited by E. Hobsbawm and T. Ranger. Cambridge, UK: Cambridge University Press, 1983.

Huang, Hao, and Bussakorn Sumrongthong. "Speaking with Spirits: The Hmong Ntoo Xeeb Ceremony," *Asian Folklore Studies* 63 (2004): 31–55.

Hudspeth, W. H. "The Cult of the Door amongst the Miao in South-West China," *Folk-Lore*, 33 (1922): 406–10.

————. *Stone Gate-Way and the Flowery Miao*. London: The Cargate Press, 1937.

Jenks, Robert. *Insurgency and Social Disorder in Guizhou: The "Miao" Rebellion, 1854–74*. Honolulu: University of Hawaii Press, 1994.

John Michael Kohler Arts Centre. *Hmong Art: Tradition and Change*. Sheboygan, WI: JMKAC, 1986.

Johns, B. "An Introduction to White Hmong Sung Poetry." In *The Hmong World*, edited by B. Johns and D. Strecker, D. New Haven, CT: Council on Southeast Asia Studies, 1986.

Johnson, C. *Myths, Legends and Folk Stories of the Hmong from Laos*. St. Paul, MN: Macalister College, 1992.

Keen, F. G. B. "Ecological Relationships in a Hmong (Meo) Economy." In *Farmers in the Forest: Economic Development and Marginal Agriculture in Northern Thailand*, edited by P. Kunstadter et al. Honolulu: University of Hawaii Press, 1978.

Keyes, Charles. "Buddhism and National Integration in Thailand," *Journal of Asian Studies* 30, no. 3 (May 1971): 551–67.

Kim, L., G. Harrison, and M. Kagawa-Singer. "Perceptions of diet and physical activity among California Hmong adults and youths." *Preventing Chronic Disease: Public Health Research, Practice and Policy* 4, no. 4 (2007). Available at www.cdc.gov/pcd/issues/2007/oct/07_0074.htm. Accessed 16 May 2010.

Kunstadter, Peter. "Highland Populations in North Thailand." In *Highlanders of Thailand*, edited by Wanat Bhruksasri and John McKinnon. Kuala Lampur: Oxford University Press, 1983.

————. "Epidemiological Consequences of Migration and Rapid Cultural Change: Non-Refugee Hmong in Thailand and Refugees in California." Paper presented at the Australian Center for International and Tropical Health, University of Brisbane, July16–17, 1992.

————. "Hmong Marriage Patterns in Thailand in Relation to Social Change." In *Hmong/Miao in Asia*, edited by Nicholas Tapp, Jean Michaud, Christian Culas, and Gary Yia Lee, 375–420. Chiangmai: Silkworm Books, 2004.

Lee, Gary Yia. "Effects of Development Measures on the Socio-economy of the White Hmong," Unpub. PhD diss., University of Sydney, 1981.

————. "Minority Policies and the Hmong in Laos." In *Contemporary Laos: Studies in the Politics and Society of the Lao People's Democratic Republic*, edited by Martin Stuart-Fox. St. Lucia: University of Queensland Press, 1982.

————. "Household and Marriage in a Thai Highland Society," *Journal of the Siam Society* 76 (1988): 162–73. Available at www.garyyialee.com.

————. "The Religious Presentation of Social Relationships: Hmong World View and Social Structure," *Lao Studies Review* 2 (1994–1996): 44–60.

————. *Dust of Life*. St. Paul, MN: Hmongland Publishing, 2004.

————. "Bandits or Rebels? Hmong Resistance in the New Lao State," 2005a. Available at www.garyyialee.com.

———. "The Shaping of Traditions: Agriculture and Hmong Society," *Hmong Studies Journal* 6 (2005b).

———. "Hmong Postwar Identity Production: Heritage Maintenance and Cultural Reinterpretation." In *Cultural Heritage in Postwar Recovery*, edited by N. Stanley-Price, N. Rome: International Centre for the Study of the Preservation and Restoration of Cultural Property, 2007.

———. "Refugees from Laos: Background and Causes," 2008. Available at www.garyyialee.com.

Lee, Nyiaj Pov. *Vim Leej Twg (Because of Who)*. Bonnyrigg: Rooj Ntawv Hmoob, 1985.

———. *Lub Neej Daitaw (A Dependent Life)*. Bonnyrigg: Rooj Ntawv Hmoob, 1986.

———. *Neej Kua Muag (A Tearful Life)*. Bonnyrigg: Rooj Ntawv Hmoob, 1989.

———. *Txoj Sawvlhub (The Love Chain)*. Bonnyrigg: Rooj Ntawv Hmoob, 1990.

Leepreecha, Prasit. *The Hmong Proverbs*. Chiangmai: Social Research Institute (in Hmong and Thai), 1994.

———. "Kinship and Identity among Hmong in Thailand." Unpub. PhD diss., Seattle: University of Washington, 2000.

———. "Ntoo Xeeb: Cultural Redefinition for Forest Conservation among the Hmong in Thailand." In *Hmong/Miao in Asia*, edited by Nicholas Tapp, Jean Michaud, Christian Culas, and Gary Yia Lee. Chiangmai: Silkworm Books, 2004.

———. "The Role of Media Technology in Reproducing Hmong Ethnic Identity." In *Living in a Globalized World: Ethnic Minorities in the Greater Mekong Subregion*, edited by Don McCaskill, Prasit Leepreecha, and He Shaoying. Bangkok: Mekong Press, 2008.

Lemoine, Jacques. *Un Village Hmong Vert du Haut Laos*. Paris: Centre National de la Recherche Scientifique, 1972a.

———. "L'Initiation du mort chez les Hmong," *L'Homme*. XII (1, 2, 3): 105–34; 85–125; 84–110 (1972b).

———. "Shamanism in the Context of Hmong Resettlement." In *The Hmong in Transition*, edited by Glenn Hendricks, Bruce Downing, and Amos Deinard. New York: Center for Migration Studies, 1986.

———. *Entre la Maladie et la Mort : Le Chamane Hmong sur les chemins de l'Au-delà*. Bangkok: Pandora, 1987.

———. "Les Hmong et les Yao." In *Montagnards de pays d'Indochine dans les collections du Musée de l'Homme*, edited by Christine Hemmet. Paris: Editions Sepia, 1995.

———. "What Is the Actual Number of the (H)mong in the World?," *Hmong Studies Journal* 6 (2005).

———. "To Tell the Truth," *Hmong Studies Journal* 9 (2008).

———, and Christine Mougne. "Why Has Death Stalked the Refugees?" *Natural History* 92 (1983): 6–19.

Lewis, J. A. "Hmong Visual, Oral and Social Design: Innovation within a Frame of the Familiar." Unpub. MA diss., California State University, Sacramento, 1993.

Lewis, Paul, and Elaine Lewis. *Peoples of the Golden Triangle*. London: Thames and Hudson, 1984.

Lin Yueh-hwa (Lin Yaohua). "The Miao-Man Peoples of Kweichow," *Harvard Journal of Asiatic Studies* 5, nos. 3–4 (1940).

Livo, N., and Dia Cha. *Folk Stories of the Hmong of Vietnam, Laos and Thailand*. Englewood, CO: Libraries Unlimited, 1991.

Lombard-Salmon, Claudine. *Un Exemple d'Acculturation Chinoise: La Province du Gui Zhou au XVIIIe Siècle*. Paris: L'Ecole Française de l'Extrême-Orient, 1972.

Long, Lynellyn. *Ban Vinai: The Refugee Camp*. New York: Columbia University Press, 1992.

Lyman, Thomas A. "A Note on the Ethno-Semantics of Proverb Usage in Mong Njua (Green Hmong)." In *Hmong/Miao in Asia*, edited by Nicholas Tapp, Jean Michaud, Christian Culas, and Gary Lee. Chiangmai: Silkworms Books, 2004.

MacDowell, M. *Stories in Thread: Hmong Pictorial Embroidery*. Ann Arbor: Michigan State University Museum, 1989.

Mareschal, Eric. *La Musique des Hmong*. Paris: Musée Guimet, 1976.

Margary, A. R. *The Journey of Augustus Raymond Margary, from Shanghai to Bhamo, and Back to Manwyne*. London: Macmillan, 1876.

Mark, L. L. "Patrilateral Cross-cousin Marriage among the Magpie Miao," *American Anthropologist* 69, no. 1 (1967): 55–62.

Marx, Karl. *Precapitalist Economic Formations*. Edited by E. J. Hobsbawm. New York: International Publishers, 1965.

McCarthy, James. "Across China from Chin-kiang to Bhamo," *Proceedings of the Royal Geographical Society* 8, no. 1 (1879): 489–509.

McCoy, Alfred. *The Politics of Heroin in Southeast Asia*. New York, London: Harper & Row, 1972.

McKinnon, John, and Jean Michaud. "Introduction: Montagnard Domain in the South-East Asian Massif." In *Turbulent Times and Enduring Peoples: Mountain Minorities in the South-East Asian Massif*, edited by Jean Michaud. Richmond, VA: Curzon Press, 2000.

McLuhan, Marshall. *The Gutenberg Galaxy: The Making of Typographic Man*. Toronto: University of Toronto Press, 1962.

McMahon, Daniel. "Identity and Conflict on a Chinese Borderland: Yan Ruyi and the Recruitment of the Gelao during the 1795–97 Miao Revolt," *Late Imperial China* 23, no. 2 (December 2002): 53–86.

Mickey, M. P. *The Cowrie Shell Miao of Kweichow*. Cambridge, MA: Peabody Museum, 1947.

Morley, D., and K. Robins. *Spaces of Identity: Global Media, Electronic Landscapes and Cultural Boundaries*. London: Routledge, 1995.

Mottin, Jean. *Eléments de Grammaire Hmong Blanc*. Khek Noy: Don Bosco Press, 1978.

———. *Fêtes du Nouval An chez les Hmong Blanc du Thäilande*. Bangkok: Don Bosco Press, 1979.

———. *History of the Hmong*. Bangkok: Odeon Store Ltd., 1980a.

———. *55 Chants d'Amour Hmong Blanc*. Bangkok: Don Bosco Press, 1980b.

———. *Allons Faire le Tour du Ciel et de la Terre: Le chamanisme des Hmong vu dans les textes*. Bangkok: Don Bosco Press, 1982.

———. "A Hmong Shaman's Séance," *Asian Folklore Studies* 43 (1984): 99–108.

Moua, Mai Neng, ed. *Bamboo among the Oaks: Contemporary Writing by Hmong Americans*. St. Paul, MN: Minnesota Historical Society, 2002.

Numrich. C. H. *Living Tapestries: Folk Tales of the Hmong*. Lima, OH: Fairway Press, 1985.

Olney, Doug. *A Bibliography of the Hmong (Miao)*. Minneapolis, MN: University of Minnesota Southeast Asian Refugee Studies Project, 1983.

Parsons, R. Keith, and P. Kenneth Parsons, trans. *Songs and Stories and a Glossary of Phrases of the Hua Miao of South West China*. Available at www.archives. ecs.soton.ac.uk/miao (accessed 18 May 2010).

Peterson, Sally. "A Cool Heart and a Watchful Mind: Creating Hmong Paj Ntaub in the Context of Community." In *Pieced by Mother: Symposium Papers*, edited by J. Lasansky. Lewisburg, PA: Oral Traditions Project, 1988a.

———. "Translating Experience and the Reading of a Story Cloth," *Journal of American Folklore* 101, no. 399 (1988b): 6–22.

Pfeifer, Mark. *Hmong Related Works, 1996–2006: An Annotated Bibliography*. Lanham, MD: Scarecrow Press, 2007.

Pollard, Samuel. *The Story of the Miao*. London: Henry Hooks, 1919.

Proschan, Frank. "Peoples of the Gourd: Imagined Ethnicities in Highland Southeast Asia," *Journal of Asian Studies* 60, no. 4 (2001): 999–1032.

Race, Jeffrey. "The War in Northern Thailand," *Modern Asian Studies* 8, no. 1 (1974): 85–112.

Ranard, D. A. *The Hmong: An Introduction to Their History and Culture*. Washington, DC: Center for Applied Linguistics, 2005.

Romero, Simon. "From a Hinterland, Hmong Forge a Home," *New York Times*, December 22, 2008. Available at www.nytimes.com/2008/12/22/world/americas/22guiana.html.

Rubin, W., ed. *Primitivism in 20th Century Art: Affinity of the Tribal and the Modern*. Boston: Little Brown, 1984.

Ruey, Yih Fu. "The Magpie Miao of Southern Szechwan." In *Social Structure in Southeast Asia*, edited by G. P. Murdock, G.P. Chicago: Quadrangle Books, 1960.

———. "The Miao: Their Origins and Southwards Expansion," *Proceedings of the International Conference of Historians of Asia* (Second Biennial Conference), Taipei, 1962.

Savina, François-Marie. *Histoire des Miao.* Hong Kong: Imprimerie de la Société des Missions-Etrangères, 1924.

Schein, Louisa. "Importing Miao Brethren to Hmong America: A Not-So-Stateless Transnationalism." In *Cosmopolitics: Thinking and Feeling beyond the Nation,* edited by Bruce Robbins and Pheng Cheah. Minneapolis: University of Minnesota Press, 1998.

————. *Minority Rules: The Miao and the Feminine in China's Cultural Politics.* Durham, NC: Duke University Press, 2000.

————. "Homeland Beauty: Transnational Longing and Hmong American Video," *Journal of Asian Studies* 63, no. 2 (2004a): 433–63.

————. "Hmong/Miao Transnationality: Identity Beyond Culture." In *Hmong/Miao in Asia,* edited by Nicholas Tapp, Jean Michaud, Christian Culas, and Gary Yia Lee, 273–290. Chiangmai: Silkworm Books, 2004b.

————. "Eastwood's Next Film Features Hmong American Cast: Exclusive Interviews from the Set of Gran Torino," *Asian Week,* 3 October 2008. Available at http://www.asianweek.com/2008/10/03/eastwoods-next-film-features-hmong-american-cast-exclusive-interviews-from-the-set-of-gran-torino/. Accessed 19 July 2008.

Schell, Justin. "Art Note: Intergenerational Exhibit Remixes Hmong traditions," *TC Daily Planet,* July 12, 2008.

Seagrave, Sterling. *Yellow Rain: Chemical Warfare—The Deadliest Arms Race.* London: Sphere Books, 1981.

Siegle, Evan. "Wisconsin man charged with murder in Hmong hunter's death," *USA Today* (16 January 2007). Available at http://www.usatoday.com/news/nation/2007-01-16-hunter-homicide_x.htm. Accessed 23 May 2010.

Skinner, George William. "Marketing and Social Structure in Rural China," *Journal of Asian Studies* XXIV, nos. 1, 2, 3 (November 1964; February and May 1965).

Smalley, William, Chia Koua Vang, and Gnia Yee Yang. *Mother of Writing: The Origin and Development of a Hmong Messianic Script.* Chicago: University of Chicago Press, 1990.

Smith, J. C. *The Hmong: an Annotated Bibliography, 1983–1987.* Minneapolis, MN: University of Minnesota Southeast Asian Refugee Studies Project, 1988.

Sutton, Donald. "Ethnicity and the Miao Frontier in the Eighteenth Century." In *Empire at the Margins: Culture, Ethnicity and Frontier in Early Modern China,* edited by Donald Sutton, Pamela Crossley, and Helen Siu (eds). Berkeley: University of California Press, 2006.

Symonds, Patricia. *Calling in the Soul: Gender and the Cycle of Life in a Hmong Village.* Seattle: University of Washington Press, 2004.

Tapp, Nicholas. *Sovereignty and Rebellion: The White Hmong of Northern Thailand.* Oxford and Singapore: Oxford University Press, 1989.

————. *The Hmong of China.* Boston: Brill Academic Publishers, 2003.

————. "Hmong Diaspora." In *Encyclopedia of Diasporas: Immigrant and Refugee Cultures around the World (Vol. 1. Overviews and Topics),* edited by Melvin

Ember, Carol R. Ember and Ian Skoggard. New York, Boston, Dordrecht, London, Moscow: Kluwer Academic/Plenum Publishers in association with the Human Relations Area Files (Yale University), 2004.

———. "The Consuming or the Consumed? Virtual Hmong in China." In *Consuming China: Approaches to cultural change in contemporary China*, edited by Kevin Latham, S. Thompson and J. Klein. London and New York: Routledge, 2006.

———. "Transporting Culture Across Borders—the Hmong." In *Asian and Pacific Cosmopolitans: Self and Subject in Motion*, edited by Kathryn Robinson. Basingstoke and New York: Palgrave Macmillan, 2007.

Thang, N. V. *Ambiguity of Identity: The Mieu in North Vietnam*. Chiangmai: Silkworm Books, 2007.

Tomforde, Maren. *The Hmong Mountains: Cultural Spatiality of the Hmong in Northern Thailand*. Hamburg: Lit Verlag, 2006.

———. "The Hmong Mountains: Space and Culture in Northern Thailand." In *The Impact of Globalization and Trans-Nationalism on the Hmong*, edited by Gar Yia Lee. St. Paul: Center for Hmong Studies, Concordia University, 2007.

Tsing, Anna. "Contingent Commodities: Mobilizing Labor in and beyond Southeast Asian Forests." In *Taking Southeast Asia to Market: Commodities, People, and Nature in the Neoliberal Age*, edited by Joseph Nevens and Nancy Peluso. Ithaca, NY: Cornell University Press, 2008.

Van, Dang Nghiem. "The Flood Myth and the Origin of Ethnic Groups in Southeast Asia," *Journal of American Folklore* 106 (Summer 1993): 304–337.

Vang, Chia Koua, Gnia Yee Yang, and William Smalley. *The Life of Shong Lue Yang: Hmong "Mother of Writing."* Minneapolis, MN: University of Minnesota Southeast Asian Refugee Studies, 1990.

Vang, Lue, and Judy Lewis. *Grandmother's Path, Grandfather's Way*. Rancho Cordova: Zellerbach Family Fund, 1990.

Vang, Song. "Stir-Fried Pop Culture," *TC Daily Planet*, 11 January 2008. Available at http://www.tcdailyplanet.net/article/2008/01/11/stir-fried-pop-culture.html.

Wanitpradit, Apit, and Nathan Badenoch. "Traditional Knowledge for Contemporary Watershed Governance Challenges," USER (Unit for Social and Environmental Research, Chiangmai University) Briefing Paper BN 2006-06, 2006.

Wiens, Harold. *China's March into the Tropics: Han Chinese Expansion in Southern China*. New York: Shoestring Press, 1954 (rev. 1970).

Winland, Daphne. "A Plea for Peoplehood: Religion and Ethnic Identity, Continuity and Change among the Mennonites of Kitchener-Waterloo." Unpub. PhD diss., University of York, Toronto, 1989.

Worra, B. T. *Tut Tut Diaries*. Minneapolis, MN: Unarmed Press, 2003.

————. *On the Other Side of the Eye*. Minneapolis, MN: Sam's Dot Publishing, 2007.

————. *Barrow*. Minneapolis, MN: Sam's Dot Publishing, 2009.

Wronska-Friend, Maria. "Globalised Threads: Costumes of the Hmong Community in North Queensland." In *The Hmong of Australia: Culture and Diaspora*, edited by Nicholas Tapp and Gary Yia Lee. Canberra: Pandanus Books, 2004.

Xiong, Ly T. *Hmoob Kev Lis Kev Cai (Hmong Culture)*. Spokane: Author, 2004.

Yaj, Vam Thaiv. *Niaj Txhis Piv Txoj Lus (Proverbs)*. Chiangmai: Lub Tsev Hauv Paus Ntawv, 1976.

Yang, Dao. *Les Hmong du Laos Face au Developpement*. Vientiane: Editions Siaosavath, 1975.

————. "Why Did the Hmong Leave Laos?" In *The Hmong in the West: Observations and Reports* (Papers of the 1981 Hmong Research Conference, University of Minnesota), edited by Bruce Downing and Douglas P. Olney. Minneapolis, MN: Southeast Asian Refugee Studies Project, Center for Urban and Regional Affairs, University of Minnesota, 1982.

Yang, Kao Kalia. *The Late Homecomers*. Minneapolis: Coffee House Press. 2008.

Yang, Kao-ly. "Problems in the Interpretation of Hmong Surnames." In *Hmong/Miao in Asia*, edited by Nicholas Tapp, Jean Michaud, Christian Culas, and Gary Lee. Chiang Mai: Silkworm Books, 2004.

Yang, Kou. "An Assessment of the Hmong New Year and Its Implications for Hmong-American Culture," *Hmong Studies Journal* 8 (2007).

Yang, Tou T. "Hmong of Germany: A Preliminary Report on the Resettlement of Lao Hmong Refugees in Germany," *Hmong Studies Journal* 4 (2003).

Young, Robert. *Postcolonialism: A Very Short Introduction*. Oxford, UK: Oxford University Press, 2003.

Zhang Yuan Qi, Yang Shao Long, and Shen Zheng Kun. *Hmoob Nyob Paj Tawg Teb [Les Hmong de Wenshan]*. Javouhey, France: Association Communauté Hmong, 1988.

Ziff, B., and P. V. Rao, eds. *Borrowed Power: Essays on Cultural Appropriation*. New Brunswick, NJ: Rutgers University Press, 1997.

Index

About the Authors

GARY YIA LEE, PhD, is a Hmong academic from Laos who has lived in Australia since before the 1975 collapse of Laos. He received his PhD in social anthropology from Sydney University in 1981 and has published and researched extensively on the Hmong. Dr. Lee has taught at the University of New South Wales, the University of Sydney, Macquarie University, and most recently at Concordia University in St. Paul, Minnesota. His published works include *The Hmong/Miao in Asia* and *The Hmong of Australia: Culture and Diaspora*. Many of his publications can be found on his homepage, http://www.garyyialee.com. He received an honorary doctorate in 2008 and the Eagle Award in 2006 from Concordia University for his lifetime contributions to Hmong studies.

NICHOLAS TAPP, PhD, is professor in the Department of Anthropology, Research School of Pacific and Asian Studies, at the Australian National University, Canberra, Australia, where he runs the Thai-Yunnan project. Dr. Tapp has extensively researched and published on the Hmong for 30 years. He received a PhD in social anthropology from the School of Oriental and African Studies, London University, in 1985, and since then has taught at the Chinese University of Hong Kong and at Edinburgh University. His published works include *Sovereignty and Rebellion: The White Hmong of Northern Thailand* and *The Hmong of China: Context, Agency, and the Imaginary*, which won the Choice Outstanding Academic Title award in 2002. In 2010, he also was recipient of the Eagle Award from Concordia University for contributions to research and writing on the Hmong.

CPSIA information can be obtained
at www.ICGtesting.com
Printed in the USA
BVHW011619131220
595023BV00016B/14